Virginia Woolf

Women & Fiction

Virginia Woolf

Women & Fiction

The Manuscript versions of A ROOM OF ONE'S OWN

Transcribed and Edited by
S. P. Rosenbaum

PUBLISHED FOR THE
SHAKESPEARE HEAD PRESS
BY BLACKWELL PUBLISHERS

First published 1992

Reprinted 1992

Blackwell Publishers
108 Cowley Road, Oxford, OX4 1JF, UK

238 Main Street
Cambridge, Massachusetts, 02142, USA

Library of Congress Cataloging in Publication Data

Woolf, Virginia, 1882–1941.
Women & fiction: the manuscript versions of A room of one's own / Virginia Woolf; transcribed and edited by S.P. Rosenbaum.
p. cm.
Includes bibliographical references.
ISBN 0-631-18037-0
1. Woolf, Virginia, 1882–1941 - Authorship. 2. Fiction—Women authors—History and criticism—Theory, etc. 3. Women and literature—Great Britain. 4. Women authors—Economic conditions. 5. Women authors—Social conditions. I. Rosenbaum, S. P. (Stanford Patrick), 1929– . II. Woolf, Virginia, 1882–1941. Room of one's own. III. Title. IV. Title: Women and fiction.
PR6045.072Z474 1992
823'.912—dc20 91–38730
CIP

British Library Cataloguing in Publication Data

A CIP catalogue record for this book is available from the British Library.

Typeset in Times on 10/12pt.
Printed in the USA.

This book is printed on acid-free paper.

Contents

List of facsimiles vii

Preface ix

Introduction: Towards the Literary History of *A Room of One's Own* xiii

Explanation of the Transcription xliii

The Fitzwilliam Manuscript

Women & Fiction 3
II 37
Chapter Three 65

The Monks House Manuscript 103

The Fitzwilliam Manuscript Continued

Chapter 4. Cont. 125
Chapter Five 137
Conclusion 167

Appendices 175

Introduction 176
1 Variant Opening, Monks House Papers 177
2 Notes for Conclusion, Monks House Papers 179
3 Typescript Excerpts, Monks House Papers 180
4 "Women and Fiction," *Forum*, March 1929 195

Notes 203

List of Facsimiles

1 The Fitzwilliam Manuscript, opening folio 2

2 The Fitzwilliam Manuscript, chapter "II" opening 36

3 The Fitzwilliam Manuscript, "Chapter Three" opening 64

4 The Monks House Manuscript, opening folio 102

5 The Fitzwilliam Manuscript, "Chapter 4 Cont." opening 124

6 The Fitzwilliam Manuscript, "Chapter Five", opening 136

7 The Fitzwilliam Manuscript, "Conclusion", opening 166

Preface

In April 1990, while finishing the second volume of my literary history of the Bloomsbury Group, I came across a letter of Leonard Woolf's mentioning that Virginia Woolf might have given one of her manuscripts to the Fitzwilliam Museum in Cambridge or the Bodleian Library in Oxford. The letter was written the year after her death, and a helpful footnote by Frederic Spotts, the meticulous editor of Leonard Woolf's letters, informed me that a manuscript entitled "Women in Fiction" and identified as "the first draft of what became *A Room of One's Own*" was indeed owned by the Fitzwilliam.

A Room of One's Own was the only book Virginia Woolf published in her lifetime for which no substantial manuscript had yet been discovered. Only twenty or so pages of what seem at first to be notes and fragments were to be found in the Monks House Papers now at the University of Sussex. The 1928 talks at the two Cambridge women's colleges out of which the book grew have not survived; they were probably recast as an article entitled "Women and Fiction" (not "Women in Fiction") that Virginia Woolf published in March 1929, before bringing out *A Room of One's Own* in the autumn.

I assumed, before visiting the Fitzwilliam Museum, that their manuscript was that for the article, not the book. (An entry in the *Location Register of Twentieth-Century English Literary Manuscripts and Letters* had described it as a "lecture" that had been incorporated into *A Room of One's Own*.) But the dark blue box that a librarian of the Fitzwilliam brought to me contained well over a hundred sheets in Virginia Woolf's not easily readable hand. This was too long for a lecture. The first page with its title and the subsequent chapter divisions made it clear that here at last was the manuscript of *A Room of One's Own*. It had been donated by Leonard Woolf, who described it in an accompanying letter as the first draft of the book, but even he misread his wife's writing and took the ampersand in the title *Women & Fiction* as the preposition *in*.

For nearly half a century the holograph draft of what may be Virginia Woolf's most famous work had lain virtually unread in the Fitzwilliam Museum's library. ("It is mentioned in our annual report for 1942," I was told, and so it is.) Now with the kind permissions of the copyright holders Quentin Bell and Angelica Garnett, of the Syndics of the Fitzwilliam Museum, and of the University of Sussex it is possible to publish the manuscript entitled *Women & Fiction* - or rather the manuscripts, for the Fitzwilliam holograph is actually made up of two different drafts, as the introduction and notes to this edition show.

That a man, and a professor at that, should be editing the manuscripts of *A Room of One's Own* has its ironies. But these have been eased for me through the help of two authorities on feminism and on Virginia Woolf. Naomi Black, who understands the complexities of modern feminism so well, and Susan Dick, the fine editor of the manuscripts of *To the Lighthouse* and *The Complete Shorter Fiction of Virginia Woolf*, both compared very carefully the emerging transcription with copies of the manuscript and suggested innumerable improvements. The finished transcript was checked with great care and perceptiveness by Barbara Bauer, who corrected it in many ways. And Brenda Silver deciphered several stubbornly illegible passages. To Paul Woudhuysen, the Keeper of Manuscripts and Books at the Fitzwilliam, and his efficient staff I am very grateful for their knowledge and courtesy. Elizabeth Inglis of the University of Sussex Library has been, once again, indispensably helpful with the Monks House Papers. I am also indebted to Kate Perry, the archivist at Girton College, for material relating to Virginia Woolf's talks there and at Newnham. For time to do research I am very grateful as well to both the Killam Program of the Canada Council and the University of Toronto. Lesley Abrams, Anne Olivier Bell, Christine Donald, James M. Haule, James King, Ann Phillips, Samuel Rosenbaum, Susanna Rosenbaum, Philip H. Smith, Jr., Irene M. Spry and J. H. Stape have also helped in various ways. Finally, Andrew McNeillie, the editor of

Women & Fiction at Blackwell Publishers, has brought to this edition his good sense, tact, and great skills as an editor of Virginia Woolf's diaries and essays.

Soon after she finished drafting *Women & Fiction* Virginia Woolf wrote a short biography of Mary Wollstonecraft in which she said of works like *A Vindication of the Rights of Woman* what readers have come to feel about *A Room of One's Own*: "they seem now to contain nothing new in them - their originality has become our commonplace". The drafts of *A Room of One's Own* allow us to defamiliarize the text and re-experience the originality of a work so influential that it has become our commonplace. In *Women & Fiction* the narrative structure of *A Room of One's Own* is clearly visible yet almost every sentence of the book was revised in some way during the course of composition. Again and again Virginia Woolf rewrites her text as she strives to fuse the diverse forms of lecture and fiction, feminist argument and literary criticism, polemic and prophecy. *Women & Fiction* reflects, like *A Room of One's Own*, the fantasy of *Orlando*, which she had just published, and the mysticism of *The Waves*, which she was about to write. Yet the study of its composition differs from those of Woolf's novels because *A Room of One's Own* is a more discursive work. In its manuscript versions one can watch Woolf creatively developing her arguments through reasoning and association in images and scenes. The revisions in her drafts raise those same questions that the narrator begins to ask in *A Room of One's Own* as she goes to look at the manuscripts of Milton and Thackeray in a men's college library: "whether the alterations were for the benefit of the style or of the meaning. But then one wd. have to decide what is style & what is meaning. . . ." For the narrator these questions end when she is prevented from seeing the manuscripts. Thanks to the copyright holders and institutional owners, any reader can now ask such questions of *Women & Fiction*.

Toronto — S. P. R.

Introduction

Towards the Literary History of *A Room of One's Own*

"By a miracle, I've found all the pages," Virginia Woolf wrote to Ethel Smyth three years after the publication of *A Room of One's Own* (*Letters*, V, 136). She wanted to donate the manuscript to the nearly bankrupt London and National Society for Women's Service, whose secretary was Philippa Strachey, a sister of Lytton. The Society asked her to sell it for them if she could in America. Unsuccessful efforts were made first by Vita Sackville-West, who was lecturing in the States, and then by Woolf's American publisher Donald Brace. The Huntington Library in California expressed interest, a wealthy collector said he would rather have the manuscript of *Flush*, but in the end Virginia Woolf was advised to try and sell the manuscript in England. There the matter seems to have dropped.

While making some enquiries as to the whereabouts of his wife's manuscripts after her death, Leonard Woolf received a request from the Director of the Fitzwilliam Museum in Cambridge, for something of Virginia Woolf's. Leonard responded appropriately and with great generosity, giving back to Cambridge (but not to Newnham or Girton, not to King's, and certainly not to Trinity's library) the manuscript that had its beginning there. He described the gift as the first draft of *A Room of One's Own* - the manuscript Virginia had been unable to sell for Pippa Strachey's society.

The Fitzwilliam manuscript bears the title *Women & Fiction* and consists of 134 holograph leaves. It is divided into five chapters plus a conclusion, and bears various dates between March and April, 1929. A closer examination reveals, however, that Virginia Woolf had not, as she thought, miraculously found all the pages. The Fitzwilliam manuscript is really two manuscripts. The rhetoric of interruption in *A Room of One's Own* together with the disconnectedness of its composition sometimes makes it difficult to recognize breaks in the manuscript's progression. But it is self-evident that the heading "Chapter 4. Cont." (p. 125 in this transcription) is not simply a continuation of the third chapter that it follows. The manuscript paper - described here in the notes to the transcription - is also different.

The third chapter of the Fitzwilliam manuscript is continued, however, in an untitled, undated manuscript of twenty leaves to be found in the Monks House Papers now at the University of Sussex. (Also to be found in the Monks House Papers and included here as appendices 1 and 2 are a brief variant opening for *A Room of One's Own* and a page of notes for the conclusion of *Women & Fiction*.) The paper of the Monks House manuscript is the same as the Fitzwilliam manuscript, except for the last few pages. But discontinuities remain. The fourth chapter of the Fitzwilliam manuscript does not carry on from the Monks House manuscript. It refers, for example to the imaginary novelist Mary Carmichael, who had been called Chloe in the Monks House manuscript. Parts of the drafts for *A Room of One's Own* are therefore still missing and must be presumed lost. To make matters more complicated, some scenes in the Monks House manuscript have been redrafted again in the following Fitzwilliam leaves. These different drafts, it is clear from the dates in the Fitzwilliam manuscript, were all made within days of each other, for the entire drafting of the book that became *A Room of One's Own* was completed in a little over a month. One reason for this remarkable speed, as Virginia Woolf noted in her diary, was that "the thinking had been done & the writing stiffly & unsatisfactorily 4 times before" (*Diary*, III, 218–19, 221–2). To understand the creative evolution of *A Room of One's Own*, we need to trace the literary history of these earlier efforts from the talks in Cambridge through the article 'Women and Fiction' to the writing of the book *Women & Fiction* and its revision into *A Room of One's Own*.

The Cambridge Lectures

On Saturday, 20 October 1928, Virginia and Leonard Woolf, together with Vanessa Bell and her daughter Angelica, drove from London to Cambridge where Virginia was to read a paper to the undergraduates of Newnham College. She had been invited nearly a year before and planned to come in May. The first version of her paper had been prepared in the spring, interrupting the writing of *Orlando*. But illness and the pressure to finish that book led her to postpone until the autumn both Newnham and Girton (the only other Cambridge college where women could study) which had also asked her to speak.

The Woolfs were staying with Pernel Strachey, the Principal of Newnham and sister of Philippa and Lytton. Virginia arrived nearly an hour late for the college dinner at which she was to speak. To make matters worse, according to the subsequent recollections of E. E. Phare, she brought her husband along and upset the seating arrangements. Phare thought the dinner at Newnham, though never a gourmet meal, suffered considerably from the late arrival of the guest of honour, and she recalled how uncomfortable the depiction of Fernham's poverty had made the students feel (*A Newnham Anthology*, p. 174). Phare, who went on to become an authority on the poetry of Marvell and Hopkins, was the president of the Newnham Arts Society, under whose auspices Virginia Woolf was to speak. Her report of the paper in the Newnham magazine *Thersites* is worth quoting because the paper or papers that Woolf read at Newnham and later at Girton no longer exist, and Phare's is the only contemporary account of what Virginia Woolf actually said that evening. One can glimpse through this summary the symbolism of rooms, the prevalence of male standards and style that figure so importantly in *A Room of One's Own*, and also a little of the book's ironic self-consciousness.

> Mrs Virginia Woolf visited us on Saturday, Oct. 20th, and spoke in College Hall on "Women and Fiction". The reasons why women novelists were for so long so few were largely a question of domestic architecture: it was not, and it is not easy to compose in a parlour. Now that women are writing (and Mrs Woolf exhorted her audience to write novels and send them to be considered by the Hogarth Press) they should not try to adapt themselves to the prevailing literary standards, which are likely to be masculine, but make others of their own; they should remake the

> language, so that it becomes a more fluid thing and capable of delicate usage.
>
> It was a characteristic and delightful lecture and we are most grateful to Mrs Woolf for coming to us, as well as to Miss Strachey for consenting to preside over the meeting. (No. 87, Michaelmas Term, 1928)

Half a century later, almost the only thing Phare could remember from the talk was the praise of a poem by Stella Gibbons, but she also recalled how well disposed Woolf seemed to her audience of young intellectual women, and how formidable. Another listener, U. K. N. Carter, recollected Woolf's conversation after the paper - how she surprised the young woman with a compliment on her dress. But it was the look that remained most vividly with Carter: "the look held a hint of a smile, a hint of compassion, but it was above all an absolutely ruthless look; my pretty frock was no proof against it" (*A Newnham Anthology*, p. 175).

The next day there was a luncheon party in the rooms of George "Dadie" Rylands that had been decorated by Carrington and overlooked the beautiful Backs and the Cam. Rylands had recently been made a fellow of King's College after having served as an assistant at the Hogarth Press. According to Leonard Woolf's diary, the other guests were Lytton Strachey and John Maynard Keynes. The party was thus a thoroughly Bloomsbury affair. Rylands thought later that one of the guests may have been E. M. Forster (who had given his famous *Aspects of the Novel* lectures at Cambridge the year before and was also a fellow of King's at this time). Rylands doubted, however, that the cooking of his college could have produced various partridges and a brown-flecked counterpane of sauce, as *A Room of One's Own* has it. He hoped that there had been two wines but thought it unlikely (*Recollections of Virginia Woolf*, p. 144).

The accounts of lunch and dinner in *A Room of One's Own* have entered into the mythology of Oxbridge, and it is sometimes forgotten that, while based on Woolf's experiences at Cambridge, they are fictive descriptions. (The book's reversal of the order in which Woolf had the meals is a small but interesting illustration of how she transformed autobiography into art.)

The following Friday Virginia Woolf again went to Cambridge to speak, accompanied this time by Vita Sackville-West. In the afternoon she visited her nephew Julian Bell, an undergraduate at King's, and contrasted in her diary the next day the splendour and luxury of his surroundings with Newnham's and Girton's. She stayed at a hotel with

Sackville-West where they had dinner with two students from the Girton ODTAA Society. (ODTAA was an acronym, taken from the title of a recent novel by John Masefield, and stood for "one damn thing after another".) The guests paid for their own dinners, to the relief of the students, Woolf thought, and afterwards were shown the cold, ugly corridors and convent-cell rooms of the college. ODTAA was quite different from the Newnham Arts Society. More exclusive and informal, it discussed topics that were not limited to literature and the arts. The society was modelled to some extent on the Cambridge Heretics Society and also on the more famous male Cambridge Conversazione Society, better known as the Apostles. The Mistress of Girton, it appears, was not a member of ODTAA and did not attend Woolf's paper. In the original invitation for Woolf to speak, some reference had been made to the women's society in her 1921 sketch "A Society". Woolf in her unpublished reply expressed the hope that ODTAA was a considerable improvement over the society of her sketch. But the connection is illuminating because "A Society" satirizes the ignorance of women, Oxbridge, women and fiction, chastity, and war - all concerns that prefigure those in *A Room of One's Own* and later *Three Guineas*.

The only contemporary record of what Virginia Woolf said at Girton is the author's: "I blandly told them to drink wine & have a room of their own" (*Diary*, III, 200). This does not sound quite like her Newnham paper. Woolf referred to both the Newnham and Girton talks as one lecture in her diary and again in the opening note to *Women & Fiction*, where she added that it was too long to be read in full. In the note to *A Room of One's Own*, however, Woolf says there were two lectures, or papers as she called them, both of which were too long. In her diary the day she returned from Cambridge, Woolf also recorded the "sense of tingling & vitality" she got from such talks but indicated as well that her Girton lecture may not have been completely successful. Preparing it had been a "long toil". Her impression of the audience was of "starved but valiant young women. . . . Intelligent eager, poor; & destined to become schoolmistresses in shoals. . . . I felt elderly & mature. And nobody respected me. They were very eager, egotistical, or rather not much impressed by age & repute. Very little reverence or that sort of thing about" (*Diary*, III, 200–1). In their recollections several Girton undergraduates who heard Woolf's paper suggest, like Phare at Newnham, that Woolf may have misjudged her audience. Her bleak view of their academic life and prospects did not persuade some of the readers of *A Room of One's Own* who had heard the original papers that theirs was an underprivileged gender. At Girton in particular there were three impressive, if not irreverent, young literary women in the audience who were certainly not going to become schoolmistresses.

The poet Kathleen Raine, in a review of M. C. Bradbrook's short history of Girton, remembered that they were both present at Woolf's paper forty years before. She found Woolf's criticism of her alma mater a little absurd. (Like almost all the accounts of Woolf's talks, Raine's does not distinguish between the paper she heard and the book into which it was made.) In her autobiography Raine also indicated another circumstance that made Woolf's Girton lecture different from her Newnham one. "With Virginia Woolf had come her friend Victoria Sackville-West: the two most beautiful women I had ever seen. I saw their beauty and their fame entirely removed from the context of what is usually called 'real' life, as if they had descended like goddesses from Olympus, to reascend when at the end of the evening they vanished from our sight" (*The Land Unknown*, p. 22). Raine, herself a strikingly beautiful undergraduate, had read none of Woolf's novels, but she had probably heard something about *Orlando*, which was partly based on the circumstances of Vita Sackville-West and published the week before. *A Room of One's Own*, she felt, laid claim to unimaginable luxuries; to escape parental vigilance she had done her writing in tea-shops before temporarily realizing the dream of a room of her own at Girton. (After Cambridge Julian Bell took her to see his aunt about a job at the Hogarth Press, and this time Raine felt none of the great writer's mana was present. No job was forthcoming.)

M. C. Bradbook rose to be Professor of English at Cambridge as well as Mistress of Girton. Her short history of Girton briefly mentions Woolf's paper and *A Room of One's Own* immediately after a much longer and rather misleading discussion of the lesbian aspects of Rosamond Lehmann's Girton novel *Dusty Answer*. The Cambridge of the novel was Virginia Woolf's, Bradbrook says elsewhere in commenting on the book's style. *Dusty Answer* had been published the year before Woolf's talk and seems to have created something of a sensation at the College. At the time of Woolf's visit in the company of Orlando's model, literary lesbianism was in the news with the banning and forthcoming trial of Radclyffe Hall's *The Well of Loneliness* - events that would be reflected in the lesbian nuances of *A Room of One's Own*. Whatever the perceived relation of Woolf's talk to Lehmann's novel was, Bradbrook recalled in 1969 that "we undergraduates enjoyed Mrs Woolf, but felt that her Cambridge was not ours" (*"That Infidel Place"*, pp. 112–16). In 1932 (when she was twenty-three) Bradbrook had been more severe. The first issue of that famous Cambridge critical scourge *Scrutiny* contained a short dismissive essay by her that asserted Woolf's delicate perceptiveness of style was maintained "at the cost of some cerebral etiolation". "Camouflage" was Bradbrook's term for the fictive art of *A Room of One's Own*: its arguments were "clearly serious and personal and yet they are dramatized and surrounded with all sorts of disguises to avoid an appearance of argument" ("Notes on the Style of Mrs Woolf", *Scrutiny*, I, 38).

Another undergraduate who heard the Girton paper was Queenie Roth. A friend recalled that she impressed Woolf, who was going to send her a pamphlet (Gwendolen Freeman, *Alma Mater*, p. 87). Roth was not about to be a schoolmistress either. She remained in Cambridge as the wife and collaborator of F. R. Leavis, whom she married the next year. In 1935 she sent Woolf a *Scrutiny* review that praised the introductory letter to *Life as We Have Known It*, but Woolf did not recognize her name (*Letters*, V, 425). Later in the year Q. D. Leavis referred in passing to the "crudely" manifested feminism of *A Room of One's Own* but still had praise for some of Woolf's other work (*Scrutiny*, IV, 329–30). *Three Guineas* outraged her, however, and she fiercely attacked both book and author.

The Article "Women and Fiction"

Virginia Woolf was still thinking about Newnham and Girton in November as she considered what to write after *Orlando*. Early in the month she appeared in court prepared to testify on *The Well of Loneliness*, but evidence of literary merit was ruled inadmissible and the book declared obscene. (Forster wrote to Leonard Woolf that Virginia, as the author of *Orlando*, ought not perhaps to have attended the trial.) The mood of *Orlando* remained with her as she recorded in her diary the desire to write something else of fun and fantasy that gave things "their caricature value. . . . I want to write a history, say of Newnham or the womans movement, in the same vein." But in the same entry she also speaks of wanting to begin the book that would become *The Waves* (*Diary*, III, 203). The next book she published was *A Room of One's Own*, in which elements of both *Orlando* and *The Waves* are to be found. But this was not the next book she completed.

For three years now Virginia Woolf had been trying to write a book on the theory of fiction for the Hogarth Press Lectures on Literature series that Leonard Woolf and George Rylands were editing. The success of Forster's Cambridge lectures provided a stimulus for the book because Virginia thought, as she said in her two reviews of *Aspects of the Novel*, that Forster had not paid enough attention to the *art* of fiction. She had begun "Phases of Fiction", as the book was called, in 1926. But she became bored with it and wrote *Orlando* instead. Woolf took up "Phases of Fiction" again and finished drafting it before going to Cambridge in October, 1928. She rewrote it in November and December, and still had 10,000 words to write, when another book on fiction intervened instead.

The idea of making a book out of her Cambridge lectures does not seem to have occurred to Woolf until the following spring. She had written an article on the subject of the lectures at the end of the year, while working on "Phases of Fiction", and sent it off to the *Forum* in America, where it was published in March the next year (see appendix 4 for the text). Woolf had followed a similar procedure with two previous talks to students about reading and writing that are among her most significant critical essays. A 1926 paper read to a girls' school was published as "How Should One Read a Book?" and then revised as the final essay and critical credo of the second *Common Reader*. In 1927, the year before she read her Cambridge papers, Woolf had gone to Oxford (accompanied by Vita Sackville-West) to speak to a mixed group of undergraduates about "Poetry, Fiction, and the Future", as she called the published article. That paper is almost a manifesto for the kind of novel she would write in *The Waves*. And later in 1931 she would give a speech on professions for women that continues the concerns of her Cambridge talks and links *A Room of One's Own* to its sequel, *Three Guineas*.

Woolf entitled her *Forum* article "Women and Fiction". This would also be the working title for *A Room of One's Own* as well as the heading for the paper that the speaker is trying to write in that book. If one counts the talks to Newnham and Girton as separate papers, then this was the fourth time she addressed the subject. (The first was the version prepared the preceding spring.) The article was illustrated with drawings of Sappho, Austen, Murasaki, who are among the women mentioned in the text, and George Sand, who is not. (Perhaps that was as close as the illustrator could come to George Eliot, whom Woolf does refer to.)

The *Forum* was a distinguished New York review that took its title seriously and tried to provide a non-partisan medium for intellectual debate and contemporary literature. In 1928 the editor, Henry Goddard Leach, had published Woolf's "Slater's Pins Have No Points", which she described to Sackville-West as a Sapphist story whose point the editor had not got (*Letters*, III, 431). A serialization of André Gide's novel *The School of Women* was begun in the same issue as "Women and Fiction", and an essay by Valéry promised at the end of Woolf's text for the next issue. The preceding issue of the *Forum* in which Woolf's article was announced carried a piece by William Allan Neilson, the President of Smith College, arguing that the liberal arts of women's colleges should be the same as men's because educators ought "to provide for all degrees of masculinity in female minds and all degrees of feminity [sic] in male minds, as for all other varieties of human nature" (the *Forum*, LXXXI, 103). The only grave disadvantage of women's colleges, he maintained, was their lack of generous benefactors.

"Women and Fiction", while not too long to have been read as a lecture, is probably as close as we can now come to what Virginia Woolf said at Cambridge. E. E. Phare's account tallies with it (though in the matter of wine Woolf's own comment about her Girton paper does not). The article begins in the best Cambridge tradition by considering the ambiguities of meaning in its title. The past, present, and future of women and fiction are all touched upon as Woolf refers to the obscurity of women's lives, the intermittent history of their literary work, the problems of style and value in women's writing, the artistic dangers of resentment, the increasing literary interest in women's relations with one another, the two kinds of modern novelist (Woolf calls them the gadfly and the butterfly in the article), and the possibilities for a more poetic fiction. Running through all of these issues is an insistence on the determining influence of the writer's environment. At the end the author calls for what has so long been denied to women: "leisure, and money, and a room to themselves". Not until Woolf had finished a draft of the book would she shift the final phrase to the impersonal singular "a room of one's own".

More revealing for the literary history of *A Room of One's Own*, however, is what the essay "Women and Fiction" does not say. The situation of women at Oxbridge is unmentioned, and the anger of men unnoticed. There is no reference to the androgynous state of mind that, according to Woolf, a good writer needs. It may seem unlikely that her account of women's colleges was influenced by Neilsen's piece in the

Forum, which appeared before she had begun to write her book, but the coincidence of his concern with their disadvantage is arresting. "Women and Fiction" also has little or none of the comedy, the satire of *A Room of One's Own*. There was humour in the lectures, as Phare's brief summary indicates. (William Empson, who met Woolf when he was an undergraduate at Cambridge, remembered becoming quite ill from laughing so hard at her jokes.) And there is nothing fictional in the article - no narrator or novelist named Mary, nothing about Shakespeare's sister.

Woolf says in her note to both *Women & Fiction* and *A Room of One's Own* that they are "based" on the paper or papers read at Cambridge. A comparison of the article "Women and Fiction" with *A Room of One's Own* makes the nature of this basis clear. It shows how the experience itself of coming to Cambridge and reading a paper to a woman's college on women and fiction became the narrative basis for the book that Virginia Woolf would begin to write some five months later. With the recovery of the manuscript versions of *A Room of One's Own*, it is now possible to follow this modernist transformation through the beginnings, endings, interruptions, repetitions, cancellations, insertions, and marginalia of Virginia Woolf's creative process.

The Writing of *Women & Fiction*

Early in 1929, the Woolfs visited Vita Sackville-West and her husband Harold Nicolson in Berlin, where he was serving as a diplomat. After their return Virginia Woolf was ill: for three weeks she lay in bed, and for perhaps another three could not write. It was a creative illness. She had wanted to begin *The Waves*, but the subject of her Cambridge papers and article forced itself on her again in a new form now, which she described as half talk and half soliloquy. Woolf began making up *Women & Fiction* in her head as she lay in bed. Then in what she called "one of my excited outbursts of composition", the book was drafted in about a month. "I used to make it up at such a rate," she noted when beginning her revisions in April, "that when I got pen & paper I was like a water bottle turned upside down. The writing was as quick as my hand could write; too quick, for I am now toiling to revise; but this way gives one freedom & lets one leap from back to back of one's thoughts" (*Diary*, III, 218–19, 221–2). It was too quick also for any easy deciphering of her manuscript. The scrawl of her handwriting illustrates the extraordinary speed with which *Women & Fiction* was written. Woolf's novels were usually written in bound quarto notebooks; the morning's work would be revised when she typed it up in the afternoon. *Women & Fiction*, however, was written on loose-leaf paper and not typed up until the holograph draft had been completed. There are no indications in the manuscript or her diary that she referred to the Cambridge lectures while composing the book that was based on them.

The first date in the manuscript of *Women & Fiction* - "Wed. 6th March 1929" - appears at the start of "Chapter II". The opening chapter is undated and undesignated even as a chapter. In the note that describes its basis in a paper read at Newnham and Girton, *Women & Fiction* is not called an essay, nor is there any mention of expanding the paper, as there is in *A Room of One's Own*. Woolf may not have known yet where her essay-story was going as she began it. The opening words pick up the original title, to which the speaker-narrator keeps returning. *Women* indicates a dangerous subject, and *Fiction* lands her in the swamp and maze of literary criticism. The license of fiction is invoked and illustrated with the image of a medieval pedlar, a device used by Woolf in one of her earliest stories. Mary Beaton, Seaton, and Carmichael are all mentioned but none is developed much as a persona. There is less emphasis on the fictiveness of the narrative at the start of *Women & Fiction*; college names are undisguised, for example. But the conclusion that will be symbolized in the revised title is present from the beginning. Watching Virginia Woolf create the narrative that seeks arguments for women having "money & a room to themselves" (p. 5) is among the most absorbing aspects of reading *Women & Fiction*.

The episodes of walking on the forbidden grass and being turned away from the library, of the luxurious luncheon party and the bleak fare at Newnham, were all drafted in the first chapter of *Women & Fiction* together with observations on the wealth of men's colleges, on the nature of luncheon parties and poetry before the war, and on the causes of the comparative poverty of women's colleges. The process of drafting involved more than crossings out, insertions, and marginalia. It was an interruptive process. The writing starts, stops and repeats. A number of pages are unfinished, breaking off sometimes in the middle of a sentence or a series of notes. The next page often starts over again, sometimes in the middle of a sentence. The drafts of *To the Lighthouse* and *The Waves* were to some extent also written in this way, but the process seems to have more significance in the writing of what became *A*

Room of One's Own because its narrative is so discontinuous. The very writing of the manuscript seems to illustrate the interrupted lives that women lead. Some of the most abrupt changes in the finished book, such as the sudden appearance of soup in the midst of a reverie on some terrible reality, are present from the beginning. The seasonal dislocation in the first chapter, where the speaker prefers to describe the beauty of spring even though it was October, is originally heightened by anachronism. In *A Room of One's Own*, the reference to the great Newnham classicist Jane Ellen Harrison is an anachronistic fantasy, for she had died in April 1928, but in *Women & Fiction* the more descriptive allusion is fancifully extended back almost a generation to include the well-known dons Verrall and Sidgwick.

Some passages in the first chapter, and not always important ones, are reworked a number of times. Five versions appear in the manuscript of the joke about the professor who is said to gallop if someone whistles. Woolf heavily revised the complaint about luncheon parties in novels that describe talk instead of food. Sometimes the first version of a familiar episode or phrase is revealingly different in small details. Freud is mentioned to avoid explaining how a train of thought was started by the sight of a Manx cat. The narrator's anonymous hostess at Newnham is first described as going to Australia to farm ostriches and then identified as a science lecturer named Mary Seton (as the name is now spelled). Finally, after leaving the college at the end of the chapter, the speaker briefly becomes another of Virginia Woolf's night walkers, experiencing a sense of isolation after escaping from some thraldom. "The day's skin is neatly rolled off; thrown into the hedge" (p. 34). In *Women & Fiction* it has not yet been described as "crumpled" with accumulated impressions and emotions.

The second chapter, now so designated and also dated, was written in six days. As in *A Room of One's Own*, it consists of a walk through Bloomsbury to the British Museum for a comical attempt to research the causes and consequences of the financial disparity between the sexes. Reflections follow, at lunch and during the walk home, on the angry power of the patriarchy and the advantages of an independent income for a woman. The general resemblance of the British Museum scenes in the manuscript to those of the book is illustrated by the similar satiric list of topics in each. Elsewhere there are various differences of detail, such as Professor X, the author of a great work on the mental, moral, and physical inferiority of women, who is given a German beer-hall setting, but not the title of "von".

More remarkable, however, are the revisions in the second chapter that reveal Woolf thinking about anger. The word appears, is crossed out, then reinserted on page 41. The narrator's doodle on pages 44–5 of the very angry professor leads to speculation as to the causes of his anger. The narrator's anger is admitted and explained, but for ten pages Woolf tries to answer the question of why men are angry. In *Women & Fiction* these thoughts occur in a French restaurant - described twice before being dropped - whose excellent cooking continues the concern with food in chapter 1. A pencilled note at the bottom on page 49 gives the conclusion that will be amplified several pages later: "Anger:/desire to be superior./ importance to have some one inferior." Evidence of partiarchal power in the restaurant is supplied by a newspaper (identified here as the *Evening Standard*), as in *A Room of One's Own*. And a looking-glass theory of male psychology is accompanied by a digression on men as bores, which illustrates the sex's superiority complex. Then Woolf introduces a passage on an amazing tribe of women in Central Asia who have a poet equal, perhaps, to Shakespeare. At first this tribe is read out as a fact from the newspaper, to the irritation of a young man lunching nearby. On the next page it is rewritten as a hypothetical example of male rage and deception, for if such a group were found to exist, men would either destroy the women's works or claim them as their own. These thoughts the narrator offers to her audience, again on the understanding that they are all women, for "there are many things that no woman has yet ⟨dared to say⟩ said to a man" (p. 57). The tribe, without this qualification, survived into the typescript of *A Room of One's Own* before finally being deleted.

The aunt whose legacy frees the speaker from women's jobs and allows her to think of things in themselves is, like her niece, unnamed in *Women & Fiction*. Nothing can take away the £500 a year as long as the narrator does not gamble in the stock market. This reservation was also deleted in *A Room of One's Own* (which ironically was then published just days before the great crash of October 1929). With that income she is spared the acquisitive torments of men, torments which indicate that in this respect their privileged education was more imperfect than women's. The sky and trees are no longer blocked by - Woolf originally wrote the cryptic phrase "Milton's bogeyman", then changed this to "the large & imposing figure of Professor X" (pp. 60–1). In *A Room of One's Own* she returned to her Miltonic allusion and substituted for Professor X the large, imposing gentleman Milton recommended for her perpetual adoration. She remembered the cancelled bogeyman, however, and brought him back in her revised conclusion to her book. At the end of the chapter a contrast, which remains only implicit in *A Room of One's Own*, is made between domestic rooms where "there was quiet & thought & happiness" and the "flying chaos & terror" of the street (p. 61).

Drafting *Women & Fiction* as fast as her hand could write (and faster in places than can now be read), Virginia Woolf took less than ten days between 12 and 22 March to produce the long third chapter. But just when and where chapter 3 ended and chapter 4 began in *Women & Fiction* can now no longer be determined. The third chapter returns to the narrator's unwritten paper on women and fiction and then moves back and forward between history and fiction. From G. M. Trevelyan's account of the situation of women and the extraordinary heroines of Shakespeare and later writers, a composite being emerges. Recorded history is a little dull for women, however, and the speaker wishes some of her audience would try using the two great searchlights of history and literature to write biographies of average Elizabethan women. Calling them "lives of the obscure" (a title Woolf herself had already used) is still an advisable dodge in October 1928. The passage about the need for biographies of the obscure is then reworked again, and references are repeated to the Pastons and others as nearly the only sources for them.

Without such lives of the obscure, the speaker is forced into fiction, and the result is a remarkable illustration of Virginia Woolf's creativity as she drafts a version of her famous myth of Shakespeare's sister. Born in Warwickshire around 1564, the woman is given the name of Shakespeare's mother, Mary Arden, as an afterthought (p. 73). The brief life of this additional Mary in *Women & Fiction* contains most of the essentials that will be reworked into Judith Shakespeare's life, except for an episode in which she is beaten by her father for gallivanting about the woods dressed as a man. There is also a cancelled passage asking how the end of her story can be told genteelly. Its evolution in her draft indicates that the fiction of Shakespeare's sister was not part of Woolf's original Cambridge talk. After going on for a page about how other women writers have been hindered from pursuing their art, Woolf breaks off and begins the third chapter again from the beginning. Here and elsewhere, the manuscript of *Women & Fiction* consists of overlapping drafts.

The revised beginning of chapter three brings it closer to the published book. Some of the details from Trevelyan as well as the life of Mary Arden are skipped over and then put back in *A Room of One's*

Own. The revised story of Shakespeare's sister is left unfinished; it ends not with her death but in a discussion of chastity, the difficulties of women writers, and the possessiveness of men again. Then Woolf comes back to a fundamental concern of both *Women & Fiction* and *A Room of One's Own*, which is the state of mind best suited to the creation of literature. Shakespeare is the standard. The writer is compared to the carrier of a precious jar through a crowd. Examples of indifference and hostility to men writers are cited to suggest how much more discouraging is a woman's situation, and how important it is, as Emily Davies realized when founding Girton, for women to have rooms of their own. Trying to explain the result of a discouraging environment on artists, Woolf returns to Shakespeare's state of mind, and jots down the single word "incandescent" in the margin opposite a reference to *Antony and Cleopatra* (p. 90). This play and image will recur in the theory of creativity that is so important in *Women & Fiction* and *A Room of One's Own*. Shakespeare's creative mind consumed all the personal impediments, the grudges and grievances, that remain in the work of Jonson, Donne, or Milton, which may explain why we have less sense of his personality than theirs. For three pages Woolf tries to describe Shakespeare's state of mind in the imagery of metallurgy.

The thought that such a molten state of mind was impossible for any woman of Shakespeare's time begins a new paragraph on page 92. In *A Room of One's Own* this is where the fourth chapter begins. But in the manuscript, chapter three continues on for another half dozen pages with discussions of pre-nineteenth-century women writers. Winchilsea, Newcastle, Osborne, and Behn are all referred to, but more briefly than they will be in the revised text. The quotations to be used are identified just by first line and page number. These women are the forerunners of Jane Austen, George Eliot, and the Brontës, whose masterpieces are first likened to waves of the sea and then more familiarly described as the result of thinking in common for many years. With the debts that these nineteenth-century novelists owed to their predecessors, the first part of Woolf's Fitzwilliam manuscript stops in the middle of a page - one-third of the way through what will be chapter 4 in *A Room of One's Own*. The second part of the manuscript picks up the story in the middle of what will be chapter 5, some thirty pages later in the book.

The gap between the two parts of the Fitzwilliam manuscript is partly filled by twenty leaves of the undated Monks House manuscript. In it Woolf continues, on the same paper as the Fitzwilliam manuscript, some time between 12 and 22 March, the survey of women writers from

Aphra Behn into the nineteenth century, as in *A Room of One's Own*. There are significant differences in both organization and detail between this version of the manuscript and *A Room of One's Own*, however. The discussion of *Jane Eyre* does not immediately analyze the awkward break in sequence that is attributed a little later to Charlotte Brontë's indignation. It is interesting to follow Woolf in the Monks House manuscript while she works tentatively towards a moral aesthetic of the novel as a structure of emotional relations depending on the author's integrity for its maintenance. One can begin to see here how her concerns with feminism, creativity, and the future of the novel all come together. Sometimes Woolf's judgements are blunter in *Women & Fiction*; Rochester's description in *Jane Eyre*, for instance, is "the portrait of a man by a woman who is afraid of men", (p. 108), rather than one drawn in the dark and influenced by fear. The much commented upon statement "for we think back through our mothers if we are women" first occurs as a parenthetical remark (p. 109). Woolf does not yet work into her argument the quotations of men hostile to women's literary aspirations that will appear later in her manuscript and book. Without saying yet that the form of a woman's novel should be adapted somehow to her body, Woolf speculates through her narrator on the kind of poetic novel women may write. In *A Room of One's Own* this marks the beginning of the fifth chapter, but in the Monks House manuscript only a line-space separates it from the preceding discussion.

Virginia Woolf begins her section on contemporaries by noting the variety of books now written by women. She then digresses to describe how a visit of Emily Davies and Barbara Leigh Smith to a family of six middle-class girls moping around the table led to the founding of Girton and the writing of such books. Suddenly the speaker blushes for her topic of women and fiction, apparently because such enquiries into only one sex "sterilise & embitter" (p. 112). Then in the remaining ten leaves of the Monks House manuscript Woolf's narrator describes and reflects upon a novel written by a woman, an Oxford graduate with £300 a year, who was born at the beginning of the century. The narrator jumps into the middle of the book to get a sense of its style, which is described as plunging up and down like a boat, using too many words, putting in the wrong things and leaving out the right ones. Still, the novelist was not trying to write a realistic novel, the typical detail of which is satirized. But the test of the book will be the novel's final situation. The work does conclude successfully, but before we reach the end, Woolf drafts some of the most interesting pages of *Women & Fiction*. In these passages on the possibilities of contemporary fiction by women she continues the double fictive frame of her book by describing her narrator's reaction to this imaginary novel as she reads it. The novelist's sentence "Chloe liked Olivia . . ." (p. 114) changes the current of the narrator's thought. Changes in current - from the first interruption on a college lawn to the last scene outside her window when a young couple come together - are one of the fundamental metaphors by which Woolf organizes her book. They are also a source of the work's humour and irony.

In *A Room of One's Own* the speaker prefaces the suggestive ambiguity of the phrase "Chloe liked Olivia . . ." by breaking off to be sure there are no men, no magistrates like the one who judged *The Well of Loneliness* obscene, hiding in cupboards. Originally, however, Woolf's comic interpolation follows the phrase, which is given as "'Chloe like Olivia; they shared a ---"' (p. 114). The pages of the book stick together at this point, and before she can separate them to read the next word, which is only "laboratory", a fantasy trial, verdict and book-burning flash through her mind. After some cancellations a more serious current of thought is started, which has to do with the immense literary change that Chloe's and Olivia's relationship signifies. Until Austen wrote, all great women in literature, such as Shakespeare's jealous Cleopatra, were seen primarily in relationship with the other sex. If Chloe likes Olivia and can write - these last crucial words are inserted by Woolf - then Olivia offers readers the extraordinary opportunity of illuminating a cave where no one has been before. Woolf stops in the middle of a sentence and page here, and starts again on different paper with Chloe, who is somewhat confusingly both a character in the novel and its author. (There is no mention of Mary Carmichael.) Chloe has the great opportunity of observing the obscure lives of organisms like Olivia, whose life is "so highly developed for other purposes, so extraordinarily complex, so sensitive . . ." (p. 117). Woolf will return to these words in the second part of the Fitzwilliam manuscript, and extensively redraft the part that follows them in the Monks House pages.

The Monks House version of this section has to do with what Chloe's novel might be about. As a naturalist-novelist (the more interesting contemplative kind is not mentioned), she watches and writes about various rooms and lives of women, such as the ancient lady, seen crossing a street with her daughter, whose life of Monday and Tuesday has passed unrecorded, or the vagrants, whose faces reflect so differently the meeting of a man or a woman. Chloe might even write about shopping rather than golf or shooting, and thus win the approval of the anonymous critic who said recently that "female novelists should only aspire to excellence by courageously acknowledging the limitations of their sex" (p. 121). Woolf took the partial quotation from the August 1928, issue of the new periodical *Life and Letters* that her Bloomsbury friend Desmond MacCarthy had started editing and to which she contributed. Woolf had been disagreeing in print with MacCarthy about the capabilities of women since 1920, when she criticized a review of his on some books about women (*Diary*, II, 339–42). That criticism anticipates the arguments of *A Room of One's Own*. MacCarthy's remark in *Life and Letters* comes at the beginning of his review of a young woman's novel. Its autobiographical relevance appears in a further part of the quotation that was omitted by Woolf: "If, like the reporter, you believe that female novelists should only aspire to excellence by courageously acknowledging the limitations of their sex (Jane Austen and, in our own time, Mrs Virginia Woolf have demonstrated how gracefully this gesture can be accomplished). . . ." After the publication of *A Room of One's Own*, in which Woolf used the same elliptical quotation, MacCarthy wrote in *Life and Letters* that he was horrified to find his unhappy sentence used so acidly when it was inspired by a wholehearted admiration of Woolf's work. He went on to praise her again, but still concluded obtusely that we should applaud the way she recognized her limitations. Later, however, he delighted Woolf with his favourable review of her book in the *Sunday Times*.

Twice Woolf gives the partial quotation in *Women & Fiction*, mocking the reviewer who knew the limitations of women writers but did not specify them. Were they allowed to describe shops, for example? (The reviewer is compared with the bishop who, in an anecdote referred to a number of times, was certain no woman could equal Shakespeare and no cat go to heaven.) The narrator finally comes back to the last scene of Chloe's novel. It represented something about the immensity of the soul, but had little to do with sex. Thus we come back to the start of the speaker's thoughts about women and modern fiction, and at this point, which corresponds to the end of chapter 5 in *A Room of One's Own*, the Monks House manuscript also ends.

The discrepancies in chapter division between *Women & Fiction* and *A Room of One's Own* remain in the second part of the Fitzwilliam manuscript. Virginia Woolf began the chapter, which she headed "Chapter 4. Cont." on 22 March 1929, continuing for ten leaves a chapter whose beginning is not indicated in the surviving manuscripts. Further evidence that part of the draft of *Women & Fiction* is missing appears with the reference several pages later to the novelist Mary Carmichael. Where Chloe the novelist turned into Mary is now unknown. How much material has been lost is uncertain; it may be only five to ten pages. The second part of the Fitzwilliam manuscript begins again with the words that had been used to describe the "highly developed", the "infinitely intricate" capacities of Olivia, though they are not the exact words used in the Monks House manuscript (pp. 117, 125). The narrator is vexed that she has slipped into praising her own sex, especially when there is yet no way of measuring their ability. All she can do is note the dependence of great men upon women. The account of this is close to that in *A Room of One's Own*, but it was not part of the original draft in the Monks House manuscript. The rooms of these women are then emphasized, and here one can watch the central symbol of the book emerging. The valuable differences of the sexes are stressed, and, in a remark later cut, the speaker says that nothing would please her more than if some explorer discovered yet another sex somewhere. Next, the different rooms and lives of women that Mary Carmichael will have to represent are described, as in the Monks House manuscript. But instead of a discussion of whether she is allowed to describe shopping, a brief description of a shop is given. Returning to Carmichael's untitled novel, the speaker comments on her abilities and discusses the challenge of the last scene at greater length than in the Monks House draft. A racecourse metaphor is repeated and extended to include the men of Cambridge and the authors of books and reviews (MacCarthy's phrase echoes again) who advise and warn from the sidelines. Woolf's narrator places a bet and urges the novelist to ignore the men and think only of the jump itself, which she successfully does. The chapter ends, as in *A Room of One's Own*, with the prediction that in a hundred years Mary Carmichael will be a poet.

It took Virginia Woolf four days to write the continued fourth chapter. On 26 March, five months to the day after giving her paper at Girton, she began the fifth chapter of *Women & Fiction*. In just one week she drafted both it and the concluding chapter - a total of thirty-four manuscript pages. The structure of chapter 5, which becomes approximately the first half of chapter 6 of *A Room of One's Own*, is generally similar to that of the book, though much more disjointed and tentative. The chapter opens with the narrator observing a London street scene. She begins to sketch a theory of androgynous states of mind, and then considers masculine self-consciousness in the work of several unandrogynous modern writers. At the end of the chapter the narrator returns to the description of creative states of mind. The writing of the fifth chapter of *Women & Fiction* was far from being straightforward, however. Much of its interest lies in watching Woolf's attempts to create a scene that will lead her to reflections on the unity of mind required for good writing. The culminating scene of *A Room of One's Own* in which a couple get into a taxi begins in *Women & Fiction* with a girl in patent-leather shoes whom a taxi-driver chooses to pick up instead of a man. Reworking the scene, trying to describe first the sexual current that sweeps all along the street and then the relief experienced at seeing the girl greet a young man, Woolf's narrator tries to explain what she means by unity of mind. Again there are allusions to Tennyson, Rossetti, and Shakespeare.

Three more or less distinct drafts of a plan for the soul can be traced in the writing of this chapter as the narrator tries to write the first sentence of her paper on women and fiction. Only the last version mentions Coleridge and androgyny. In the first version (pp. 142–5), the lack of repression felt by the speaker as she sees a young woman and man together leads to the realization that she can think back through her mothers or her fathers. She can make herself an inheritor of her civilization or an alien in it. Instead of letting her consciousness flow undivided, she can for some special purpose accentuate the dominant sexual half of her brain, as the narrator had been doing in thinking back only through her mothers. A brief fantasy intervenes of some primeval woman who regrets her destiny of having to people the jungle instead of being free to swing through the trees. Towards the end of the first version the sexual imagery of a marriage is used to describe the creative process as one in which the author draws the curtain and sinks into oblivion. While the male and female halves of his brain mate, he may look at stars, pull the petals from a rose, or watch swans. (The pronouns are Woolf's.) The imagery recurs again at the end of the fifth chapter, as it does just before the conclusion in *A Room of One's Own*.

The street scene of a young couple meeting also begins the second draft plan of the soul's male and female powers (pp. 146–50). The narrator turns to books by living authors, identified as Messrs A, B, C, and D, to try out her theories on men's writing. She begins by noting with some irony that despite all their advantages, men write books that lack the power of suggestion. A self-centred male's novel is mentioned, then the work of Kipling and Galsworthy, before Woolf begins the section again (pp. 151ff.), this time referring to Coleridge and the androgynous mind of Shakespeare. After the suffrage campaign is identified as the cause of modern sexual self-consciousness, the text takes up again the ego-phallic novel of an author identified as Mr A. The reworked account is essentially that of *A Room of One's Own*, including allusions once more to Victorian poetry; the characters of the novel are not named, however, the speaker's confession of boredom is more defensive. In his review of *A Room of One's Own*, MacCarthy thought the novelist was a gifted contemporary and clearly recognizable under his initial. Woolf, writing to express her pleasure at the review, asked if he meant D. H. Lawrence, and added, "He was not in my upper mind; but no doubt was in the lower" (*Letters*, IV, 130). Just who, if anyone, might have been in her upper mind she does not say. (Lawrence's *Lady Chatterley's Lover* had been privately printed in Italy in 1928, and at the end of the year his old friend S. S. Koteliansky told Woolf, who had probably not read the novel, that it was disgusting (*Diary*, III, 217).)

After referring to the critic Mr B, whoever he may be, the narrator of *Women & Fiction* moves on to Mr C, who turns out to be Churchill. She feels crushed by the furniture of his rhetoric - the size of the sentences, the weight of the metaphors. Victorian preachers were less vociferous. Works by Galsworthy and Kipling are criticized next, and in more detail than in *A Room of One's Own*. Their purely masculine values bore her horribly and thoughts of Mussolini's Italy follow. A list of androgynous and masculine writers, to be discussed in *A Room of One's Own*, is jotted down on the back of a manuscript page at this point. Then Woolf suggests again that the cause of all this literary cock-a-doodling lies in the work of reformers like the founder of Girton. (In *A Room of One's Own* she blames no individuals.) This leads once more to the narrator's blank page headed "Women & Fiction", and for a dozen lines she tries to formulate what will eventually become the first sentence of the paper - that it is fatal for writers to think of their own sex. Once more she tries to imagine the violence as well as the calm, unself-conscious freedom of Shakespeare's state of mind while creating a scene in *Antony and Cleopatra* or writing a line like "Daffodils that come before the swallow dares". The marriage-night metaphor is used again to conclude the chapter.

The last chapter of *Women & Fiction*, entitled simply "Conclusion", corresponds to what follows the dropping of the persona in chapter six of *A Room of One's Own*. The manuscript's conclusion is briefer than that in the book, however. Woolf had jotted down notes for her conclusion in a reading notebook (see appendix 2), used them at the start of her chapter, then cancelled them. Anticipated objections to her insistence on money and a room of one's own (the phrase first appears in the manuscript here) start with the material one rather than the comparative merit of the sexes, as in the book. The same quotation from Quiller-Couch is invoked as a reply to anticipated criticisms. Woolf began a reference to Florence Nightingale, crossed it out, and then expanded it in the book. Justifying the necessity of women's books leads to the speaker's admittedly selfish complaint about the monotony of her modern reading and the need for books to influence each other.

The important discussion of what Woolf's narrator means by reality and unreality follows from the attempt to justify the existence of good books, and it differs significantly from *A Room of One's Own*. In *Women & Fiction* the narrator attempts twice to justify its indefinable intuitive basis before giving up and just illustrating what she means. As in *A Room of One's Own*, Woolf connects the experience of reality with the mystical moments that the speaker has experienced at Cambridge and in London. Masterpieces express reality too, and the list in the manuscript includes *Lycidas* and *War and Peace*, which is cancelled. Examples of the effects of unreality are more extended in *Women & Fiction*; they include muffling, swaddling, drugging, numbing, and being knocked senseless or into torpor. There is no escaping unreality. Civilization requires it but one can fight with pen, brush, piano, or talk. We are close here to Bernard's final efforts in *The Waves*. Nowhere else in Woolf's writing, except perhaps in the late "A Sketch of the Past", does she attempt to describe so explicitly the mystical enmity of unreality that she associated with what she called her madness.

There are no perorations in *Women & Fiction*, no disagreeable quotations from men, no references to liking women and wondering again if a magistrate is in the cupboard. The women of the audience are called upon to get to work - not to write fashionable books, but to conspire, anonymously perhaps, to bring Shakespeare's sister back to life. This they can do if they are free to regard human beings in themselves, to look past Milton's bogey at reality. Such an effort, the speaker maintains, "is worthwhile". These are the last words of both *Women & Fiction* and *A Room of One's Own*.

The Revision of *A Room of One's Own*

Virginia Woolf finished *Women & Fiction* in London on the 2 April 1929. The next day she went to Monks House to arrange for a new room of her own - two rooms in fact, a bedroom opening into the garden with a sitting or work room above - to be added onto Monks House. Ten days later she complained to her diary that *Women & Fiction* had been written too quickly and now she was toiling over revisions. But she thought it had conviction and predicted "some sale" for this book of "half talk half soliloquy" (*Diary*, III, 221). After a month of revising the manuscript as she typed it up, Woolf announced, again to her diary, that the final version was finished, but she was now uncertain whether it was a brilliant essay or a mass of opinions "boiled down into a kind of jelly, which I have stained red as far as I can" (*Diary*, III, 223). Leonard was to read it after tea. But still the process of revising continued.

The revisions of *A Room of One's Own* were apparently made while Woolf was trying once again to finish "Phases of Fiction". (In the reading notebook that contains the page of notes for the conclusion of *Women & Fiction* Woolf actually started a page on "Phases of Fiction" under the heading "Women & Fiction" then struck it out.) She was trying to complete the rewriting of this other book on fiction even as it was being serialized in America. In her letters she was calling it her dullest and most hated book. At one point in its writing Woolf jotted down the final title for *A Room of One's Own* and a new opening that emphasized the speaker's train of thought. (See appendix 1.)

Woolf was dismayed when Harcourt Brace suggested in the middle of May that "Phases of Fiction" be published in the autumn of 1929 and *Women & Fiction*, as it was still being called, kept over until the following spring (*Diary*, III, 227). On 16 May, however, Leonard wrote firmly to Donald Brace in an unpublished letter that his wife preferred to postpone "Phases of Fiction" until the next year and bring out *Women & Fiction* under a different title in the autumn of 1929. This is the first mention of a change in title.

In the event, "Phases of Fiction" was never published as a book. Woolf felt she had been wrongly pressured by her husband and Rylands into writing it for the Hogarth Press. Despite the title, "Phases of Fiction" is far less historical than *A Room of One's Own*. Forster's aspects had been elements of the novel, but Woolf's phases were kinds of novelists classified as truth-tellers, romantics, character-mongers, comedians, psychologists, satirists, fantastics, and finally poets. Some women writers are discussed - Radcliffe, Austen, Eliot, Emily Brontë - but few of the novelists considered really fit into their categories. Woolf's phases also fail to meet her objections to Forster's *Aspects of the Novel*, for there is little analysis of the art of fiction in them. Forster had argued in the introduction to his Cambridge lectures that the novel was a mirror unaffected by such things as the women's movement because subject matter had nothing to do with the mirror's acquiring a new coating of sensitiveness. He amusingly imagined all the novelists writing their novels together timelessly in the Reading Room of the British Museum. In the book that Woolf developed from her Cambridge lectures, however, women are depicted as writing their novels in parlours or bed-sitting rooms. The British Museum is where the speaker goes to find out why women are poor and why men are angry. *A Room of One's Own* is, in its way, a more direct and effective response to *Aspects of the Novel* than "Phases of Fiction" was.

Sometime after Leonard Woolf wrote to put off the publication of "Phases of Fiction" as a book, Virginia sent Harcourt Brace the typescript entitled *A Room of One's Own* now in the Monks House Papers at Sussex. Just how hard she had toiled to revise *Women & Fiction* into *A Room of One's Own* can be shown through a brief chapter by chapter comparison of the typescript with the manuscripts of *Women & Fiction* and also with the published book. Much of the typescript is identical with this final version, but there are also numerous, significant holograph additions and cancellations. Some of the chapter divisions of the typescript are still tentative, and a few pages present overlapping passages. The most interesting variants in the typescript have been included in appendix 3. They show that even at the typescript stage, *A Room of One's Own* was still in the process of composition.

The most obvious difference between the manuscript and the typescript is, of course, the new title's emphasis on the work's principal symbol. In chapter 1, still undesignated as such, Woolf incorporates into her typescript the new opening and reworks the speaker's novelistic solution to the problems of lecturing on women and fiction. The frame story of the three days (revised to two in the book) that preceded the Cambridge paper is established, the image of the pedlar dropped, and some of the Cambridge names are disguised, including Jane Harrison's which is reduced to her initials. Footnotes are added to document the history of women's colleges. One interesting addition is the passage on how child-raising makes it impossible for women like Mary Seton's mother to acquire the kinds of fortunes men have amassed or inherited. The revised first chapter ends with a recapitulation of the day's incidents.

In revising the second chapter of *Women & Fiction*, Virginia Woolf introduced a comparison of research with the aloe that flowers once in a hundred years, and this harkens back to a similar comparison of the plant with a don's life in her sketch "A Society". The descriptions of the kind of men who attend to women and of the student working next to the narrator have not been muted in her revisions. Footnotes are added again for sources on men's opinions of women, and some of the literary allusions are dropped, as is the description of the cooking in the restaurant where the speaker has lunch. Also deleted is the digression on male bores. But Woolf retained the Asian tribe of women whose achievements rivalled those of Shakespeare and Einstein (p. 181). She cut it only when revising the typescript for the book. In the typescript Mary Beton is given now as the aunt's name that is also the speaker's. Another addition to the manuscript involves Desmond MacCarthy again. About a month before she gave her Cambridge papers, Woolf listened to MacCarthy expressing his irritation at Rebecca West's saying that men were snobs. She retorted by criticizing his condescension in *Life and Letters* about the limitations of women novelists (*Diary*, III, 195). How the later remark was worked into *Women & Fiction* has been discussed, but now in her revisions Woolf took up the earlier comment, included a description of West as "arrant feminist", and then ascribed it all to "Z, most humane, most modest of men" (*Room*, p. 53). The remark is introduced again at the revised opening of chapter 4. Woolf also revised the account of male acquisitiveness, adding an observation on how large groups of people are driven by instincts beyond their control. (This, incidentally, was one of the central tenets of Leonard Woolf's political theory.) At the end of the typescript's second chapter Virginia Woolf resolves the chaos and terror of the London machine into a fiery fabric with flashing eyes; in the book it is defined further as a hot-breathed tawny monster.

Chapter 3 of the typescript is quite close to the final version of *A Room of One's Own*. The details of Mary Arden's life are worked into Judith Shakespeare's. A comparison of the artist to a jar-carrier is omitted, the portrait of Oscar Browning developed more astringently, an allusion to Lady Bessborough brought into the text from the back of a page, and a collection of opinions on male superiority called cock-a-doodle-dum is imagined. The beginning of chapter 4, which is missing from *Women & Fiction*, starts in the middle of a page, rather than at the head of it, as the second chapter had. Woolf's continuing uncertainty about chapter divisions reappears at the end of the next chapter.

Her revised discussions of women writers in chapter 4 are more detailed, especially in the analysis of *Jane Eyre*. Additional references to other writers appear. An allusion to Mary Wollstonecraft is dropped, but the significance of Dorothy Osborne's letters is developed. There is no indication in the typescript of the gap which is to be found in the Fitzwilliam manuscript at the point where nineteenth-century women and fiction begin to be considered. The prevalence of masculine values is emphasized, and then MacCarthy on the limitations of female novelists is brought in and criticized together with another quotation, from T. S. Eliot's *New Criterion*, in which the reviewer of Dorothy Wellesley's *Matrix* (in the Hogarth Living Poets series) asserts that a metaphysical obsession is particularly dangerous in a woman. From this Woolf turns to the discussion of men's and women's sentences, giving holograph examples of both in the typescript (pp. 181–2). The woman's sentence, taken from *Pride and Prejudice*, was deleted from the final version of *A Room of One's Own*. At the end of the chapter Woolf reworked in her own hand the remarks on the future form of women's writing (pp. 182–3).

That Virginia Woolf had not yet sorted out the organization of the book in her typescript is apparent from the brevity of chapter 5 and the confusion over the numbering of chapter 6. The fifth chapter is only five pages long. It begins with the various kinds of books which modern women write (she later included Vernon Lee on aesthetics) then suddenly veers into a unique fantasy on Florence Nightingale that exists only in the typescript. There is nothing like it in *Women & Fiction*. In her best *Orlando* manner, Woolf imagines a shell from the Crimean War crashing through the drawing room door of Nightingale's house; out steps the lady with a lamp, which marks the end of women's servitude. Quotations from Nightingale's *Cassandra* follow. Harriet Martineau is mentioned, and then Woolf brings in the anecdote from the lives of Davies and Smith that she had used in *Women & Fiction* when beginning to discuss modern women's books (pp. 110–11). There the chapter ends.

Two chapters 6 are to be found in the typescript of *A Room of One's Own*. In the first Woolf's speaker continues, as in the fifth chapter of the final version, her discussion of living writers by analyzing Mary

Carmichael's novel. Now called "Life's Adventure", the novel also has named characters and a style that fears sentimentality and breaks the sequence like a switchback railway (instead of the earlier tossing boat). The satire of realistic fiction in the manuscript is removed, and the reaction to Chloe's liking Olivia changed. Woolf also adds to the discussion of women's friendship in fiction a reference to Meredith's *Diana of the Crossways*. But no indication is to be found in the typescript of the discontinuity between the end of the Monks House and the beginning of the second part of the Fitzwilliam manuscripts. There is, as well, considerable evidence of Woolf's rewriting in the typescript. The speaker now distinguishes between the naturalist and contemplative species of novelist. She criticizes the multiplication of books on Napoleon, Keats, and Milton, while the lives of obscure women go unrecorded. Woolf also added a passage about the spot in the back of the head that only the opposite sex can describe. References to Thackeray and Flaubert are reworked and new allusions made to Juvenal and Strindberg.

The second chapter 6 of the typescript corresponds to the sixth chapter in the book, yet the substantial differences between them indicate the degree to which Woolf would revise her typescript again for the final printed version of *A Room of One's Own*. The crucial scene of the young couple getting into a taxi is more succinctly described in the typescript, and to it Woolf added a remark about the union of men and women making for the greatest happiness. She eliminates the passage on the primeval woman and confines the marriage-night metaphor of creation to the end of the chapter. Her theory about the mind's unity becomes the familiar one of *A Room of One's Own*, except for the retention of the botanical term "gunandros" as a companion for "androgynous" (p. 186). The remainder of the chapter's first part, where the theory of androgyny is tested on some modern men's books, is quite different in detail from both the manuscript and the published book. Mr A, for example is referred to as a descendant of Oscar Browning, and his female characters are described not only as boneless but also as "jelly fish adapted to his lust" (p. 186). Churchill is reduced to his initial; the ridicule of his rhetoric now likens his metaphors to stuffed Wagnerian ravens and his ideas to poor little things rigged up in rouge and brocade - all of which she then drops again from the book. Another passage follows in the typescript describing a banquet at which the narrator wanted to shout the praises of unknown women in response to the Prince of Wales's extolling of fishermen. Woolf revised the more extended criticism of Galsworthy's Forsyte books in the typescript before finally cutting it from her book. She retouches the description of Fascist Italy and works into the text from the margin the list of androgynous and unandrogynous writers, to which a comment on Shelley's sexlessness is added. Also revised before being cut is a description of the violent state of mind that Shakespeare's composition of *Antony and Cleopatra* must have involved.

A line in the typescript separates these discussions from the conclusions that Virginia Woolf now brought in from the last chapter of *Women & Fiction*. Only later in revising the typescript for the book did she accomplish the transition by abandoning her narrative persona. The conclusions of the typescript nevertheless differ significantly from those of the manuscript. Woolf crossed out a beginning that defended the symbolism of money and rooms by citing Quiller-Couch on the material conditions required for the writing of poetry. In her second attempt she moved closer to the book by recapping the episodes of the previous few days. She added a scornful criticism of the comparative merits of the sexes before coming to the Quiller-Couch quotation again, and after it made an allusion to Florence Nightingale. In defending the value of good books, she altered the description of reality, which she refuses to define; she gives instead more examples of it but deletes the illustrations of unreality in *Women & Fiction*.

In the typescript Woolf introduces the peroration called for by the conventions of male eloquence, and then evades it by urging her audience simply to think of things in themselves. She does not stop with an emphasis on ends, the means to which are £500 and a room of one's own, but goes on to remark in the typescript that current writing calls for something very unpleasant when a woman addresses women. Another joking allusion is made to the magistrate of *The Well of Loneliness* trial who may be yet lurking in a cupboard. And then one more ironic quotation, which Woolf had used before in her writing, is given about how women will cease to be necessary when children cease to be wanted. The raising of these topics at the end of *A Room of One's Own* makes its criticism of the patriarchy's sexual standards stronger than that in *Women & Fiction*. Indeed there is little in the manuscripts to suggest that Woolf is softening or censoring her text to make it more acceptable to male readers, as is sometimes claimed about her revisions. At last, after urging young women on to the next stage in their sex's career, Woolf returns once more to fiction for the final invoking of Shakespeare's sister.

During the last two weeks of June 1929, Woolf worked at correcting what must have been the typescript of "that much corrected book, Women & Fiction" (*Diary*, III, 237). It is odd that she should revert to its original title on the same day - 30 June - that she signed the contract for *A Room of One's Own* with Harcourt Brace (*Letters*, IV, 71). Two days later Woolf began the first draft of *The Waves*.

The proofs for *A Room of One's Own*, which allowed more opportunity for change, were corrected in July and August. They do not appear to have survived, but Woolf's correspondence indicates that she had to send Harcourt Brace revised proofs containing additional alterations in the first two chapters or so (*Letters*, IV, 76). On 19 August, more than four months after finishing her manuscript, she opened her diary to record "the blessed fact that for good or bad I have just set the last correction to Women & Fiction, or a Room of One's Own. I shall never read it again I suppose. Good or bad? Has an uneasy life in it I think: you feel the creature arching its back & galloping on, though as usual much is watery & flimsy & pitched in too high a voice" (*Diary*, III, 241–2). The next day she expressed her delight with Vanessa Bell's cover which showed a view though a curtained arch or window of a room with a clock on the mantle. The clock's hands form a "V", and Woolf thought that would cause a stir (*Letters*, IV, 81). The published dust-jacket of the Hogarth Press first edition also has a blurb describing *A Room of One's Own*. From what is known about the operations of the Hogarth Press, it is reasonable to assume that this description of the book has authorial status. Woolf would continue to comment publicly and privately on the book and its reception, but the summary on the dust-jacket can be given here as, in a sense, the last act of the book's composition. Its opening comment's generic paradox, the description of the author as an outsider, the emphasis on the relation of the sexes and hopeful forecast of a freer future for women are all completely characteristic of Woolf's writing and thought.

> This essay, which is largely fictitious, is based upon the visit of an outsider to a university and expresses the thoughts suggested by a comparison between the different standards of luxury at a man's college and at a woman's. This leads to a sketch of women's circumstances in the past, and the effect of those circumstances upon their writing. The conditions that are favourable to imaginative work are discussed, including the right relation of the sexes. Finally an attempt is made to outline the present state of affairs and to forecast what effect comparative freedom and independence will have upon women's artistic work in the future.

Note on Sources

The edition of *A Room of One's Own* used here is the first English one published by the Hogarth Press on 21 October 1929. B. J. Kirkpatrick's *A Bibliography of Virginia Woolf*, 3rd edition (Oxford, 1980) is the indispensable source for the history of Virginia Woolf's writings. References to the equally indispensable editions of Woolf's letters and diaries are to *The Letters of Virginia Woolf*, edited by Nigel Nicolson and Joanne Trautmann, 6 volumes (London, 1975–80) and *The Diary of Virginia Woolf*, edited by Anne Olivier Bell and Andrew McNeillie, 5 volumes (London, 1977–84). Also essential are the *Letters of Leonard Woolf*, edited by Frederic Spotts (New York, 1989) and Brenda R. Silver's *Virginia Woolf's Reading Notebooks* (Princeton, New Jersey, 1983).

A Newnham Anthology (Cambridge, 1979) was edited by Ann Phillips. Leonard Woolf's diaries are in the Monks House Papers at the University of Sussex. George Rylands's recollections have been included in *Recollections of Virginia Woolf*, edited by Joan Russell Noble (London, 1972). ODTAA is defined in Eric Patridge's *A Dictionary of Slang and Unconventional English*, 8th edition (New York, 1984). Woolf's sketch of "A Society" is reprinted in *The Complete Shorter Fiction of Virginia Woolf*, 2nd edition, edited by Susan Dick (London, 1989). Kathleen Raine's review of Bradbrook's history appeared in the *Daily Telegraph*, 30 January 1969; her second volume of autobiography is entitled *The Land Unknown* (London, 1975). M. C. Bradbrook's history is *"That Infidel Place": A Short History of Girton College, 1869–1969* (London, 1969). Q. D. Leavis's attack on *Three Guineas* appeared in *Scrutiny*, VII (September 1938), 203–14. Gwendolen Freeman's *Alma Mater: Memories of Girton College, 1926–29* was published by Girton College in 1990. Desmond MacCarthy's remarks on Woolf occur in the August, 1928 and December, 1929 issues of *Life and Letters*; his *Sunday Times* review, which Woolf clipped for her *Three Guineas* scrapbook, appeared on 26 January 1930.

Explanation of the Transcription

In this transcription the Monks House manuscript leaves have been inserted between the third and fourth chapters of the Fitzwilliam manuscript. The manuscripts have then been repaginated sequentially at the bottom of each page. (The pencilled page numbers in the Fitzwilliam manuscript were added by someone other than Virginia Woolf; the Monks House manuscript is unnumbered.) Part titles before each chapter indicate the manuscript that is being transcribed in the chapter. Italicized running heads have also been supplied for the manuscript.

The general form of the transcription here is a simplified version of that used in the editions of holograph drafts for *The Waves*, edited by J. W. Graham, and *To the Lighthouse*, edited by Susan Dick, (University of Toronto Press, 1976, 1982). Virginia Woolf's spelling and punctuation, or the lack thereof (she regularly omits apostrophes), are reproduced as they are in the manuscripts. The line arrangement, paragraphing, and page divisions are also followed. When too long for the width of the page, the lines are doubled back and indented, as in the printing of poetry.

Woolf's holograph insertions above, below or within lines are represented by being enclosed in angle brackets. The insertions usually appear after cancellations that they replace, unless the sense is made clearer by putting them before the cancellations. Marginalia clearly marked for inclusion in the main text have also been inserted this way. Otherwise they are usually represented approximately where they occur in the manuscripts, and in smaller print than the main text. It has not been possible, however, to follow the line breaks in the marginalia very closely. Insertions within insertions have been transcribed simply as insertions. Substantial insertions or comments on the backs of the manuscript pages are given as separate pages with a bracketed page number and verso indication above the regular page number. Brief verso passages have been included in the margin of the page they face and identified in the notes. Passages written in pencil have also been identified in the notes.

Holograph cancellations are represented by struck-through characters. Vertical or oblique slashes cancelling entire passages have also been represented by struck-through characters. Cancelled fragments of words have not been reproduced unless they contribute to the sense of a passage. Various blots, lines, and squiggles have also been omitted. Cancellations within cancellations have been transcribed simply as cancellations.

Doubtful readings in the transcript have been followed with a question mark and enclosed in square brackets. A blank in square brackets marks an illegible word or phrase; a cancellation line in brackets indicates an illegible cancellation. The occasional square brackets used by Virginia Woolf in her manuscript have been replaced by braces (wavy brackets).

". . . The handwriting has become in its distraction indecipherable" says the narrator of *A Room of One's Own* as she tries to make out from her notes whether the age of puberty in the South Seas is nine or ninety. This comment, expanded from the manuscript, may reflect the author's difficulty as she revised her manuscript by typing it out. It certainly describes her editor's. Much of the handwriting in the Fitzwilliam and Monks House manuscripts is difficult to decipher, and some of it impossible, as the facsimiles show. The transcription of many words and phrases, cancellations and insertions depend on their context and must remain tentative.

Explanation of the Transcription

Summary of Signs in the Transcription

<example>	=	insertion
~~example~~	=	cancellation
[example?]	=	uncertain reading
[~~example~~?]	=	uncertain reading of a cancellation
[ ]	=	illegible
[——]	=	illegible cancellation
{example}	=	enclosed in square brackets by Woolf
[page number *verso*]	=	the back of the previous page

***Collation of* A Room of One's Own *and* Women & Fiction**

The proliferation of editions of *A Room of One's Own* makes it impractical to collate them with the pages of *Women & Fiction*, but the following table indicates approximately where the chapters of the book may be found in the manuscripts.

A Room of One's Own	*Women & Fiction*
Chapter I	Chapter I, 3–34
Chapter II	Chapter II, 37–62
Chapter III	Chapter III, 65–92
Chapter IV	Chapter III, 92–110
Chapter V	Chapter III, IV Cont., 110–134
Chapter VI	Chapter V, Conclusion, 137–174

The Fitzwilliam Manuscript

Women & Fiction

Women & Fiction ×

× Based on a paper read to the Arts Society at Newnham & the Odtaa at Girton, October 1928. The paper proved too long to be read in full; & the parts then omitted have been restored, with some alterations

The words hang like a collar round my neck. It is obviously that to write of women & fiction ~~only~~ would require many many volumes; one can see even from a distance that the subject is dangerous. From bars ~~should be between~~ lies [illegible] ~~[illegible]~~ is ~~bitter~~ dangerous. Neither man nor woman has ever written ten words on the subject without throwing signs of ~~some~~ ~~[illegible]~~ frozen in their veins. ~~It~~ ~~[illegible]~~ to them, if we mitigate the ferocity of the first word "women" by adding "& fiction" we ~~are~~ landed in the dismal swamp of the everlasting maze ~~[illegible]~~ literary criticism. One will have to say something about the present & the past & the future of a form of art which lends itself less than any other to examination owing to its vast size, its immense ~~[illegible]~~ ~~[illegible]~~ fertility, its incredible ~~[illegible]~~ admixture of splendour & ~~[illegible]~~ mains.

I propose to slip the collar from my neck ~~at~~ first quickly by ~~taking~~ ~~that~~ ~~thought~~ saying that I offer you ~ nothing, disclaim ~~any~~ all infallibility. I propose to ~~order of literary, notes~~ ~~or comments~~. What I offer is simply raw material for you to fashion ~~[illegible]~~ pedlar, the sort of pedlar who went in the Middle Ages from village to village with ~~[illegible]~~ laces & coloured kerchiefs; who ~~[illegible]~~ at the cottage door, ~~[illegible]~~

Women & Fiction [x]

[x] Based on a paper read to the Arts Society at Newnham
& the Odtaa at Girton, October 1928. The
paper proved too long to be read in full; & the
parts then omitted have been restored, with some
alterations.

The words hang like a collar round my neck. It is
not only that to write of women & <of> fiction ~~only~~ would
require many many volumes; one can see, even from a
distance, that the subject is dangerous. Iron bars
~~should lie between us~~. Sex ~~reaches out its~~ is
~~bites~~. ~~dangerous~~. <bite> Neither man nor woman
has ever written ten words on the subject
without showing signs of ~~some~~ ~~some~~ frozen in their
veins. ~~If I try to~~ Then, if one mitigate the ferocity
of the first word "women" by adding "& fiction"
one is landed in the dismal swamp of <the everlasting maze>
~~words of~~ literary criticism: one will have to
say something about the present & the past & the future
of a form of art which lends itself less than any other
to examination owing to its vast size, its immense
~~vitality, its~~ fertility, its incredible ~~idiocy & its~~
admixture of splendour & ~~poverty~~ misery.

I propose to slip the collar from my neck
~~in~~ quite openly by ~~stating~~ ~~that though~~ saying that
I hereby disclaim ~~any~~ all <pretence of> infallibility. I offer you a
~~series of scenes, of notes, of comments~~ I propose to
What I offer is simply raw material for you to
<I am not a lecturer - a professor. I am a writer a> strolling
~~mendicant~~ peddlar, the sort of person who
went in the middle ages from village to village
selling [reels of?] laces & coloured [ballads?]; who
gossiped with the women at the cottage doors, & was

& was welcome for his ~~news~~, <gossip>, even ~~if it was only hearsay & half~~
when it was false, rather than for his wares.

make what you will of,

what I offer is <a hidden basket of odds & ends for you to buy, or reject, to use or to> raw material for ~~your inspection~~ you to
~~use or rejection.~~ And I want to use all the
liberties of fiction, drawing scenes, telling stories, making up dialogues,
because I believe that when ~~a question is~~
one is talking about a subject that is in dispute
~~the one must~~ <it is a help to> have the whole scene before one;
~~to draw conclusions from,~~ ~~& not only~~
~~what the speaker~~ to be able to visualise the
~~person's~~ circumstances, & surroundings <of the person who is giving his opinion> so as
to get ~~at for oneself~~ ~~at~~ the ~~reason that~~
~~Emotional~~ supplement what he is saying <wh. is sure to be only partly true, with what he is not saying, & may indeed scarcely [suspect?].>
~~with~~ from other sources.

by observing what is going on round him.

Here then ~~am~~ was I (Mary Beaton, Mary Seaton,
Mary Carmichael or anybody else - that is not
a matter of any importance) sitting on the
banks of the Cam, a week or two ago, in fine October
weather lost in thought. That collar, I have spoken of,
women & fiction, the need of coming to some conclusion,
on a subject that indeed admits of none, bent my head to
the ground. To the right & left coloured bushes of some
sort like fires on the tail of ones eye, burnt
splendidly. The beautiful willows wept, in perpetual
lamentation, ~~for some~~ their hair about their shoulders.
The Cam reflected what it chose of sky &
bridge & burning tree; ~~while~~ & when the undergraduate
had oared his ~~cano~~ boat through the reflection
they closed again as if he had never been.
There one might have sat the clock round,
~~But~~ Thought - to call it by a prouder name than it
deserved - had let its line <[down?]> into the stream; &

of golden & yellow trees

~~& there it might have~~ where it swayed hither & thither
among the reflections, letting the water lift it, & sink it
till - lo & behold! there was a bite: ~~I drew to the~~
~~surface~~ <perhaps I had caught> a conclusion. Laid on the grass
it looked
small, insignificant, the sort of fish a good fisherman puts
back so that it may grow fat - worth catching: but I
offer it to you, because if I do not ~~give it to you now~~
keep it till the end of the ~~evening~~ paper, where it rightly
belongs, you will be so dazed with boredom that
you will not notice that it is ~~a conclusion: a little~~
a fish at all - a conclusion; ~~Money & rooms~~ to
them~~selves: that is~~ "~~What is~~ <It is> absolutely ~~essential then~~,
~~Rooms~~ necessary that they should have money, & a room to
Money - themselves" I said aloud, beginning under the stress of this
a room to vast, this epoch making claim to walk
themselves - rapidly across the lawn in the direction
of some gate.

with truly
again all
coloured
all life

absurd
though it
sounds

put ~~it~~ back in~~to~~ the water & ~~let it swim & splash among~~ the
~~other contents of the mind~~ swimming & floating, diving
among the contents of the brain it ~~appeared~~ seemed <wonderful
&> strange
beautiful; ~~it made~~ everything ~~seemed to~~ rocked & swayed; &
life seemed filled of excitement & importance - ~~In such~~
~~moods~~ with such <the> ~~vast~~ <thrown into such by little
fish> commotion taking place, in the
waters of the mind it is impossible to sit still; &
Do we not all instinctively jump to our feet &
stride hastily in the first direction that seems to ~~open~~
offer an open field? It was thus that I found myself
walking with extreme rapidity across a grass plot:
<Up> ~~There sprang~~ from the earth, <sprung> a man's figure. ~~His~~
~~arms~~
his arms were wide open; <~~He wore a semi~~ -evening dress;~~ white~~
shirt front & ~~swallow~~ tail coat,> ~~& his face expressed more~~
~~horror more righteous indignation than~~ He was, I
think, a Beadle. ~~That a woman should be walking~~
His face expressed horror & indignation. He waved his arms
~~toward the~~ path. [even?], I felt more the light of
instinct than of reason, a Beadle; & I, again
instinct rather than reason supplied the explanation, was a
woman; & this, was turf; & that was a path; &
& only the Fellows & Scholars of Trinity or Kings or
whichever it was have the right --- <to walk on> ~~In obedience to~~
the turf; ~~not~~ ~~foot~~ the path being good enough for me.

My mind was a blank. What had sent me so audaciously <hastily>
~~trespassing~~ upon <racing across> the turf I could not remember.
The spirit of
peace descended upon me; for <if> the spirit of peace ~~seems to~~
~~brood~~ dwell, ~~in these ancient~~ anywhere it is here, in the
Courts of Cambridge on a fine October morning.
Naturally, strolling ~~past~~ <~~through~~ by> those grey walls <colleges,
those ancient halls> one's thoughts turned
~~to the~~ past; ~~& one began to try Ephemeral do they make us~~
~~view, & the agitation whatever it may have been, was~~
~~smoothed out as completely as a to the past;~~
The present seemed smoothed & flattened; one's mind
indeed, ones body, seemed stilled & encased <enclosed> in a
miraculous
<cabinet> case, through which no sound comes; & one ~~had~~ has
leisure ~~to think back to~~ what~~ever scene of all those~~
~~that~~ settle down upon whatever meditation is most in

a [perhaps?] I had noticed it for the first time

temper with the moment. On this occasion the chance that
there had been placed quite lately ~~perhaps~~ a tablet in the Kings
<Parade>
~~memory~~ stating that Charles Lamb stayed ~~in here~~
~~some rooms in the Kings Parade~~ made my mind
settle upon him. "Saint Charles" said Thackeray
putting a letter ~~to~~ of Lambs to his forehead. <I am giving you
the course of my thoughts> Indeed he
must have been the most lovable of men. His
Essays are superior even to Max Beerbohms, which is
saying a great deal, because of that wild flash of
imagination, that lightning crack of genius in the
middle of them which often leaves them flawed &
imperfect in comparison with his. Lamb then came

but higher, now [perhaps?]

to Cambridge (I ~~am~~ <continued> ~~giving~~ you the course of my
thoughts)
~~some time~~ perhaps a hundred years ago. Certainly he wrote
an essay which may have been written here perhaps about

seeing the manuscript of one of Milton's poems. Was it Lycidas.
Lamb said how it shocked him to ~~see~~ think that ~~one~~
the words could possibly have been different. <from what they>
It seemed a
sort of sacrilege that Milton had dared to alter his own
poetry. This led me to ~~try~~ remember what I could of
Lycidas, ~~with a~~ view to - & to amuse myself with wondering
what could have been bettered, where Milton had thought
twice. It then struck me that the manuscript which Lamb
had looked at, I too could look at. It was only a few
hundred yards away, over there in Trinity Library.
One could follow Lambs footsteps across the court & in at
~~the door~~ up the stairs. Moreover, it occurred to me,
putting this plan into execution, there is also the
manuscript of Thackerays Esmond there.
~~People~~ ~~The~~ Critics often say that this <Esmond> is his best novel.
For my
own part, it is, if I remember written in an affectedly
Eighteenth Century style; which hampers one; only
perhaps the Eighteen Century style came quite naturally
to Thackeray - a fact that one might prove <ascertain> by
looking at the manuscript & seeing whether the
alterations ~~where~~ for the benefit of the style or of the
meaning. <But then one wd. have to decide> what is style & what
is meaning is
furling his | however - here I was at the door which leads into Trinity
wings & | Library. I must actually have opened it, for there issued
instantly like a guardian angel, (save that he had no wings
barring the | & a most studious air) a kind, deprecating, silvery gentleman;
way; <[a man | ~~whose~~ <his> voice was <very> low & [plaintive?] & pliant; ~~but~~
in ?]> | ~~whose~~
~~voice said nevertheless, authoritatively, undeniably.~~
~~Enter not here, without the~~ that ~~only~~ Ladies
& saying in | are only admitted to the library if accompanied by a
Fellow of the College or provided with a note <letter> of
introduction.

~~Its <Its> Not for the likes of me, I said again; & vowed that never should~~
~~would I darken the~~

That Trinity Library has been cursed by a woman is
a matter of complete indifference to Trinity Library.
Venerable & calm, with all its treasures & its memories <books & its manuscripts>
safely locked up
it slept complacently as I beat my retreat; ~~(for who~~
would want to read Lycidas ~~in the presence of a don?)~~
& there for ever, as far as I am concerned, <Trinity Library> it will continue
to sleep. ~~One does not read manuscripts & in the~~
~~presence of a second person.~~

Still an hour remained before luncheon, & what
I ask you who know Cambridge so much better than
I do, could one do? ~~Walk on gravel paths.~~ Sit in
the Backs, walk on the paths? Certainly it was a
lovely autumn morning, & there was no hardship
in spending ~~the time an hour in~~ <strolling about the court> strolling <about> ~~through Trinity &~~
~~Kings~~ <strolling by the river> in ~~the sunshine,~~ dreaming.
<But I passed.> Some service was
a foot, & ~~as I passed the Chapel~~ & the organ was
<com>plaining magnificently as I passed the door of the chapel.
~~Yet one felt that the organ itself was lapped in ease; &~~
Even the sadness <of the> Christianity was more a <sadness at his>
recollection of some sorrow than sorrow itself; even the
organ itself seemed lapped in peace ~~& ease.~~ I had no
wish to go in; even had I the right; ~~for~~ <&> this time it might
have been the verger <[now?]> who would have asked one
~~for the~~ for ones baptismal certificate; or a letter of
introduction from the Dean. But the outside of these

magnificent is often ~~more as~~ more beautiful than the inside.
Moreover, it was enough amusement to watch the congregation
~~running~~ <going> in & out, ~~for~~ like bees at the mouth of a hive,
~~There is a certain oddity about the dignitaries of~~
~~University towns which The mixture of cap & gown~~
~~trousers & boots is always strange. dignitaries,~~ many of
them in cap & gown; some wheeled in bath chairs; others
~~of~~ not past middle age but creased & crushed, into shapes so
singular that one was reminded ~~of some~~ of those giant
crabs who move with difficulty across the sand of an
aquarium. A ~~however~~ It is one use of a University
perhaps to protect & cherish types that have become
obsolete elsewhere. <None of these ~~people~~ could live long in the
Strand> ~~The <An> irreverent desire came <to me> into my~~
~~to me~~
~~to whistle, because it used to be said that there used to be a~~
~~Don somewhere who of an old story <wh. says if you whistle~~
~~certain.> that~~ many ~~Dons~~
~~run if you whistle. There was however, something~~
It is sitting over Greek texts ~~eight~~ for ten hours a day that
bends them thus. They are a race ~~who~~ so unworldly &
remote that ~~it would be~~ they deserve reverence, not ridicule.
And here I checked ~~the~~ the desire which had risen in me
to prove the truth of an old story: if one whistles suddenly
old ~~Mr.~~ Professor ----- ~~always~~ breaks into a ~~canter~~ gallop.
All sorts of stories

All sorts of stories came back into my mind of the singularity
<oddity> of
professors; ~~<their oddity & their> how one used to break into a
gallop if you whistled; &
another for it looked as if there were a sanctuary where
still the~~ but before I had ~~time to~~ summoned up the courage to
whistle - it used to be said that at the sound of a whistle
old Professor ---- <always> broke into a gallop, the venerable &
congregation had gone inside. But the outside of the Chapel
remained. As you know, the <its> high roof <back> ~~of that
Chapel~~ can be
seen, <and> riding ~~like a ship~~ at anchor for miles away across
the fens. Once, presumably, this court, with all its
trim lawns, ~~&~~ <its> the massive buildings, & the Chapel
itself was fen too, where the grasses waved & the ~~swallows~~
swine rootled. Since stone would be rare in these parts, <here>
teams of ~~oxen~~ horses & oxen must have hauled it
~~over~~ on wagons from far counties; & then with infinite
labour, the great grey blocks against which I am now so
comfortably leaning, were poised in order one upon another; &
then the painters brought their glass for the windows; & the
masons were busy for centuries perhaps up on that roof,
with putty & cement, spade & trowel. Every Saturday
somebody must have paid their wages too; an ~~infinite~~
unending stream of gold & silver, even of precious stones
must have flowed perpetually to keep the stones coming
& the masons working, ~~to provide dinners for the men,~~
& ~~then, when the halls & chapels were ready, food for the~~
to level & ditch & drain. It was the age of faith, &
money ~~was not~~ was poured liberally into this thick
Cambridge soil to make a house of learning. Money

flowed in from the King, from the nobles; <[new laws now were in
order?]> later ~~when the~~

like all its

the ~~endowments were magni~~ fellowships, lectureships,
all were splendidly endowed; & when the age of reason
had come, the same flow of gold was directed to this
particular patch of ground, flowing now not from the
coffers of the King & the great nobles, but from merchants, from
city companies, from ~~great~~ men ~~of busin~~ who had made
fortunes from ~~the~~ the manufacture of chemicals, (their wills are
published in the Times)
perhaps, worked to endow thus the science which had
given them prosperity. Hence the laboratories, the
observatories, the splendid equipment of scientific
instruments ~~on~~ which now stand here, where ten
centuries ago, the grasses waved & the swine rootled.
Certainly, as I ~~made my way~~ <strolled round the> court, the
<days of the fen> ~~pavement~~ seemed
solid enough. Men with trays on their heads went busily
from staircase to staircase. ~~A gramophone was~~
~~Kreisler played The Kreutzer Sonata was~~ played on the
~~<The> gramophone.~~ was heard in the windows. It was
impossible not to reflect ---- The reflection was
cut short ~~by the~~ the clock struck. There was ~~not~~ <hardly>
~~really~~ time ~~to walk &~~ find one's way to luncheon. ~~Indeed I~~
~~was a little late.~~

these foundations of gold & silver are solid [land?], the pavement seemed to have vanquished the fen.

~~Nor will you wish <will> me to describe that luncheon;~~
It would be pleasant now to make use of ~~that~~ the
novelists privilege which I claimed ~~for myself~~
& to ~~continue~~ write a page or two of brilliant
dialogue. For surely ~~any~~ that particular party
consisting as it did of Mr. M. Mr. P. Mr. T.
Mr. L. & Mrs. H. must have said

~~<much that was very> many amusing~~ witty, <things> or profound,.
~~Indeed, to be~~
~~frank with you, they may have, but novelists are far too~~
~~apt in~~ But

which one could pass off as a truthful account of what was
actually said. ~~Unfortunately~~
Here one should by rights break into a brilliant passage of
dialogue -
The novelist has a way of making us believe that
luncheon parties are ~~of often very~~ <invariably> memorable
~~occasions~~
~~when things are said for something brilliant~~ <either for what>
was said, or for what was ~~done. As I am not speaking~~
~~now as a novelist, I will confess that the memorable~~
Why the novelist never ~~describes what he must know to be~~
~~praises the food, I cannot imagine. It i~~s
But as a matter of fact ~~they consist largely of eating.~~ <it is only
the> Food
plays <in what one remembers:> an enormous part in them.
Duckling & salmon -
~~that is what one~~ remembers. On this occasion, we began
with ~~some~~ soles ~~disguised in~~ over whom the college
cook had woven <spread> a counterpane of ~~the~~ whitest
cream, save that here & there, like the spots on a
branded milk white doe, <the salamander had> was a stained ~~of~~ brown.
After that came
the partridges. But ~~it is~~ if ~~you~~ this suggests bald
brown birds on a dish <plate> you are mistaken. The partridges
many & [various?]
came with all their retinue of sauces & <also> salads,
each in order; the sharp & the sweet; their potatoes, crisp but not
<succulent;> ~~crisp but not~~ <their sprouts, fine as rosebuds> their
~~sprouts~~; & no sooner had they
been done with, than the silent servingman, ~~in~~
~~another manifestation, perhaps of the~~ the beadle perhaps
in another <a milder> manifestation, ~~brought~~ <set [down?]> in
~~foaming &~~
wreathed in napkins a confection which rose all sugar
from the waves. To call it pudding is ~~too~~ impossible. <was an
insult>
Meanwhile, the wine glasses had been filled;

~~emptied~~, <sipped> & filled again I~~n these circumstances it is~~
~~unnecessary to brilliance is unnecessary; brilliance~~
~~would perhaps looks a little silly; but the human~~
~~spirit for so we may name that Food, wine, comfort, a~~
~~good cigar, make not for brilliance, not for~~
~~<The light not> A spirit which is not <of> brilliance, but <of>~~
~~something which is to~~
~~beside which brilliance is the There was lit a~~
~~subtler,~~ a And thus, by degrees, was lit, half way
down the spine, which is the seat of the soul, not that
hard little ~~hard~~ electric light which we call brilliance
but the <slow> yellow flame ~~of good fellowship~~ which
burn so steady & so slow, of rational conversation. of human
[intercourse?]

wh. flicker
out of the
lips

No need to hurry. No need to be clever. No need to
~~think am I being a success?~~ <be [asking?]> We are all going to
Heaven & Vandyck is of the company. ~~Perhaps you~~
~~the That is the <It is but> [state?] of mind which produces~~
unfortunately
which lends itself to How simple <[answer itself?]> the problem
of life then
became! And its rewards <how sweet> are ~~in~~ our grasp. And all
these divisions & difficulties - ~~being~~ warned off the Turf,
~~failing to see the manuscript, are trumpery little~~
~~much like bubbles. Sweet, sweet is life, & dear the~~
~~faces of our friends. & our friends how compare describe.~~
~~<Vandyck is of the company, &>~~
~~So lighting a good cigar, one sinks among cushions~~
~~by the window, & looks deep deep into the & then~~ --

as from
torches
steeped in
wine

[regularly?],

If by good luck there had been an ash tray on the
arm of the chair, one ~~would not have had to move;~~ if one had
not knocked the ash out of the window, one would not have
seen a manx cat. ~~&~~ The sight of the manx cat drove
<[ ] my mind the> - by some fluke of the ~~mind~~ <[subconscious?] soul> which I leave to Freud to
[~~say,~~?] explain - ~~that~~ to the reflection which I had been
about to make when the clock struck. At once
I had been thinking - it matters not what: but the effort to

We are all
going to
heaven,
together
~~Vandyck~~

that
abrupt that
truncated
animal

retrieve the thought changed the emotional light for me; as a
if a shade had been changed on the electric lamp.
The ~~fun~~ effect of the excellent hock may have been ~~disappe~~
giving out. What element is lacking ~~here,~~ I asked,
as I watched the manx cat crossing those famous lawns
with dignity. And I had to think myself out of the room,
many years back before the war indeed, to another lunch party;
in Cambridge too, ~~But the difference? Was it~~
~~time, or age? Perhaps. But I found myself~~
& to put before my eyes the model of another luncheon [party?]
party, all exactly like this; save for the fact that in one
there was something which the second lacked. And it maybe a
good lack, I thought: nothing can be

something suddenly seemed ~~truncated, abbreviated; in~~
something lacking; wrong; truncated, abbreviated, like
~~that cat.~~
Something seemed lacking; something seemed wrong, <different;>
as I
watched the manx cat pause in the middle of the lawn as
if it too questioned the universe. But what? To
answer that question I had to think myself out of the room
back into the past, before the war indeed, & to set
before my eyes the model of another luncheon party, held
not so very far from this one; but different. Meanwhile
the <actual> conversation went ~~on~~; <forward> ~~nor could I lay~~
~~hold of~~ any <of the [clues?]>
~~single word or gesture~~ against that ~~ghostly~~ background; &
in every way the one seemed ~~the legitimate successor~~
~~of the other, its peer,~~ ~~its~~ to <[succeed?]> ~~continue~~ ~~to be~~ the
legitimate
~~successor~~ of the other; nothing was changed; nothing impaired,
save only that in those days ~~the thing there was~~
~~something a sort of humming noise I figured it vaguely -~~
~~which went on in the depths; beneath the words; beneath~~
~~the silence, like a <there was a sound in> the silence had a~~
~~little sound in it;~~
which here <the [silence?]> - I listened; everybody was silent
for a moment -
~~the silence~~ had not. ~~It was as if in those days~~ the
~~Each sex~~ <Men & women> were singing <humming> deep down,
under its breath, a ~~little~~
~~song without~~ words; <all> ~~indeed the its~~ accompaniments
the words - which were precisely the same as the words
are today - ~~without interfering with them.~~
but they sounded different because of the
~~little~~ accompaniment. There was a book beside me,
an anthology ~~- & I opened it at Tennyson & read~~
~~looked to see if I could find the~~ What a
magnificent poet, ~~after all,~~ ~~the~~ Tennyson could be, in
his way, I said, For example,

descendant of the first its legitimate heir;

& I opened it, ~~no doubt~~ as if inspired by the memory of luncheon parties before the war at Tennyson; & read

There had fallen a splendid tear

Well, it was something like that ~~that~~ the men said; at luncheon parties before the war; <yes,> & the <this> women sang,

My heart is like a singing bird
   Whose nest is in a water'd shoot;
My heart is like an apple-tree
   Whose boughs are bent with thick-set fruit;
My heart is like a rainbow shell
   That paddles in a halcyon sea;
My heart is gladder than all these
   Because my love is come to me.

Men & women sitting over their lunches

There was something so ludicrous in thinking ~~how we <how I>~~ <~~used to say~~ people [and?] saying such things, even under their breath>
these things had been said ~~before~~ at lunch parties before the war, that I burst out laughing, & had to explain it by pointing to the manx cat, who did look a little absurd, poor beast, without a tail, in the middle of the Court. ~~And so,~~ ~~How did he lose his tail, by~~ — ~~was it natural~~ Was he really a manx cat, or had he lost his tail in an accident? The genuine manx cat is a very rare animal - you know the sort of thing <people> one says as a party breaks up, & ~~thanks~~ to this one had lasted far into the afternoon, thanks to the hospitality of our host, & the boundless

leisure ~~with~~ <with> which ~~he persuaded us at least~~ it was his art,
perhaps to seem endowed.
The beautiful October day was fading & the leaves
were falling from the trees in the avenue, as I left.
Gate after gate seemed to close <lock> gently <but> to behind
me; [ensuring?] <~~one had a~~>
were ~~vision of~~ innumerable beadles ~~with~~ <~~must be~~> fitting many
double keys into vast locks & ~~leaving securing~~ <making> that ~~vast~~
huge treasure house ~~safe for with all its laboratories &~~
~~its libraries & its chapels~~ <seem> safe for another night.
One comes out upon a road - I do not know its name - which leads
if you take the right turning up to Newnham. But there was
plenty of time. Dinner was ~~still~~ not till half past seven.
One could almost do without dinner after such a luncheon.
~~The reflection I had been about to make~~ was,
~~I had been thinking~~ It is strange how a scrap of poetry
will take <works in one> ~~possession~~ of one, making one repeat it
over &
over again, & even moving ones legs & arms in its rhythm.

There has fallen a splendid tear
From the passion flower at the gate.
She is coming my dove, my dear, -

how I trolled the words out upon the road which leads
to Grantchester I think in the end. And then, switching over
to the other measure, I sang (where the waters are
churned up by the mill)

~~Raise me a daïs of~~
My heart is like a singing bird
Whose nest is in a water'd shoot;
My heart is like an apple tree ---

Raise me a daïs of silk & down;
Hang it with vair & purple dyes;
Carve it in doves & pomegranates,
And peacocks with a hundred eyes ---

Heavens, I cried out loud as one does in the dusk, I would give all
~~that I possess to have written that~~. What poets they were, Alfred,
<& Christina, &>
~~The passage of~~
~~instantly~~ in a sort of jealousy, I suppose, for our own age,
silly & absurd as these comparisons are, I went on
to ~~ask~~ wonder ~~whether~~ <if> ~~one could~~ honestly <one cd.> say that any
living poets are as great as ~~they were~~ those two.
~~Obviously it is impossible, I thought, looking into those foaming waters, to~~
~~compare the living with the dead - make any comparison.~~
~~compare them.~~ An impossible task, for many reasons.
Indeed the very reason why that poetry goes to ones
head like wine is ~~that it~~ perhaps that it celebrates some feeling
that one used to have (at luncheon parties before the war
perhaps) but has no longer, so that one responds, easily
uncritically with a kind of sentimentality & lack of
scrutiny, because it is now no longer what one feels: <one has
forgotten what it was like to feel this> though
said with an astonishing beauty. But the living
poets express a feeling that one is actually feeling here & now:
what one feels here & now has none ~~of that~~ one resents one
hates; ~~& it has none of that~~ one cannot abandon oneself to it;
in a rapture: it is almost always painful. Living poets
One is excited; in a different way. For some reason, ~~one~~ cannot
<Since - because of the difficulty this newness>
remember ~~two words~~ more than two lines of any <good> living
poet,
however; & for lack of material But why, I
continued, moving on towards Grantchester, ~~has~~ have
we stopped singing these songs <humming these tunes under our
breath> at luncheon parties?
Why has ~~that emotion~~ have ~~Tennysons emotions -~~
<Alfred> men ceased to sing She is coming, my dove, my dear,
& why ~~have~~ women <has Christina> ceased to sing
My heart is gladder than all these,
Because my love has come to me;

[Left margin:]
such
abandon
ment
such
rapture.

but what we
used to feel;

so that one
can test it;

one [feels?];

Shall we put the blame on the war? When the guns fired in
August the 4th 1914 did the faces of men & women ~~appear to~~
Each other so ~~incredibly ugly that~~ <unromantic> that romance was
killed?
~~To some women~~ (Certainly <it was a shock to see> the faces of
our rulers ~~suddenly~~
~~seemed the reverse of all that they~~ ~~appeared ugly enough~~ --
Put the blame where one will <the war is made the scapegoat for
simply> it seems undeniable,
that the ~~particular~~ illusion which inspired Tennyson -
Christina Rossetti to sing so passionately about the
coming of their loves is ~~now~~ <far> ~~far~~ rarer <far> than it was.
~~Even then~~ <One has only to>
<read novels, newspaper; to hear people [say?]>
But why put blame? Why, ~~if indeed it was an~~ < [~~can we only~~?] if
it were an illu,>
~~illusion~~, not praise & thank the force, whatever it was,
that destroyed illusion ~~& put <set~~ is not> truth in its place.
But what <is truth - ?> sort of poetry <I asked [myself?] . . . .>
what sort of future will men &
women produce when they have ceased to find each other
romantic? <And the human race --> Fewer children were born
in England
last year than have ever been born before. . . . .
~~I put~~ These dots to mark the point where <in pursuit of that
object> lost ~~in~~ about the
future of the race & ~~the part played in human affairs by~~
~~illusion & the desire to imagine what the~~
I missed the turning up to Newnham.

show up
so
very plain
in their
light?
to women
~~particularly~~
who had
~~sent their~~
~~sons to~~
believed
in
education
& the
but yet,

It was a
horrible
shock to the
nerves. People
had other
things to
[hum as?]

~~Truth yes it is the truth that those buildings, <buildings> now so little houses, now agreeably dim & festive, with their red lit windows, are by day hideous little shops, villas,~~

~~After all,~~

~~It is no wonder if <that> one is late for dinner if one goes seeking truth along the Grantchester Road, looking at the houses, now so dim & festive, & saying are you there now, or <am I now seeing is that the truth;> were you true at nine this morning, plastered with advertisements, displaying cheap haberdashery?~~ ~~& asking~~ What is the truth about them, this evening <these houses, for example --> dimness & festivity, or the raw redness which they reveal at nine o'clock in the morning? ~~when they What is truth, & what is illusion?~~ And the willows & the river, where the mist is now rolling; & the gardens that run down to the river? ~~I spare you the convolutions~~ What is the truth about them all? I spare you the ~~convolutions of my logic~~ turns & twists of the argument; ~~for~~ & ask you to suppose that I now found out my mistake about the turning, & retraced my steps <up> ~~in~~ the ~~direction~~ <hill towards> Newnham.

~~If~~ I ~~had~~ ~~not~~ <have> already said several times that it was an October day, ~~I should now be~~ so that I ~~cannot~~ darent forfeit your respect & ~~imperil~~ <bring> the ~~fair~~ good name fiction into disrepute by changing the season & describing the lilacs hanging over the garden walls, the laburnum, & the tulips, & the crocuses. Fiction must stick to facts; & the more accurate a

this ~~novelist is the greater~~ & the ~~more~~ <accurately> a novelist <~~thinks~~
describes> knows about the
different seasons of plant & ~~flower~~ tree the more we honour him.
Therefore it is <was> still autumn, & the leaves ~~are~~ <were> still
yellow &
dropping if anything a little faster than before because it was
(7.18) now evening & ~~the~~ a ~~little~~ breeze (from the <south> west to be
in fact precise) had risen; but ~~it is~~ for all that ~~it spring in~~
~~my mind.~~ there ~~is~~ <was> spring somewhere.

My heart is like a singing bird
  Whose nest is in a water'd shoot;
My heart is like an apple tree
  Whose boughs are bent with thick-set fruit ---

singing themselves over & over in my head
perhaps the words of Christina Rossetti were partly
responsible for the foolish fancy - ~~do not for a moment~~
~~believe~~ that it was any<no>thing but a fancy of mine - that
the ~~purple~~ lilac was shaking its flowers in the
~~little front yards~~ over the <garden> walls. ~~The walls were~~
A wind was blowing, from what quarter I know not,
but it was lifting the ~~little half~~ half grown leaves
so that there was a flash of silver in the air.
It was the time between the lights when colours
undergo ~~that~~ <a> strange intensification; - [kindles?]
purple & golds burn ~~into win~~ ~~beds~~ in window
panes, like a [flash?] like the beat of an excitable heart.
~~Dusk comes~~ <came> ~~down the road in white~~ spouts
& for some reason, - the beauty of the world, <[suddenly is?]>
~~revealed~~
suddenly in such a & yet to pass - ~~all those~~
~~contrasts &~~ is as much <truly> sorrow as laughter.

~~The garden~~
~~Indeed,~~
here I came in at ~~the~~ your gardens ~~at in~~ by the wrong door -
I ~~where one is~~ has two voices of ecstasy & ~~sorrow.~~ <pain>. The
gardens of Newnham ~~I~~ lay before me - wild & open <all untidy,
unruly>
~~It seemed~~ flowery with many trees, & in the long grass,
starting up
there were daffodils, & blue flowers; all unkempt,
not very orderly, but blown hither and there, while in
the ~~generous~~ glass windows, so curved <like the window & curved
like a ship>
<any> ~~of~~ generous <waves of red brick> burnt here with red here
with silver
~~the~~ as ~~the~~ with the raked & changing spring sky.
Somebody was swinging in a hammock, strung between two
~~trees, & if I do not mistake, her book was only held by its~~
~~by & from her attitude I should doubt that she was~~
~~reading. Indeed she said, to somebody who &~~
somebody was racing across the grass; & somebody was
banging on a piano; & then ~~popping~~ in & out, or up
as if for ~~on a little errand which~~ <~~It is~~> [~~was~~?] just to get a breath of
a glimpse of air on the way ~~to~~ somewhere, popped - was it
the [green?] Mr Verrall? Mr Sidgwick? Jane Harrison? <yet ~~some~~>
~~You know perhaps how venerable, how intoxicating~~
such <[was?]> venerable - & perhaps lovable would be the better
word -
some such figure I saw in the ~~rampant~~ spring evening
& saw with what strange mixture of reverence &
laughter; so little did they claim - even of those

claim ~~anything~~
though changed to a stranger (& I ~~have no right to talk openly anything~~
was a stranger; here, as in Trinity or Kings) with the
~~sort of mocking derision which women, when they have ceased to be young, & yet have won a great name; as Jane Harrison had, & never spend a penny on the proper up keep of their name, for no one ever serves them~~ inspire in the young, the irreverent, the of their own sex. She went in & --

Greatness - witness the great forehead, & ~~luminously~~
humility; witness the shabby dress - Perhaps it was
~~Jane Harrison herself~~. with her great <fore>head, her shabby
~~clothes~~. dress. ~~She went in, &~~ perhaps Jane Harrison
herself. ~~I did not know. I was a~~ All was dim - &
~~wrapped in a red of~~ yet intense too, as if the scarf which the
spring <dusk> had thrown over ~~that~~ <the> garden was ~~torn gashed~~, in
rent asunder ~~&~~ <by> starlight or sword light - [as?] ~~I crossed the grass to the [steps?]~~ The flash of some terrible reality
~~leapt~~ leaping out of the spring, ~~to its~~ ~~such~~ Youth -
~~Confused feelings in youth~~--- Here was my soup.

& [that whether?] my best [having?] <u>fables</u> I have been making up about the spring

~~For as I need not point out to you that in in fact~~
~~wh. all this~~ ~~It was, as I have said, half an October evening;~~ For I need not remind you that it was, in truth,
October, & dinner was ~~on the table~~ ~~being served~~ <was on the table>
~~First there was soup;~~ The maid had just set down
before me a plate of soup. {Then there was beef. {Then there
was prunes & custard; & then there was biscuits & cheese.}
There was nothing to stir the fancy ~~to~~ in that soup.
a plain, transparent liquid, through which one could have seen

any pattern that there might have been on the plate. But
there was none. The plate was plain. Next came the beef &
~~two vegetables, cabbage~~ <with> greens & potatoes. - a homely
trinity, suggesting some ~~sodden market day in the~~ a
somehow the rumps of cows in a muddy market; ~~the~~
greens, curled & yellow at the edge, are of so little account
that many are trodden ~~into~~ under foot. <so> ~~&~~ ~~Not there~~ is
~~anything to complain of it~~ is human nature's daily food; &
<a general sense of [~~say~~?]> & catering & bargaining, <& women
with bags &> on a Monday morning. ~~the~~ It
~~To complain of~~ There was no reason to complain of
human natures daily food, however, seeing that the
supply was sufficient, & coal miners doubtless were sitting
down to plain bread & cheese, <to the bread without the cheese>
their wives. . . And if
anybody goes on to complain that the prune, even when
mitigated by custard, is an uncharitable vegetable,
stringy ~~like~~ <as> a miser's purse, & exuding ~~upon any~~ a
~~yellowish~~ liquid which ~~only~~ seems to prove that even the
which ~~though resembles the~~ <such as doubtless> might run in
misers' veins,
who have denied themselves wine & warmth for
eighty years & yet not given to the poor, & he ~~is~~
also ~~to be~~ should reflect that there are
~~doubtless very poor~~ people, ~~who~~ <whose> ~~mere~~ charity~~able~~
<suffers> &
Than he is <& the prune, sturdy> who ~~like~~ prunes. <them. Then>
~~The~~ biscuits ~~& the~~
cheese ~~which~~ were ~~set~~ <next> before us; ~~in dishes like~~
~~clover leaves, of all clover leaves were white~~
& ~~nobody in~~ & the water jug was passed round,
because it is in the nature of biscuits to be dry - &
that was all. Everybody scraped their chairs back,
the swing doors swung violently to & fro, &

[Margin: a general sense of catering & bargaining.]

soon the hall was swept & tidied; & made ready for
breakfast next morning. Down corridors & up staircases
the youth of England went banging & singing. And
was it for a guest, a stranger, ~~one who has never paid given~~
~~<paid>~~
~~<a> penny to the Cause College or been received anything from it~~
~~but to complain when who has~~ (for I have no
more right here than in Trinity or King's or Christchurch)
to say 'The dinner was not good', to say (we
were now <alone> in a sitting room) ~~which where As there is only~~
would it not be a <pleasant> convenience to dine alone sometimes,
up
& to prove — here - , to search & probe, ~~as~~ into the
mine — economies & <[ ] your> barenesses of a house which
[are all?] — to the stranger, ~~shows~~ <wears> so fine a front of gaiety &
courage? Nothing <of course not.> ~~could~~ be said openly. But the
truth is this: <The> Human ~~nature is~~ frame being what it is,
~~not made up of body in this here & brain, there~~
~~heart & in wit, affection, there, but & heart~~
imperfect — ~~the affection, the emotions, in another compartment, since~~
rudimentary — ~~on the contrary, the heart & body & brain are all~~
now, — all in one, body & brain & heart <the emotions> all mixed up ~~if~~
~~you~~
together, - though in a more perfect state they will <not in
separate compartments as they will be in a million years or
so>
doubtless be separated - as things are, at the moment,
if one has not dined well, first one is ~~tired & then one is~~
one cannot think well, & then one cannot love
well, & finally one cannot sleep well - in
short, It is true that my friend, now alas
translated as they call it in higher circles to
Australia, where she is doing very well &

~~where she~~ & keeps a horse of her own & sends me from time
presents of ostrich feathers, plucked apparently at
great personal risk from giant birds (she has taken
~~up ostrich farming)~~ had even in those <severer> days a secret
cupboard where she kept a squat bottle & little glasses)
so that we were able ~~to light a very small fire in~~ the
~~spine~~ repair some of the damage of the day's living - (but
there should here been sole & partridge first) &
thanks to this, we did manage ~~to sit over the fire~~
till two ~~or three in the morning.~~ to talk a little, over the fire,
about the immortality of the soul.

We drew up to the fire & ~~discussed gossiped, talked~~, slipped quite
freely
in & out ~~of all those~~ among ~~this & that, here~~ all those
objects of interest & curiosity which ~~have a few months absence~~
grow up, when one has not seen a ~~person~~. <friend> for some
months,
when people who ~~have interests in common are separated~~. <like
each other are separated
~~& are & become When they come together~~ --
how somebody has married, & somebody been divorced, &
somebody written a book, had a baby, <or> been corrupted, left
England in a temper; <huff> ~~with~~ all those speculations upon
human
<nature> character & the nature of the world ~~whats such & the
permutations & combinations of things whats such~~
which spring from them. ~~It was~~ <among> ~~in the flow of such
things
that there that I became aware that~~ While these
things were being said, I became aware of a current setting
~~in, which floated some which was working influencing
the talk; a as so often happens of a current directing
the talk, one of those a which sprang from some
as if in the deeper layers of my mind, I was being from the
depths, if we like to call themselves them so; of a
something antecedent to this the present moment an~~
<these> influence; an overmastering desire ~~to~~ as if suddenly all
this
odds & ends were being swept along in the same
current towards one end. ~~An very elementary exercise in
self analysis was enough to reveal the last that~~
One might be talking about the ~~tendency of old men to~~
curious fact that ~~Jane~~ so & so had settled down at last
on a farm to with a woman who was -
but ~~in my on~~ The important ~~thing was~~
but the real interest of everything (to me, at the moment) was

of wh. we
become aware
when we meet
which grew
upon ~~the~~
~~absence of~~
~~one of~~
~~when two~~
two people
who like
each
other are
separated;
& come
together,
very
interestingly,
when they
must age -
underneath
surface
facts,
& growing
in thought,
& strength

this: for many centuries king & nobles had laid gold
under the foundations of Trinity, Kings, ~~Queen~~ Christchurch, Balliol
& the rest; What did <kind of digging had been> Newnham &
Girton stand on?
Clay & gravel? The mind is often ~~the mastered~~ thus
possessed by ~~pictures,~~ scenes, things that have an astonishing
power to carry on a life of their own, with words & voices,
which overpower rational conversation, & ~~make~~ <colour> steep the
~~soul~~ (forgive me for using obsolete words) ~~in an~~ <the ~~whole~~ soul
benefit of this> ~~An~~
~~elementary exercise in analysis will show that one was~~
~~comparing dinner & lunch. was~~ These two opposing
pictures, ~~form~~ one made in the morning, the other in the
evening, had me at their mercy; & until I could expose them
both to Mary Seton, all disinterested talk was at an end.
Briefly I told her about the masons who had been up all
those years on the roof of Kings, <the Chapel> & the sacks of
gold & other
precious objects that Kings & Queens had shovelled deep into
the courts & under the pavements! ~~What was the case here? <And~~
~~what had happened here!>~~
~~Founded in the year 1880; It was a case of wringing a~~
~~few what a few thousands from the advanced; the buildings stand~~
~~on~~
~~them But What was the case here?~~

& the partridges & the wine.

(A few thousand scraped ~~from the~~ collected wrung with
difficulty in the 80ties. Enough to carry on with; but
not enough for sittingrooms & so on.) What was beneath
(here greed got the better of good manners) beef & prunes.
~~About~~ <In But you know the story.> Somewhere about 1870
Lady Stanley of Alderley
& other ~~well~~ women who had the education of their sex
at heart collected sufficient funds - It was a prodigious

effort, & if there was not money enough to do everything
that one could wish - it would be ungrateful, greedy,
[unfilial?] & greedy & all the rest of it to wish that the
funds had permitted of <private> sitting rooms for everybody; of
sofas;
of servants carrying tin dishes upon their heads; of
wine and partridges; of leisure; of contemplation:
How vividly her words brought before me ~~the ground~~
~~gashed in~~ [&?] fields gashed by spades [when ?]; workmen
~~in~~ with straps tied round their corduroy trousers; & sitting
~~perched about in~~ <in> in all sorts of temporary offices, or the
sitting rooms of private houses, Lady Stanley, Miss Clough
perhaps, ~~women~~ women with paper before them; baskets;
envelopes; little speeches & leaflets being put into
envelopes; circulars sent off; names collected; & somebody
reading out Mr & Mrs, I have obtained a promise - or
[Mr?] So & So has written to say - or a meeting was held.
this April & so on.
~~Yet without leisure & contemplation~~ -
And, ~~am~~ irritated as one can be even at an imaginary
scene, at ~~the waste~~ of all this effort to get a
few thousand pounds, ~~all this bitterness into the bargain,~~
[ ]. The waste of good time, I ~~naturally~~ burst out to
Mary Seton, the science lecturer, ~~about the~~ upon the
~~ridiculous~~ <reprehensible> poverty of our sex: its inability, when
the need arose, to bestow here 100,000 there 50
thousand, or whatever is needed to make a
make a college rich, & endow its fellows, & build
observatory, laboratory, library - all that the
mind wants when it is thinking, & the body when

is growing & the heart when it is seizing ~~in~~ as it does in these
[years?], a thousand thoughts & desires & wild loves which
tear it asunder in the spring. No money.
What had our mothers busy doing then, not to acquire wealth?
Marys mother, Mrs. Seton, had been} Powdering their noses
looking in at shop windows? Flaunting in the sun at
Monte Carlo? Mary's mother - there she was over the
fireplace - ~~had at that brought~~ may have been a wastrel,
~~if~~ it is true; in the intervals of bearing thirteen
children,) up in Scotland to her husband the Minister; but
her gay & dissipated life had left <far too> little trace on her.
She was a homely body; in a plaid shawl, which
was fastened by a large cameo; & a spaniel of the
sort that walks very slowly, dripping from the mouth, was
cuddled against her side. ~~A~~ & she sat ~~on~~ in a
basket chair; looking rather ~~surprised~~, <amused> as if she
was afraid from previous experience that the dog
would move. She had had thirteen children; &
~~her mother? Another seven shall we say. As for~~
~~never saved a penny.~~ Now if she had gone into
business, had made pills or artificial silk, she might have
bequeathed 100,000 to ~~found~~ - endow this & to found that.
But she did not. Nor did her mother before her. Nor
hers Either

[Margin: in her spare time (she had]

[Margin: tense amused expression when one hopes that a dog is not going to move.]

Deaneries; would have opened before us.
There would have been a nice little
post in an office. A librarianship,
a comfortable sinecure, in a
government office. A post in the
Civil Service. A diplomats career.

I pointed this out to Mary. If your mother had
gone into the City at the age of 17 & become the
head of the successful firm Seton & Co, do you
suppose she would have had time to buy peanuts
ice cream? Possibly in the summer holidays.
But no brother & sister. And you - left to the
charge of nurse from ~~9~~ 10 to 6: ~~or growing up~~ < [in?] sent to>
School & put in the charge of ~~friends~~ ~~ladies~~
charitable home in the holidays. ~~No~~

we might be sitting at our ease tonight, ~~with~~ a the
subject of our talk might be, ~~Greek~~ archaeology, the
anthropology, ~~science,~~ physics, atoms, mathematics,
astronomy, ~~Einstein,~~ relativity, geography, or
botany; ~~because or any subject~~: because our
mothers had ~~left enough money <enough>~~ for us ~~to go on studying~~
~~such subjects all our lives, with the necessary~~
~~instruments & to be~~ lectureships & professorships
& prizes & scholarships in ~~such~~ abundance ~~that given a~~
~~<any woman with a> turn for such thought, the chances are we~~
~~could have~~
~~gratified it, we should have been surely~~
any woman with a turn for such thought could have gratified it.
Only <[again?]> if Mrs. Seton had gone into ~~her lumber business~~
~~the silk trade at the age of fifteen & <founded> started the famous~~
~~Company which is now paying a dividend of 200~~
~~pays its share holders over 200 per cent, Mary~~
~~alone what is needed~~ <left> ~~to leave~~ £200,000 to a college -
had ~~been director & founder promoted companies & founded~~
~~or captained industries~~ <[there wd. have been no?]> Mary ~~would~~
~~not have been~~ <to enjoy her little plan of>
~~<higher living> in existence.~~ Floating companies, captaining
industries is are
~~obviously a while~~ <incompatible with> ~~excludes~~ thirteen children,
it is perfectly plain that she would not have left
Mary & twelve brothers & sisters: Floating companies,
captaining industries, all those labours by which men in
the past have built up great fortunes <& so [produced?]> which
they have
left, justly & wisely to their sons, are not compatible
~~with those other labours which have filled so many~~
with bring into the world families of thirteen

If your mother
had only left
money to
endow

we might
have been
looking
forward,
without undue
confidence,
to a life time
spent
honourably &
comfortably -
~~the~~ in study
Deaneries

things:

the old lady in the photograph still continued to smile~~,~~ ~~rather~~
at her spaniel. And ~~lookin trying~~ looking at her
it came into my head, that one must get to the bottom of
old lady — the matter before ~~one came down~~ <coming> to Newnham -
smile - — Girton ~~& lectured the~~ to give this lecture.
spaniel - — It was a very fine night, as I went down the hall again to my
captain of — bed <was> at the hotel; one had the curious sense that so often
industry — ~~one had escaped~~ haunts the night ~~traveller~~ walker, of
[one?] - — having escaped ~~from the~~ some intolerable [yanking?]
thralldom, <got [out?] from some street or place> of ~~seeing~~ being out at sea, alone; &
as if — arguments, bitterness, laughs all [are due wh.?] The day's
skin is neatly rolled off; thrown into the hedge. A
thousand stars ~~are~~ communicating perhaps, with one another, &
with nobody. Even the door at the hotel opened
~~not~~ by some invisible agency. Not even <the> a boots was sitting up for me.
it was so late.

The Fitzwilliam Manuscript

II

Wed. 6th March 1929

II

The scene now changes. It was still October, but we are in London ~~we live in London~~ & but the leaves were now falling ~~here~~ in London, & I must ask you to imagine one house in any street in London. The room was of no ... a room, like many thousand ~~...~~ with a window ~~here~~ looking ~~into~~ across into other windows across the same current of ~~...~~ & feet ~~...~~ (head) ~~...~~ chairs & books rugs & tables; ~~...~~ chairs & tables ... a few pictures & a few books — ~~the only~~ & laid out on the table, conspicuously a blank sheet of paper on which were written ~~headed~~ in large letters the words

Women & Fiction. Page one.

To fill that page, ~~after what I had seen over the week end at Cambridge~~, it would be necessary, ~~also~~ to ~~go to the British Museum. For it~~ find out a good deal more about certain facts. Up at Cambridge during the week end one had ~~been~~ ~~forced to~~ received ~~certain~~ impressions ... coloured all of them with a thousand accidents, which it would be necessary to strain off in order to get at the ... pure white ... fluid of truth ~~that seemed~~ — There was that curious disparity between the wealth of the ... — one ~~was~~ so prosperous, the other so poor. Has woman by nature less power of acquiring money ... than man? What does that arise from? And now ... what influence ... over the fact of poverty ... upon creation in the arts? ... at once suggested ... dependency ... [illegible]

(Left margin notes:)

Supper ... heard ... & the ... [illegible]

Recently ... [illegible]

Some ... [illegible]

Wed.
6th March
1929

. II .

The scene now changes. It ~~is~~ <was> still October, but ~~we are~~ in
~~London;~~
~~but it was in London, &~~ but the leaves were <now> falling ~~now in~~
London, & <not Cambridge> I must ask you to imagine any
<London> house in any <London> street.
~~The room was of no~~ & a room, like many thousands,
with a window ~~here~~ looking ~~into across a~~ into other
windows across ~~a~~ the usual current of ~~taxis <cabs> &~~ foot
passengers <heads>; ~~& in that room the usual chairs & books,~~
~~rugs &~~
~~tables;~~ & chairs & tables <[almost?] seen>, & a few pictures & a
few
books - ~~the only~~ & laid out on <one's> the table, conspicuously,
a blank sheet of paper ~~headed~~ <on which were written> in large
letters the words
Women & Fiction, page one.

peoples heads & the hoods of vans & motor cars,

To fill that page, ~~after what I had seen over the~~
~~week end at Cambridge~~, it would be necessary, ~~alas,~~ to ~~go~~
~~to the British Museum. For it~~ find out a good deal more
about certain facts. Up at Cambridge during the
week end one had ~~been forced to~~ received ~~certain~~
impressions <enough to stock a> ~~mix~~ <but> coloured all of them
with a
thousand accidents, <of time & person> which it would be
necessary to strain
off in order to get at the ~~essential~~ <pure white &>
fluid of truth. <liquid essential oil>
~~It had seemed~~ There was <to begin with> this curious disparity
between the wealth of the sexes - one ~~was~~ so prosperous, the
other so poor. ~~Has woman <then> by nature less power of~~
~~acquiring money & <less power of>~~ it to her own use <?> than
man? What does that arise from? And how far
~~has it influenced the whole~~ does the fact of poverty
~~tell upon~~ <[affect the?]> creation ~~in the~~ <of works of> arts? ~~Many~~
more <A thousand or>
questions ~~ramify from those two~~ at once suggested
depending from those two

Recently this impression they resolved themselves primarily to this:

some radical difference of fibre,

themselves, which could only be answered by consulting
the learned, the unprejudiced, who have removed themselves
from the strife of body & tongue, & set themselves to investigate &
~~think~~ reason & at last issued the result of their thought in
books which are to be found on the shelves of the British
Museum.

The day, though not actually raining, was dismal
enough, & the streets in the neighbourhood of the Museum,
when I made my way there, dutifully, with a note book & a
pencil, were full of coal carts, as if all the ~~Kit~~
cellars of all the boarding houses were stoking up for the
winter. ~~As usual in this quarter, dilapi antiquated~~
~~four wheelers were arriving laden with~~ <drawing up & depositing>
huge corded wooden
<boxes> ~~trunks, in which were the entire wardrobe of some Swiss~~
~~or~~
~~Italian family, seeking their fortune~~ <were being deposited on> on
the pavement, containing
presumably, seeking fortune, refuge, ~~what can what~~
~~extraordinary illusion had brought these unhappy people from~~
or some other desirable commodity in ~~hand~~ a
Bloomsbury boarding house in the winter. The usual
men paraded the streets with <plants a> barrow. Commerce
~~One~~ <walking in> has a sense in London at this hour <one has> of a
<giant> machine
getting into its stride, sending its rain & its omnibuses both -
[thither?], its men & its women - ~~all of us were being~~
~~flung~~ of a an engine ~~making things~~ being some
insignificant thread ~~or bead~~ worked by a vast power into
a pattern. ~~Here are the~~ At ten in the morning the
~~only the bare~~ ~~No~~ no pattern was visible; only the
nondescript ~~threads~~, string coloured threads. And it is

the entire wardrobe of the unhappy Swiss or Italian family.

~~admirable~~ all in keeping with the sobriety & power of London
in October <Early on a weekday morning> that ~~by~~ without any fuss
or difficulty, beyond
signing one's name, one is admitted to ~~that vast storehouse,~~
all the resources of the world's culture. {It is a fact that by
signing ones name, on ~~another slip of paper~~ <or is it now a
number> on another slip of
paper any book that has ever been written, the merest
ephemeral pamphlet, the rarest folio, will be brought on a
~~trolley~~ <fetched> from its <the> cell in the vast honeycomb which
& given into your own particular hands.} One takes a slip of
paper; one opens the catalogue at <any> ~~the~~ name or <any> ~~the~~
subject one
~~is not~~ <W - for inst> Women for instance . . . . <women & the
. . . .> These dots indicate
~~not~~ <very> imperfectly ~~but they may but I have no other~~
~~way of conveying to you the physical oppression which~~
~~seems to at once settles somewhere at the nape of the neck;~~
~~at the from the conglomeration the as if at the sight~~
~~alone of all that has been thought & written, bound & printed~~
~~& bound, on that particular point subject: Women.~~
~~Why, the nothing else can have It appears that women~~
~~have been more written about than any subject under the sun~~.
oppression, surprise, despair, exultation, <humility> horror - I
know not what -
It is a feeling that often besets the amateur investigator.
I had strolled in with a note book & pencil; &
here was I confronted with a <[instead?]> library that it would
need a life time to read & a <the brain & nerve of an elephant to
digest> I proposed to give three
hours from ten to one on an October morning.
~~It is a subject sex.~~ <It is of course understandable> Sex of
course is a subject that attracts
scientists in all countries of the world. That is explicable.
But what was to me surprising & difficult of
explanation was the number of ~~men~~ <books written not by> many
professors, many
doctors, but ~~some without any special qualification;~~
but by ordinary unqualified writers, agreeable essayists,

[Margin:] as if a cloud of insects had [returned home?];

[Margin:] What is Known about a China cup!

[Margin:] a

on the other hand, many were serious, & indeed

well known novelists, upon women. Obviously <to judge by the titles> some were frivolous
facetious; ~~others~~ <but many> were prophetic; <[many?]> expostulatory, ~~hortatory,~~
descriptive <irate> - to read the titles merely ~~gave one~~ a sense of

Earnest anger, with

innumerable schoolmasters, & <of>innumerable clergymen,
mounting their <rostrum> desks, their pulpits, & holding forth
with a loquacity which far exceeded the hour limit
upon this one subject. ~~What~~ <It was> a queer phenomenon. &
apparently - here I ~~took down the~~ consulted the letter M -
~~one <on> that~~ confined to the male sex. Women do not write
books about men - a fact that I could not help welcoming
with relief, for if I had first to read all that men have

in order to come to a conclusion -

written about women, then all that women have written
about men, should I ever come to Cambridge & deliver
this lecture at all? No, immured in some cell, ~~my~~ <the>
hair would grow to my heels, & the mushrooms sprout ~~among~~

lecture my finger

<in> my boots - So, making a perfectly arbitrary selection <from the books men write [about women?]> I
sent my slip of paper to lie in ~~in~~ the wire tray, & waited
in my stall, among the other seekers for the essential oil
of truth.

What could the ~~attraction~~ <reason> be then, I wondered
~~making~~ drawing cartwheels upon the slips of paper
that the British taxpayer provides for itself - ~~Why, if~~
~~the British Museum Catalogue is any~~ for this curious
disparity? ~~Men take~~ Why are women so much more
interesting to men than men are to women - <?> if, ~~that is~~, judge a

that by the testing

the British Museum Catalogue is ~~any but~~. ~~Yet only~~
~~the names of men encircle the proud dome of the~~
~~British Museum Reading room, I reflected;~~
~~raising my eyes to what has all the appearance of a~~
A very curious fact it seemed, & my mind wandered

to the lives of men who spend their mornings <days> writing
about women, -
~~so to the studious & impersonal faces of my fellow~~
~~students, many of whom being already provided with their~~
~~provender were hard at work making <new> books out of books.~~
~~It is not apparently a very profitable occupation~~ -

~~to picture the what;~~ Whether they were old, whether they
were young, married or unmarried, red nosed or
humpbacked - <until> ~~in~~ such frivolous ~~dream~~ thoughts were
~~ended~~ by ~~the~~ an avalanche of books <~~which~~> deposit~~ing~~ <~~ed~~>
itself ~~in~~
on the desk ~~before me~~. in front of me. Now the
trouble began. ~~People of~~ The student trained in
research has no doubt some method of knowing what his
~~selecting~~ <cleaving fast to> isolating his question <shepherding it
through all> & of disregarding all
<the difficulty & danger of its course safe with a pen:>
~~Anger~~ information that is irrelevant to it. <the anger> ~~But i~~f
~~one starts merely to find out why women are~~
~~poorer than men, & then one must know precisely~~
~~what one's question is. It should be~~ Thus in a
few hours he knows the truth. <~~he has him fast by the scruff~~>
The student by
my side, who was copying assidously from a
scientific manual, was, I felt sure, getting at the
truth. ~~<in> His page was~~ ~~If~~ But if one <is not a trained student,
or> asks of a
miscellaneous armful of books by professors, schoolmasters,
clergymen, novelists, essayists, & men of no
particular qualification, <asking> why are women poorer
than men? ~~in~~ very soon, in the space of half an hour
indeed, one is reduced to this condition (I quote
from my note book~~) which was illustrated~~
~~in~~ Women, condition of in middle ages. A

anyhow it was
flattering,
vaguely, to
feel oneself
~~Even~~
~~recognizing~~
~~Even~~
~~a simple~~ such
~~attention~~
object of such
attention -
provided
always that
the
provided that
it was not
entirely
bestowed by
~~the~~
crippled &
~~little~~ the
very small
men with
earnest
faces,

in the Feejee Islands.
Natural inferiority of,
Worshipped as goddesses by
Lacking in moral sense,
<Greater conscientious of,>
Attractiveness of,
Age of puberty among South Sea Islanders,
Offered as sacrifices, to,
<Small> Size of brain of,
~~Greater~~ ~~susceptibility~~ <depth>~~ of to [ ]~~
~~subliminal keeness of smell,~~
<Profounder sub-consciousness ~~life~~>
~~More conscientious than men~~
~~Lower moral sense,~~
~~Beauty of,~~
Less hair on the ~~chin~~ <body> of,
Mental, moral & physical
inferiority of,
Love of children of,
Greater length of life of,
Reproductive cells of,
Weaker muscles of,
~~Love of,~~
~~Hate of~~,
Higher education of,
Shakespeares opinion of,
Popes opinion of,
Dean Inges opinion of,
Lord Birkenheads opinion of,
La Bruyeres opinion of,

~~Here, at last,~~ having copied out all this ~~conscientiously~~, I could not help writing, Query:

Why, then, why, did Samuel Butler say that wise men
never say what they think of women? For
apparently they talk of <never say any>~~no~~thing else: ~~here is for~~
~~instance~~ <there is>
~~Pope, "Most women And I copied out, this~~
~~will show how But Pope for instance says,~~
~~Most women have no character at all, &~~
~~La Bruyere says And no one would not complain~~
~~of that~~, But what is so unfortunate - if one is
seeking truth - is that they ~~will not~~ <never seem to agree> always
say the
~~very opposite~~. Here is Pope.
Here is La Bruyere. Turn up any heading,
for instance, Education of, & the same contradiction [presents?]
Here is ~~the great educationist~~ Thomas Day, ~~advising~~
a very clever & ~~advanced~~ man, who made a speciality of
Education -- ~~It~~ advising Mr Edgeworth not to teach his
daughter anything, & here is his contemporary
Dr Johnson saying . . . Here are the ~~nature~~
of ~~saying~~ denying that women have souls, & the
German tribe of, ~~was~~ saying that they have something
divine in them. ~~<So it goes on > Their brains are shallower; &~~
~~their~~
~~consciousness is deeper. They are more rudimentary &~~
~~more complex.~~ Goethe says one thing, Lord Birkenhead
<another.>

~~It is another proof~~

~~The~~
It was all very confusing; ~~but that~~ & rather humiliating, ~~for~~
~~the student reader next door was writing getting on very~~
~~well with his research, I felt sure;~~ for while the reader next
door was making the neatest abstracts, ~~often~~ headed <as I cd see
over my shoulder> with an
A. B. or a C, or a 1 2 or 3, & so on, my own
note book ~~book~~ was the wildest scribble of contradictory
jottings, ~~none of them~~ in which I was still quite
unable to find any answer to my question: why are women
poorer than men? Is it because they have less
hair on their bodies, or because in the Feejee Islands
the age of puberty is - I ~~entirely forget~~ could not even read
the figure. ~~Ninety?~~ Nine? or Ninety? ~~Ridiculous!~~
~~It was all so silly, & such a waste of time;~~
I ~~was so~~ thoroughly <& fully> out of conceit with my own powers
of research; ~~that & this~~ must excuse me for
[the rest?] leaving unopened a whole handful of books whose
seemed titles seemed to indicate that they dealt with
written to ~~women or~~ W (as I now called her) - in the future.
If I cannot <am unable to> grasp the truth about <or> W. <was>
in the past, or
W. <is> in the present, ~~what is~~ why bother about W. in the
<will be> future? ~~I asked; &~~ ~~So~~ And, so, taking my
pencil I began - in listlessness, in desperation, ~~to~~
~~draw~~, where I should have written, very neatly, under
headings, like my neighbour, a conclusion, to draw
instead the face & figure as they appeared to me
of Professor X ---writing his great book

on the mental, moral, & physical inferiority of the female <sex> to
the
male. He was not, in my picture, attractive to women;
that <u>he</u> is he with a great jowl,
he was heavily built, & wore, <with> a pair of spectacles which
he kept on taking off & putting on, ~~as he argued (at a table in a~~
~~bier halle) perhaps <the [unfriendly?   ]> on this very subject;~~
& his face - the
red ink <wd. have> c~~a~~ome in handy - was <as red as a> inflamed.
For ~~The Professor~~
was, in my picture, very angry; - had <was> his wife
twitted him for being such a great lout of a man; only
fit for a common foot soldier while her Hans -
(here was Hans, ~~coming in~~ very slim & elegant in a coat
with an astrachan collar) or was it simply that he
had failed to get some post in the university, owing to the
machinations of the <some> wife of --- or had he simply
been laughed at (to adopt a Freudian theory) in his
cradle by a pretty girl? Even as a baby the Professor
in my sketch, was not what one could call an attractive
child - & something like a [~~and~~?] <And this is the reason why>
taking a sheet of
paper from the [case <in front>?] he ~~heads it~~ <writes> very
angrily. The
mental moral & physical inferiority of the female sex.
& palms it off upon the world as the fruit of
disinterested, cold, scientific truth. Plainly the
A very interesting

Whatever the reason, the professor was made to look <very angry>
far from
attractive & ~~very angry~~ in my sketch. It was an idle
way of finishing an unprofitable morning~~'s work~~ <work> ~~But~~
Yet it is in our idleness, in our dreams, that the truth
<~~submerged~~> sometimes
appears. A very elementary exercise in ~~analysis~~
psychology not to be dignified by the name of
psycho-analysis, ~~made it apparent,~~ showed me,
that ~~this~~ <the> sketch ~~had~~ of an angry professor ~~had~~
had been made in anger. But why anger? Hope,
confusion, amusement, boredom, - those were the
emotions that one could name. <had succeeded each other> Had
anger been lurking
among them? ~~Appar~~ <Undoubtedly> The sketch said yes. It
referred me unmistakably to the book which demonstrated
the mental, moral, & physical inferiority of women.
~~And To prove With the fact~~ On being plainly faced
with the fact ~~that one had been of one's anger & the reason for~~
<~~of~~ that one had been angry, & with a particularly bitter>
~~it~~ anger leapt into the open, like a flame when the
leaves that smother it have been moved. <are brushed aside> My
heart leapt; my
cheeks burnt. This fool dared ~~to~~ say - &c &c. The actual
<charge is not>
~~The actual charge against him <the fool> is not interesting;~~
~~What~~
~~<was> is interesting was & a moments thought was enough to~~
~~explain the sufficiently for ordinary purposes the~~
~~As~~ Soon the flame sank, & one was able to ~~say~~
sort out the elements, & to recognise the fact that,
however foolish it may appear, ~~no~~ one does not like to be
told that one is mentally, morally & physically inferior to
the ~~little~~ man in the next ~~stall~~ chair. ~~A~~ Nor is
there anything remarkable or discreditable in that
~~flame of~~ anger. It is only human nature, I reflected,
~~running my pencil~~ drawing cartwheels & circles
over the angry professors face till he looked like a
burning bush, or a flaming comet - a~~n~~ impersonal <apparition>
a regular but quite impersonal object ~~which roared no~~

[Margin notes:]
comes to the surface
~~Emerges~~

on looking at the note book

or new notes throughout the way.

Moreover it pointed

& the cause,

apparition without any human significance whatsoever

Anger then had died down; <&> there sprang <[instead?]> from its
ashes, ~~however~~,
another ~~another~~ emotion ~~which <where> eager & energetic, which might be~~
~~called temper spirit seemed to~~ with a strong resemblance
allied to to curiosity. My own anger <heat> was explained; but
how explain <the ~~temper~~ heat> the professors'? For ~~now that~~
~~it came~~ to <~~to~~ it of the more interesting ~~to~~>
~~analys<e>ing emotions <left by> roused by reading apart from the~~
~~results (which were ridiculous) is more profitable~~
~~sometimes then to tabulate results which in this case~~
~~were ridiculous. For often the emotion left by reading are~~
~~more important than the results.~~ For when it came to
analysing the ~~emotions~~ <[impression?]> left ~~by reading~~ these
books,
there was ~~one that seemed to~~ always this one; that ~~some~~
~~emotion had been mixed up with~~ them; they had been
written in heat. The heat might show itself in ridicule; ~~or~~ in
~~satire;~~ <sentiment> ~~or in~~ <in> moral earnestness; in reprobation; in
in admiration; <in glory;> but heat there always was.
~~It was their heat that had generated my heat.~~ Had
they written coldly, impartially, dispassionately of women,
as the author of that scientific manual there had
written of the atomic theory or whatever it was,
no heat would have been <[generated?]> roused in me; my mind
would have burnt with a white light instead of a red.
~~What~~ ~~But why~~ <& my note book in> All my notes were
invalidated
by that fact. ~~And, by the same showing, their books,~~
~~were invalidated too.~~ One would have accepted
their conclusion, ~~whether they were ag~~ disagreeable,
~~Whether they were~~ <or> agreeable. As it was,
every note in my note book was worthless ~~& for the~~
& for the same reason, the books on the desk were
worthless; worthless scientifically, though humanly
full of amusement, interest, instruction, boredom & the
rest of it. Therefore they must be

because they were written not in the white light of reason but in the red light of anger but they were written in a red light of ~~not in~~ And not in white light light of reason

returned to the central desk, & ~~the formality completed with which cancelled my responsibility as a reader~~ restored to their shelves
Still curiosity remained; ~~asking why the Professors (to lump all them together) were angry?~~
~~the professors Thinking back over that morning's skippings~~
<work>
~~reading~~ That the ~~professors~~ <gentlemen in [pink?]> ~~should be~~
& novelists &c. should be amused by W., in love with her,
~~curious about~~ her, concerned for her morality, &
influence full of warnings, & good advice, & theories, &
speculation seemed ~~neither~~ natural enough;
Men, ~~for one thing,~~ must make a living, & the
Why anger? - ~~My own anger~~ The causes of my own anger
were not far to seek; & could be named straight off:
vanity, injured vanity had ~~given rise to it.~~ <was ~~the cause of it~~
at the root of it> ~~But~~
~~I found it very difficult to~~ Now the professors (to ~~give them~~ lump them in one) were amused & sarcastic & interested
& argumentative; ~~they were~~ full of good advice -
theories & warnings & speculations as is natural
among <quick witted> men ~~who have to make a living by writing, find a good But some were angry.~~ All
this was easy to understand; But some were angry.
Why angry? why angry? I repeated, standing
under the Colonnade & wondering where ~~in the neighbourhood was a good~~ place <was> ~~to lunch at. there used to be a place~~ where they cooked chicken
not divinely but in the tradition of the small French inn:
with butter & lots of vegetables, strewn about it: also
they had fresh rolls; Camembert cheese, & a very
tolerable glass of burgundy. Before the war,

when ~~the~~ one used to hum under one's breath,
Come into the garden Maud or whatever it
was.
Confound the professors! ~~I said~~. They have made me forget
how the poem goes. The professors are angry.
~~with women~~. Their style, their facts, prove it. But why were
the professors angry? There ~~is~~ <was> a puzzle that ~~will~~ <wd> last
all the time it takes to ~~bring a plate of chicken~~
~~cook a wing of chicken~~. bring <me> a wing of chicken & a roll of
bread

from the kitchen to the table.

~~That men should be angry with women - that the~~
~~rich should be angry with the poor~~.
If women <had> told men that they were mentally &c
inferior to ~~men~~ women, ~~then the profs~~ men might <will> be angry:
but it was the other way round. ~~Also~~ <And> men were rich, & had
all the power in their hands - the press, for example.
The lunch edition of the Evening Standard lay on the ~~table~~:
~~plush~~ chair. "Judge - on shamelessness of Women."
That was given a more prominent place than it would have
had if the paper was financed, edited, sub-edited by women -
And judges are men. And

"All, all are men, women & all" as Miss H. Hitchen exclaimed.

Anger:
desire to be superior.
importance to have
some one inferior.

Still curiosity remained, seeking to define further that
emotion of the Professors <wh. cd. not be called> ~~which~~ was not
curiosity or love,
but might be called, provisionally, anger. ~~Why anger,~~
The causes of my own anger were not far to seek; vanity,
injured vanity was at the root of it. ~~But the~~ But
why should they be angry? Why should ~~professors~~ <they> be
angry? I repeated, standing under the colonnade &
wondering where that shop was, kept by a Frenchman,
where they cooked chickens in the tradition of the small
French Inn ~~with butter & vegetables~~; & made coffee,
~~very strong & very~~ as fragrant as coffee smells, & very
strong. The professors were angry; ~~their style~~
~~their arguments proved it; but for what reason &~~
what ~~was it that~~ <the cause> ~~one meant by anger What was the~~
~~emotion one called anger~~? Here was a puzzle that
would last all the time it takes to be served with
food in a small restaurant somewhere near the
British Museum. ~~For, here was a copy of the~~
The lunch edition of ~~the~~ the evening paper ~~suggested that~~ <might>
threw ~~its~~ <some> oblique light on the subject perhaps. ~~Judge~~---
~~had commented in~~ ~~Obviously it is a patriarchy,~~ <The latest
score;>
~~the evening paper which is perpetually flashing in ones~~
eyes a Judge - <in the divorce court> commented on the
shamelessness of
women. The latest scores were to hand of <a> ~~cricket~~
game of cricket in America. A film actress had been
lowered from a peak in California & <hung> ~~was shown~~ in
mid air. Sir Austen Chamberlain was at Geneva.
A sheep had given birth to a lamb with a dogs head.
~~There was And so on~~. Nobody could doubt

if anger
was the
word for it,

nothing can
keep
anger out of
~~one's~~ <their>
style;
~~but why~~? if it
is in the mind;
[warmly?]

~~that England~~ Even from ~~so this~~ <this> haphazard ~~comment which~~
<~~review~~ statement>
~~an evening paper makes upon the progressives that England~~
~~the power of the~~ of current affairs that the judges & the
cricketers & the ~~statesmen~~ <politicians> were in the ascendency;
~~the government of England is patriarchal; the judge could~~
~~comment was there to comment; the woman to be commented on;~~
~~was commenting, the cricketer play hitting, players, The Foreign~~
~~Secretary controlling, <was dictating> the skill of the cricketer~~
though
film actress might hang by a single rope over peaks &
Lady -- looked lovely last night in <[ ]> pale ~~mauve~~ blue
Nobody in ~~their~~ <his> senses could doubt the rule of the
~~patriarch;~~ professor: {Yet the professor was angry -
~~But the paper was his, & the~~ } He had all the power, all the
money all the influence: he was ~~ed~~ sub-editor, ~~sub~~
Editor, owner of the evening paper; he was Foreign Secretary -
made treaties; he was judge & commented upon women; he
was cricketer & <[& hit runs?]> & he ~~was~~ owner of race horses &
~~he was~~
the ~~man who had~~ had millions to leave to charity in
education as he ~~chose~~. he was ~~th~~ millionaire & ran
industries. ~~Yet he was angry. It It <But> was foolish <annoying>~~
~~though~~
~~to use a word that did not precisely fit. He was~~
~~The~~
~~It might be an essential part of this power:~~
~~that is, it might be necessary to believe with~~
~~extravagant force in~~ The patriarchy: when, that is
Yet when it came <[judging?] from his bias> to writing books
about women he was
undoubtedly annoyed. {Perhaps this arrogance was
the natural result of having power <being a patriarch> - ~~one~~
~~observes~~
~~it is a familiar fact that the~~ very rich are often
<irritable> unamicable because they live in a state of
~~with~~ suspicion, ~~lest the~~ that ~~other people~~ want their
the poor want their money.}

This anger might be a natural result of his power. He might
think of women as the rich think of the poor - ~~they~~ with
suspicion, with hostility. ~~But~~ That ~~surely was a~~
~~superficial account of the~~ might ~~go a little way to~~
<[serve help?]> explain the anger of professors <[~~has for~~?]> with
women; but not <the [explanation?] was> ~~far~~
<not satisfactory. Indeed not truly with truth>
~~enough.~~ wholly. What was in the mans mind when
he insisted <so warmly> upon their inferiority? That
Really, it seemed to me possible that the poor man
was not thinking about women at all; he was
very probably well disposed to them; the kindest of
fathers, the best of husbands; ~~for~~ what was
troubling him <perhaps ~~not~~ not curiously> was this - the ~~necessity of being~~
~~extreme~~ necessity he felt <was under> to be superior: <to>
someone. ~~I must~~
~~believe, he kept on saying to himself, thus I am superior~~;
Life for both sexes, is there can be no need to say ~~is~~
arduous, difficult, a perpetual struggle. If I can
It calls for gigantic ~~powers~~ courage, ~~self con~~ <industry> &
strength.
~~have~~ The most valuable ~~factor is our~~ weapon in the
~~struggle~~ <[house?]> is not sword or axe, however: it is ~~simply~~
self-confidence. And ~~my con~~ this imponderable
quality, ~~which~~ is generated ~~far more~~ <much more> quickly
& ~~copiously~~ <more easily & might in fact> by ~~thinking~~ that one is
'superior' to somebody
~~that one has always with one living in the same roof <[house?]>~~
~~under the a creature who in whose eyes one has only to~~
~~look to see oneself perhaps twi whom one~~
~~who serves two invaluable purposes: she is~~
~~smaller The first,~~ by seeing other people small
than by being actually large oneself. Hence the
enormous importance to a professor, <or> a patriarch, of
of ~~an inferior race~~ & believing that half the
human race is ~~naturally inferior to them.~~ Smaller

[Margin: as possible thieves & ~~revolu~~ rebels,]

by nature than they are. It is of immense importance that the
patriarch should be able to have in his home, at breakfast &
dinner, a mirror - two mirrors to be precise - ~~which~~
into which he has only to look to see himself twice his
natural size. That was probably the cause of the
war, ~~when one comes to think of it;~~ the Kaiser looked into

Both Napoleon & Mussolini it is to be observed had & have the [consent of men?] & of women; both - felt the necessity of an inferior sex to his [pride?] in order to keep going at all.

eyes of the Kaiserin; the Czar into the Czarina's eyes; in
both they saw themselves far, far bigger than they could
ever have been in ~~an~~ a looking glass ~~that kept its~~ of
right proportion <so> that they began boasting & bragging; &
~~& the more they brag the more essential it is to keep~~
~~<find> their sense of inferiority alive: so that we always get~~
pretending that they were mailed fists, <or professors the finger
of destiny> or whatever the
phrase was, much as Mussolini is doing in Italy
now & Napoleon did a century or so ago in France.
~~This would account for the fact which so in~~.
This looking glass theory would serve to explain some of those
psychological puzzles which so frequently perplex any ~~the~~
~~ordinary one~~ in ordinary life. Why for example is it
~~utterly entirely out of the question~~ <impossibly> ~~to~~ for a
woman to
~~offer criticism of his intellect to~~ criticise a man, intellectually?
~~He may have written a bad book. But for her to say~~
~~"This is silly nonsense" is far more to invite a~~
without giving far more pain, rousing far more anger than is
comfortable or profitable? <~~Perhaps why~~> He sees the figure in the

Her criticism should be on her own showing less acute; less

looking glass shrink, ~~presumably~~; & it not only affects his
vanity, - & that is a quality that is scarcely measureable -
the desire of a man to be admired by women - but
it ~~makes him less~~ he sees the figure in the looking
glass shrink; & how is he to go on giving judgment -
making laws & building up fortune unless he sees
& has his fitness for life diminished;

himself much bigger than he is? The superiority complex - if one must have recourse to such ugly words - is a necessity to him. Perhaps he would die ~~if he were~~ without it, like a drug taker ~~denied~~ refused his cocaine. ~~It must be surely~~

under the spell of

that illusion ~~that keeps~~ thousands of men <not notably successful> happy & content. ~~"I am a man. I am <a> superior to being"~~ he says ~~to himself,~~ putt~~ing~~ <puts> on his coat in the morning, & ~~thus upheld he~~ go~~es~~ about his work, upheld, supported, confident, & ready to suppose that they are welcome, which is <~~be~~ on to> the best way, of being welcome, ~~though not alas, without~~ & one way, unfortunately of being, as men are, more often than women ~~an intolerable~~ <~~rather a~~ something of a> bore.

~~Luckily the chicken here interrupted what would have been~~

~~There were So one might analyse into its parts that~~

Here followed a list of bores, who were, for the sake of the theory, led to ~~their~~ this vice by the fact that they said as they dressed in the morning, "I may be-- anything you like to [call?] it; but ~~any how~~ I am a man." ~~But it was necessary to A few illustrations of the looking glass theory~~ Was one getting any nearer ~~the~~ to understanding the 'anger' of professors? ~~An~~ The anger of professors thus arises from this, that they wish to be superior, not that they wish ~~you to~~ anybody to be inferior. ~~And in support of this theory to be in part a true one, I recalled next that to be superior is, at present at any rate, the most a deep necessity, a root in the very being of the other sex, The fact that noth For angry they are. Angry Then They are Angry they are For otherwise, with all~~

Some irrational element must enter into the anger of
professors;
otherwise <with all the power in their hands, masters, kings,
judges, directors, a [ ] an.> they would talk very calmly
& coldly about
the other sex; & ~~it would not be a painful shock to them,
a fact that they wish to repudiate with every instinct in
them fights against, But ones impression has always been
that far from being calm, nothing so quickly stirs
heat as [compre?]~~ & not seem, at least, to regard it as a
calamity. The fact that the Odyssey was written by a
woman, the fact that in a forest in central asia is a
woman's ~~tribe~~ which has made the greatest contribution
to science, to art to letters that has been made since the
time of the Greeks - It is is an open question whether their
chief poetess, the poet Maya Hina is not the
superior of Shakespeare. I read out the fact
aloud ~~to a~~ & was amused to see how painfully the
~~young~~ man at the next table started, how he irritably
bethought him of some contradiction: how healthily his
desire for superiority was working. In sober
truth, I paid my bill & left. For, civilised
though we call ourselves, & rational, open minded, &
in particular able to talk freely, men & women together,
there are many things that <no> women has yet said to a man.

Would this theory work better than the other? ~~One~~ <Let us> must
turn it on to ones observations of real life. ~~For example~~
~~how about the war   The Let us see the~~ let us
turn it on to the war; & ~~say~~
Every man of action needs a mirror - two mirrors to be
precise, in which he has only to look to see himself
twice his natural size. That is why Napoleon - <in the>
<past &> Mussolini <in the [present?]> both insisted so
emphatically upon the
inferiority of women.   But

And finally - for here I must <get up> ~~find my purse~~ & pay the
bill - the looking glass theory explains a fact that used to
be prominent in the suffrage days, before the war,
leading to great irritation: I mean, that when
~~a the~~ <what seem to> irrational, ~~indeed~~ unimaginative ~~& timid~~
~~behaviour of~~ a ~~little~~ against human interests: the
strong wish on the part of one sex ~~not that~~
explain   that the other should not bring trophies to the common
the   hoard of surpassing excellence. ~~Was~~ <Were> a tribe of women
discovered in Central Asia, one of whom had written a
play better than Lear, another ~~a~~ made a discovery of [greater?]
~~into~~ importance than Einsteins, the news would be
received by the evening press with incredulity, first; later
with a passion of rage which would very
likely make away with these divine works
stealthily, in the dark of night; or substitute for
the Jane or Anne on the title page
William or George.   That is a curious fact to
contemplate - the wish

All these thoughts passed through my mind, ~~as I walked~~
& I hand them on to you, for ~~your scrutiny &~~ to do
~~what you like~~ with as our agreement is. In default of a
~~plain~~ the plain answer which I had hoped
after a morning in the British Museum to be able to offer you.
I give you these thoughts ~~trusting to you as~~ on the
understanding that ~~they are~~ the audience is entirely
of the one sex; For civilised ~~as~~ though we call
ourselves, & rational open minded & in particular
able to to talk freely, men & women together, there are
many things that no woman has yet <dared to say> said to a man.
~~Here I~~ <The bill> ~~My~~ bill <for lunch> came to five shillings &
eight pence, &
I handed the waiter a ten shilling note, & waited for the
change. It is a remarkable fact, & one that ~~often~~ still
takes my breath away ~~to find~~ <whenever I open my purse to find>
~~this~~ <the> power of my
purse to grow ten shilling notes. <Automatically I open it & there
they are.> Society gives me luncheon,
<&> clothes & a house ~~for nothing~~. in exchange for a
certain number of pieces of paper, which were given me
for no very good reason, by an Aunt who died ~~from~~
by a fall from her horse, when she was riding out to
take the air in Bombay. A solicitors letter
fell into the post-box one night about the same time
that the act was passed giving votes to women.
~~And I will confess, since it is useless to keep up any~~
~~pretence of~~ She had left me, this almost unknown
Aunt, somewhere about £500 a year. Before
that I had made my living by cadging odd jobs in

newspapers, reporting donkey shows; earning a few pounds by
addressing envelopes; reading aloud to old ladies; ~~once I~~
~~kept myself for half a year by taking typing letters;~~
~~in an office; & helping~~ making artificial flowers, & teaching
~~in a school~~ the alphabet ~~in some a~~ <to young children> in a
kindergarden.
Such were the chief occupations that were open to women
before --- ~~before the bill passed which~~ ~~those~~ <when they we> allowed them to enter
~~most of~~ the professions. I need not, I am afraid,
describe in any detail the hardness of the work; <for> ~~probably~~
you know women who have done it; nor the difficulty of
living on the money when one had earned it. ~~It was~~
But ~~there was a more one result~~ were certain other ~~effects~~,
~~of less tangible, But it had another~~ But what
still remains with me, though it is fading rapidly, is
the corrosion, the rust of the poison of fear & bitterness
which those days bred in me. To begin with, always
to be doing work one did not wish to do, that was
~~bad enough~~, & then ~~to then the~~ to do it in ~~chains~~,
like a slave, ~~with the sort of~~ flattery and fawning,
not ~~perhaps necessary, but~~ always necessary <only> perhaps,
but it seemed necessary; & the stake was too great to
risk it, if ~~a~~ archness coyness, <& the female dress> silk stockings ~~& all the~~
~~rest of it~~ would make it safe; & then the thought of
that one gift which it was death to hide - a very small one,
save to the possessor - perishing, <for an> & with it myself my soul;
~~all became &~~ all this ~~became~~ because one was in the
power of the patriarchs; became like poison, like rust;
eating away the bloom of the spring; ~~& its~~ <destroying the tree at its core.>
However, as I say, my Aunt died; & whenever I
change a ten shilling note, a little of the rust is
rubbed off by those silver shillings; & fear &

bitterness go; - Indeed, I thought, slipping the ~~pence &~~
<coins> ~~change~~ into my purse, it is ~~a~~ remarkable, remembering the
bitterness of those days, ~~how~~ what a change of temper, &

in its most

~~indeed~~ fixed income will bring about. No force in the
world, not even another war, can take from me my
five hundred pounds; ~~so safely is it invested~~. so long as
I do not gamble on the stock exchange. There it is for ever.
~~So long as I live I shall be given~~ Food & house & clothing. will
be given
~~Therefore,~~ me for ever. ~~That brings me~~, Therefore not merely
do effort & labour <cease> go, ~~but there wells up the feeling is
so acute that it is physical a~~ but also hatred & bitterness
~~What is there to~~ <why should> I need hate no <any> man; <He can
not hurt me.> nor need I flatter him.

flatter him? He has nothing to give me.

~~No longer need I buy a hat, for example, in the hope that
it will be the kind of hat that Mr. at the office
admires: I buy it for because it is a beautiful hat, or a
hat that does not spoil in the rain.~~ So
They can give me nothing; <~~nor~~> ~~they can~~ they <can> take
~~any~~<no>thing
~~from~~ me. Instantly, - within a very few days of hearing
of my Aunts death <India> - I found myself adopting a
new <true womans> attitude to ~~the~~ <all> patriarchs &
professors. ~~Poor old~~
It was not their fault, after all; ~~that they were
born like that~~; they had had, endless difficulties, endless
disabilities to contend with. Their education had been
in some ways more imperfect, lopsided, than my own.
True they had money & power, but what a ~~torment to have
so highly developed a possessive instinct!~~

but only at the cost of having in their brains

but what a torment to have bought it ~~by breeding
in oneself this~~ at the expense of owning, chained in
ones breast, that vulture, that eagle, who is always
tearing the liver & the lights in one, the possessive
instinct! Think of ~~being~~ wishing to possess

The eagle claws
other peoples land, & goods; ~~of furbishing up such <it makes an>~~
~~spending such~~
~~so killing ones sisters & cousins in order to get it from them;~~
~~of wasting ones energies in making guns & poison gas;~~
~~and of spending <passing> ones life in law courts, & sleeping after~~
~~dinner~~
~~to make money & spending making money <when> Five~~
~~hundred a year is all that one <a> human being needs~~
~~And then there~~ Indeed, who can ~~walk down~~
<walk> through the Admiralty Arch or The Sieges Allee
or any other avenue given up to trophies & cannon
~~& not feel There but for the pity a kind of pity~~
~~that it was necessary to be like that~~ - does one
envy those who collected that testimony to their power.
Or watch, in the spring sunshine, the unhappy creatures who
<[make coin at the stock exch at two?]>
make money & more money & more money still at
the command of the vulture in their breasts - Read
anywhere, the initials carved on statues in
obedience to its command, I. I I -- for the
vulture wishes forever to reiterate & to assert.--
In some such way as this I modified my
fear & bitterness into a kind of pity, or toleration;
& then, in a year or two, pity & toleration, went; &
the great release happened, which is the ~~only~~ chief
thing to be desired: one ceased to think of ~~people~~
sex at all. ~~One thought Is this right? Is this beautiful?~~
~~or simply what is this? Milton's bogeyman,~~
~~that had blocked the stars & the trees for~~
~~centuries, was consumed in the bonfire: If you~~
~~have 500 a year, you need can lunch~~
~~And this was the~~ one thought of things in themselves.
That hat, for example, do I like it, or do I not like it?
That picture - is it beautiful? That book - is it good or bad?
I am not saying that in private life the

~~What is the atom?~~ What are the stars? My aunts legacy
I may say without exaggeration unveiled the sky to me;
Otherwise ~~should I not have I should have squinted at it to my dying day behind from without it I should have been squinting now to this day, trying to see it in relation to some~~ removed for ever the large & imposing figure of
Professor X. which tried to ~~get in~~ the way. <block the heavens & earth>

Dominate ~~the~~ heaven & earth

~~The afternoon was now late dark. Lights <Lamps> were being lit, & a~~ It was now getting dark; lamps were being lit, & an indescribable change had come over London, as if the great machine ~~which had been were making something~~, after roaring ~~&~~ all day <at its work> were ~~making~~ <producing at last> some~~thing~~ ~~before ones eyes~~; something ~~at once terrible~~ & serene. ~~On the one hand, there in the houses, private life,~~ the lit rooms, where ~~book~~ there was quiet & thought & happiness; & this flying chaos & terror. of ~~the open air & the rushing~~ omnibus & train. In my little ~~back~~ street, however, domesticity ~~one was not moved to any~~ <prevailed> the house painter was still on his ladder, the nursemaid was bringing the perambulator carefully home to nursery tea. The coal heaver was letting his sack shower into the cellar - just as in the ~~morning~~, & the woman who keeps the greengrocers shop was adding up the days ~~takings in a glass~~ takings ~~at a desk~~ with her hands in red mittens to keep off chilblains. In a belated attempt to find something to ~~say abo~~ write on the

page headed "Women & Fiction" which awaited me, I made
these final ~~notes~~; <reflections> ~~who can be sure whether it is~~
~~better to be a~~
~~nursemaid or a coal heaver?~~
That it was a very difficult matter, to

Observing the sexes ~~so~~ thus employed, I made the
following reflections, - that it is <becoming increasingly
difficult to say> difficult to say which
employment is the better - the coal heavers or the nursemaids,
~~though~~ the prime ministers or the charwomans; we are
not nearly so sure of values as they were in the
nineteenth century. Which led me (here I was at my
own doorstep) to wonder what would happen when
nursemaids took to coal heaving. It is all very
~~well to say that~~ Women <~~(& clergymen & gardeners)~~> live longer
than men; except clergymen, <and gardeners>
~~probably tame pheasants live longer than wild ones; but~~
but when they do the ~~same things as men~~, heave coal &
paint house & ~~work they~~ as logically now they
must, will they not ~~perish~~ die so much younger,
so much quicker, that one will say "I saw a
woman today" as one used to say "I saw an
aeroplane?" ~~Women have been preserved, in~~
~~like~~ So I went in.

The Fitzwilliam Manuscript

Chapter Three

Tuesday 12th March.

Chapter Three.

after visiting the British Museum

Here, indoors, among the chairs & bookshelves, ~~one could~~ [on the table]
lay the blank sheet of paper, headed Women & Fiction. ~~It~~
It was disappointing not to be able to write down ~~one~~
~~single & satisfactory answer to that question — why are~~
women are poorer than men; & to ~~get on with the proper~~ [is this, or that]
leave ~~women~~ the ~~ugen~~ [woman] [fiction] & get on to the fiction;
that ~~this~~ ~~writing is somehow or other~~ [my eyes a little with] [... and]
~~writing~~, is like a spider's web, attached ~~in all sorts of~~ [either so slightly]
~~odd places to the things~~ to life ~~in~~ at all ~~sorts of~~ [... is]
~~queer way~~. four corners. Often, the attachment is
imperceptible; the achievement, Shakespeare's plays, But
~~the~~ Milton's poems, seems complete by itself.
when the web is pulled askew, hooked up here,
or with a great hole in the middle of it there, then one
~~re~~ remembers that these webs are not spun in
mid air by incorporeal creatures, but ~~are the~~
~~work of~~ ~~do depend~~ on are attached to grossly
material things, like money, & health, & ~~private~~ ~~rooms~~ [a house] ~~of one's own~~, & that
the spider is a human being. I was thinking as I
~~gravely~~ ~~angrily~~ ~~with~~ made this simile of the spider's webs,
of certain strains & holes that to my mind
still strangely disfigure the webs that made by women.
But clearly it's no use rummaging in the British Museum
for a reason, it was a futile proceeding. An
avalanche of opinion had descended on one's head. ~~And~~
the opinions ~~of men about~~ women were this that & the other
according to the temperament of the observer. But
suppose one ~~went to a person, or~~ consulted ~~an~~ someone

the usual ...

They are ... other work ... children

but in case ... on a ... ...

Tuesday
<u>12th March.</u>

<u>Chapter Three</u>.

Here, indoors, <on the table> among the chairs & bookshelves, ~~one could~~
lay the blank sheet of paper, headed Women & Fiction;
It was disappointing <after visiting the British Museum> not to be able to write down ~~one~~
~~single & satisfactory answer to that question — why are~~
women <are> poorer than men; & so ~~get on with the paper~~ <is this or that>
the reason why — leave ~~women~~ the ~~sexes~~, <woman> & get on to the fiction;
But ~~it is~~ <fiction> ~~writing is, somehow or other~~ imaginative work <each kind,>
~~writing~~, is like a spiders web, attached ~~in all sorts of~~ <in ever so lightly>
~~odd places to the things;~~ to life <at> ~~in~~ all ~~sorts of~~
~~queer ways~~. four corners Often, the attachment is
imperceptible; the achievement, Shakespeares plays,
~~the~~ Milton's poems, seems complete by itself. But
when the web is pulled askew, hooked up here,
or with a great hole in it there, <the centre> then one
remembers that these webs are not spun in
mid air by incorporeal creatures, but ~~are the~~
~~work of~~ ~~do depend on~~ are attached to grossly
material things, <like> money, & health, a ~~room~~ to merely; <& ~~privacy~~ & a [house?]> in short
the spider is a human being: I was <no doubt> thinking as I
~~provided myself with~~ <made> this simile of the spiders web,
of certain strains & holes that to my mind
still slightly disfigure the webs ~~that~~ made by women.
But clearly to go rummaging in the British Museum
for a reason, ~~to~~ was a futile proceeding. An
avalanche of opinion <hot as lava, [~~in~~----?] various as a [shower of stone?]> descended on ones head. ~~And~~
~~the opinions of men about~~ <women> were this that & the other,
according to the temperament of the observer. But
suppose one ~~went to a person, wh~~ consulted ~~an~~ some one

they are made often with great delicacy

who was not giving an opinion, but recording a fact - an
historian that is to say - might there not be a better chance
of understanding ~~the~~ something about the condition in
which women were living when they wrote, or did not write;
something <highly> important, if it is true that money & rooms,
chicken and coffee, five hundred a year & a clear view
of the sky influence spiders, of both sexes, ~~when~~ at their work.
So I went to the shelf where the sober books stand &
took down Professor Trevelyans History of England.
I found in the index "Women, position of', &
looked up the references. "Wife-beating was a
recognized right of man, & was practiced without
shame ~~a~~ by high as well as low. . . "Therefore
the wife ought to suffer & let the husband have the
word, & ~~be~~ to be master (writes a contemporary)
Similarly, the daughter who refused to marry the
p. 260-1 gentleman of her parents' choice was liable to be
locked up, beaten & flung about the room, without
any shock being inflicted on public opinion. Marriage was
not an affair of personal affection but of family
avarice, particularly in the 'chivalrous' upper classes
. . . Betrothal often took place while one or both of the
parties was in the cradle, & marriage when they were
scarcely out of the nurse's charge." That was about
1470, ~~a little~~ soon after the death of Chaucer.
Let us ~~to skip to the~~ turn to the next references to women, <[in history?]>
some two hundred years later, in the time of the
Stuarts. "It was still the exception for women of
the upper & middle class to choose their own husbands,
& when the husband had been assigned he was
lord & master, so far at least as law &
custom could make him. Yet even so" Professor

Professor Trevelyan concludes "neither Shakespeares women
nor those of authentic Seventeenth Century memoirs, like
the Verneys & Hutchinsons, seem wanting in personality &
character". No, <certainly> Cleopatra had ~~something~~ a way
<must have had a way with her;>
~~with her one would~~ was not altogether insignificant.
Lady Macbeth ~~had~~, one would think, a will of her own. <[knew
her own mind ?]>

one can imagine Rosalind [was?] ~~now an~~ was ~~was an~~ ~~an attractive agreeable girl; rather [ath tall?]~~

~~As for Chaucer's Cressida,~~ she <was> could lead a lover a
dance - Professor Trevelyan ~~has not been~~ says <speaks> no less
than the truth when he remarks that Shakespeares
women are not wanting in character. Indeed,
not being historians, we might even go farther & say that
all time is women burn ~~in the~~ <blaze in all the poetry of poets>
burn in ~~all the~~
~~down~~ all the shores of poetry <[down all the wastes?] of time> like
flaming beacons.
Clytemnestra, ~~Phedre~~, <Phedre> Antigone, Cleopatra, Lady
Macbeth; <[ ]>; Cressida, Rosalind, Desdemona; the
Kitty . . . Emma Bovary, Madame
de Guermantes - <name after name comes to mind;> they do not
seem "wanting in
~~personality~~ & character." ~~But these women are all~~
made ~~no doubt out of some~~ ~~But it is~~ ~~It~~
~~But~~ ~~To write~~ Indeed, if one ~~merely considered women in
fiction as it is written by men one would be~~
<women> had no existence, except in the ~~play~~ ~~<plays>~~ ~~poems~~
fiction
written by men one would imagine her ~~an
astonishing portent; very important;~~ very various;
with an ~~astonishing~~ beauty, force, grandeur;
unlike a man; sordid; wicked; cruel; ---
~~but the poets & the novelists are, <until a late period>
unfortunately for many <hundred years,>
<all of one sex> men for the most part, & therefore
so that we get a they write the creation is a~~
creature of ~~the~~ great interest & importance. It is

only when we come to facts that we realise ~~that the~~
how much a ~~man~~ poet colours things with his own
temperament, ~~how~~ & creates what is not <[why no?]> there. For
<[fact?] was when> the truth was, as Professor Trevelyan points
out, that
women were beaten by their husbands; that they were
locked up, beaten, & flung about the room if they
~~disobeyed~~ <refused> ~~their parents choice~~ to marry the man
~~of this him~~ were married when they were scarcely
out of their husbands charge; that they were locked up in . .
if they refused to marry the man of their husbands choice;
that they were beaten by their husbands; '& that
the husband was lord & master, so far as law &
custom could make him". A very queer
composite creature <thus> emerges; ~~from both~~ from the two
versions of the fact: ~~a she is capable,~~
~~She is capable of~~ <imaginatively> of great importance
imaginatively;
practically she is of complete insignificance. She
pervades poetry; she is almost absent from history.
She dominates the lives of Kings in feeling; in
fact she was the slave of any man who chose to marry <knock her>
<about the room> her. ~~She spoke some~~ <few> of the most
profound words, ~~in~~
some of the most inspired words in literature fall from her
lips; ~~she was~~ in real life she ~~had~~ was without education,
without money, without an atom of land that she
could call her own. We must ~~needs~~
reduce this glaring monster to human size before we
can understand ~~any~~ <anything about her> a word that she writes. It
would be a fascinating, & more, a useful, task for

for one of you, whose heart is set upon writing books, to write the
life of an average woman <say> in the time of Shakespeare.
That would teach us ~~so much~~ <what we want to know> about their
poetry;~~ that is to~~
~~say~~ why <that is> they did not write ~~any~~ But where are you
going to get the facts? ~~Here is Professor Trevelyan~~
If you go to the historians - take Professor Trevelyans
history for example - what do you find? "The Manor Court
& the methods of open field agriculture . . . . The
Cistercians & sheep-farming. . . . The crusades. . . . The
University . . . The House of Commons . . .
The Hundred Years War . . . The Wars of the Roses. . . .
The Renaissance Scholars . . . . The Dissolution of the
Monasteries . . . <Agrarian & Religious Strife> The Origin
of English Sea-power.
The Armada . . . So it goes on.
Occasionally of course one individual woman is
mentioned, an Elizabeth a Mary; but the whole
process ~~is~~ excludes women entirely; by no
possible means could ~~a woman~~ <women,> ~~have taken part in~~
average women, women who had nothing but their
brains or their character to commend them, have
taken part in any one of the great movements
which thus brought together. <constitutes the historians view of the
past.> For that reason
history often seems, to a woman, a little dull.
She may go on to ask, is it <really> true? ~~Those~~
~~That war making, that law making, those~~ was there
nothing of importance happening in England except
what gets recorded here? Had I no share in these
events? What was I about all those years?
~~Well of co undeniably~~ <we have of course the> ~~there~~
~~are the~~ Paston <letters;> the
<lives of the> the Verneys & the Hutchinsons's Obviously women

a mans view of what was important in the past.

were in existence all this time. ~~But when you come to write your life~~
~~of the average woman in the time of Shakespeare you will fin~~d
Is it not time perhaps that history should be re-written?
Or ~~shall~~ if that task sounds too ambitious, that a
supplement was added - The lives of the obscure. If it were
called by some such title as that, nobody could ~~of~~
object to it, & these little dodges are still (Oct. 1928)
advisable.

One must ~~perform that~~ ~~use the~~ unite the two ~~great~~
powers of fact & fiction, ~~& bring to bear upon the woman,~~
~~the average woman say of Elizabeths time say if it she~~
~~who is the object of our curiosity, the fact of her~~
using both ~~insignificance, legally & politically, & the [question?] of her~~
senses at ~~each~~ as we do in judging ~~real~~ <living> people, so as to
once, make a real woman of her; for if we go by the historians we
shall think her a drudge, if we go by the poets, a queen.
~~The truth about the average woman of Elizabeths age~~
The difficulty ~~is~~ however <is> soon apparent. Suppose we
want to ~~get~~ imagine the life of an average woman in
the time of Shakespeare, ~~there is hardly & the~~ <there are no> facts;
~~are~~ <that line of [investigation?] is almost non-existent>
~~negligible compared with the fiction. If we go to the~~
<consult the> historian, like Robert Trevelyan for example. ~~What~~
does,
<the> history mean ~~to him~~. <of England is to him> A ~~process~~
~~which~~
succession of events ~~which~~ in none of which, unless perhaps she
was born a Queen, could ~~any~~ a woman possibly take
part. ~~Read the~~ ~~One looks at the~~
<X> So it goes on; The whole process excludes women
entirely. X We have of course the Paston letters, the lives
of the Verneys & the Hutchinsons. But if you are
going to write the For that reason history often seems to a
woman a little queer, dull perhaps, untrue perhaps.
[~~The~~ reason?] Something seems lacking. {We have of course the Paston
letters; ~~for~~ & later the Verneys & the Hutchinsons. But}
To rewrite history would be too ambitious, a task;
but surely a supplement is needed, the lives of the
obscure it might be called, & women might
figure there <perhaps> without impropriety. But
for the moment we are occupied with a simpler
task: to find out what sort of life a woman lived in

~~the time of Elizabeth. <Shakespeare> Had she money? Had she rooms of her own?~~
~~<At> what age did she marry? How many children had she? How was she expected to take part in the work of the house?~~
~~If we knew what the life of that woman was, we should then be able to say how it was <why> that she did not write Shakespeares plays - whether from natural incapacity, or from an~~
incapacity that was [~~entered~~?] the nature of her life -

all the machinery for cooking & washing up.

One would have to go searching in parish registers; to read
through lists of births & deaths & marriages; to reconstruct houses; to
add up bills. So in time we might ~~answer~~ have
facts to ~~oppose~~ ~~com bine~~ <bined> with our fiction. & with these two
immensely valuable searchlights working side by side
we might see what has never yet been seen - a

[living brown brushes & waves ripple?]

the average woman, the middle class woman, the woman
who lived in England when Shakespeare was writing.
This piece of work, this fascinating & masterly biography,
would be, I submit, better worth writing than a
new life of Jane Austen, or, further consideration of the
claims of Joanna Baillie to have influenced Scott.
Even Miss Mitford, I think, might be allowed a centuries
sleep. For until we know how the average woman
of Shakespeares time {lived we cannot know why ~~that~~ <she>
~~she~~ did not write Shakespeares plays. And
that is the question that I am asking myself, without
any chance, so far as I can see, of an answer.

based on invaluable facts & yet imaginative all glowing with [imaginary?]

extraordinary woman ~~of~~ ~~gneius did~~ did not

There was it is true lately in existence an elderly
gentleman, a Bishop I think, who said that
in no circumstances could a woman ~~write now have~~
have written, write now, or write in all time to come
Shakespeares plays. ~~He also~~ (It was the same
authority who told a lady correspondent in Norwich that

cats do not go to Heaven, <but granted them souls of a kind)>
though cats, he added, ~~are~~
have souls, ~~Alas,~~ <But> I have forgotten what ~~his~~ he based his
decision upon; ~~perhaps~~ the smallness of womens brains,
which is now said to be no argument either way.
Thus ~~deprived of~~ with only such facts as I have quoted from
Professor Trevelyan, & a few I have picked up in ~~such
books as~~ the Paston letters & the Verneys & the Hutchinsons
(who are a little late) ~~I am forced to fabricate for
myself a fancy picture of going to imagine
I cannot come very near the truth of the averge woman
in Shakespeares time;~~ it is hopeless to try to
understand the truth about the average woman in Sh<u>res</u> time.
Therefore to imagine the extraordinary woman is still more
difficult. But let us try. Let us imagine a
very extraordinary child <Let us call her Mary Arden> born in
Warwickshire about
1564 - we need not haggle about the date. Her father
was a small tradesman, perhaps a butcher or a
dealer in wool. ; ~~He~~ <who> married an heiress <of gentle birth>
however -
~~became of some importance in the town, & the child
shall we call her Mary Arden~~ They were
therefore well off enough for the sons to have some
education. The sons went to the grammar school &
~~learnt~~ read Ovid Virgil Horace Juvenal Plautus &
Seneca & Cicero: ~~They also learnt~~ <[also?]> the elements of
Grammar Logic, Rhetoric. The sons then -
but we must remember that we are dealing with the
daughter. The daughter stayed at home & learnt sewing &
baking. The son <was rather wild in his youth, [a park?];>
marries, & has a daughter six
1582 months later, & then twins. After that the son ~~goes~~ <went>
to London & is said to have held horses at the door of the
playhouse. Very soon he got work in the theatre, &
became a successful hard working actor, living in the
~~thick of his~~ hub of the world, in taverns in inns,

she might have scribbled a few pages more in

meeting everybody knowing everybody going everywhere, learning his business on the boards, in the streets, & even getting access to the palace of the Queen. But his extraordinarily gifted sister remained at home. She was as adventurous, as imaginative, as agog to write plays & see the world as her brother. But she had no book learning. She picked up a book now & then & read a few pages. Then her mother would come in & mind the stew. Once she went gallivanting off in the woods dressed like a man. She was severely beaten that night by her father. Sickened with <~~The~~ They talked of marrying her to this>
this treatment, she made up a small parcel of her belongings, sold some ~~small~~ trinket which was all she had of valuable & took the road, one summer night for London. She was only <~~just but~~> seventeen. ~~Her mind~~ was ~~flooded~~ The birds that sang in the hedge were not more musical than she was. She had the quickest fancy, the the loveliest gift for language. <words> ~~Some think she I~~ As far as
book learning went, she had not much to seek. But how was she to make her living, how learn her crafts in London? She had her brothers [taste?] & followed him to the theatre. what use was a woman there? Could she hold horses? Could she act? Could she seek her dinner in a tavern, or roam the streets alone at midnight?
Her genius ~~<[when?]> asked all these things demanded scope, action. It asked free life with men & women. She was courageous, strong. She should have been a poet, but how shall I tell the story politely <genteely>? The very first night she asked for~~ held horses at the stage door;
She stood at the theatre door. Some one came along & - <But no one gave her horses to hold.>
there is no end to the passion & sensibility of great poets, insulted her: she was unprotected, a woman.
And she could not get work - women could not act, men said. When she asked for work, the old manager said

He was surprised
something about a woman acting & a dog dancing. It was
That insult worked in her brain. She could get no training
Could she seek her ~~tavern~~ <din> in a tavern or roam the streets
at midnight? Her genius was young still, wordy;
~~in~~ unsaleable. She fell into the power of ~~Greene, a~~
old Nick Greene, the actor manager, poet & pamphleter.
<~~She had~~ before she was 18, ~~in~~ in the peak of her prime, she bore a child>
And so - for who shall measure the heat & violence of the
poet; <heart,>
when caught & tangled in the body of a woman - <she killed herself one winters night, in>
& is buried ~~in~~ under a tomb <in one of the city churchyards> without a name.

That is somehow how the story would run. now ~~we~~ <if a woman> begin to see
why ~~the extraordinary woman of~~ <in> Shakespeares time
had did ~~not write Shakespeares plays~~. For my own part I
had entirely agree with the deceased Bishop, when he said
Shakespeares that it was unthinkable that any woman had ever had <in Shre time shd.>
genius:
Shakespeares genius. For genius like Shakespeares is not
born among ~~illiterate, working~~. labouring, uneducated,
servile people. It is not born, even today, among the
working classes. ~~Certainly~~ How could it then have
been born among women, whose work began, according
to Professor Trevelyan, almost before they were out
of the nursery; who were forced to it by their parents,
who were locked up & flung about the room if
they refused ~~to do~~ it? Shakespeares genius
could not have ~~existed under~~ come into ~~those~~
existence ~~in~~ under those conditions. But genius
of a sort must have existed even among women, as it
must have existed even among the working classes.
What happened to it? Certainly it never got itself in

those days onto paper. When however we read of a witch being
ducked or of a woman being possessed with devils, or of a
wise woman, & even of ~~the~~ a very remarkable man,
then I think we are on the track of a lost novelist,
a suppressed poet, some mute & inglorious Jane
Austen, some Emily Brontë who dashed her
brains out on the moor or mopped & mowed about
the highways, crazed with the torture her gift
had put her to.

~~Here you may accuse me of exaggeration; but unless you~~
Can Indeed I would venture a guess that
Anon, who wrote so many poems without signing them, was
<often> a
woman. It was a woman (the suggestion is not mine)
who made <often> ballads, crooning them to ~~her~~ children,
<making them to beguile> ~~over her~~ spinning, <or> while the kettle
boiled.

the nature of the art of creation
memoirs. . .

It was disappointing not to have brought home in the evening a very important statement; an authentic fact. Women are poorer than men because ---- this or that. Now ~~one~~ Perhaps now it would be better to give up hunting for reasons, asking opinions, which descend on ones head like an avalanche, hot as lava, discoloured as dishwater. It would be better to draw the blinds across the windows so that no distraction can enter in; & to light the lamp; to go to the book case & to ~~consult the historian find out &~~ to ask the historian to tell - <explain> us <under> what ~~was the~~ conditions ~~of~~ women ~~in~~ ~~fact in history~~ lived; not throughout the ages; but in one particular age - the Elizabethan. for instance.

For it is always a ~~puzzle~~ <puzzling truth> why there was no woman writer among the Elizabethans, ~~considering~~ the ~~enormous &~~ when ever other man, it seemed, was capable of a sonnet or a song. What were the conditions in which women lived, I asked myself, for fiction, imaginative work that is, is not like a pebble dropped single & solitary upon the ground, as science is perhaps; fiction is like a spiders web attached ever so slightly it may be to life at all - &c.

I went therefore to

thus letting the
two sides - that she is
dressed in blue, & wears
patent leather shoes & has a
cut on her finger ~~mix~~
mingle with the
oddities & astonishments
of the soul which
~~her underneath~~ is for
ever modifying the
blue dress . & the
blue dress [then?].

[77 *verso*]

It was certainly an odd monster that one made up by
reading the historians & the poets simultaneously <one after the
other,> --
~~a~~ a ~~woodlouse~~ <worm winged like an eagle> with the wings of an
eagle, a
a creature ~~so fair as free as light & a~~ ~~a~~ the
spirit of life & beauty ~~with~~ in a kitchen chopping up
suet. But these monsters, however amusing to the
imagination, have no existence in fact; What one
must do ~~next, is to reduce bring tha new~~ was to
~~humanise her, to bring~~ make an ordinary woman

she is a
that she is
dressed in
black <blue>
& has
two sons at
Winchester,
one works &
the other:

of her, which ~~was~~ one does, in real life, by thinking
prosaically & poetically at one & the same moment.
~~Thus keeping in touch with fact, as is essential, <that she is~~
~~[there?]> but at~~
~~the same time realising that what we knew about~~
~~anybody is only her mind being is coursing up & down her~~
~~veins & send~~ She is an immortal soul &c.
But if one ~~begins~~ <tries:> to think of the Elizabethan woman,
<like this> one is at once tripped up by the ~~poverty~~
scarcity of facts. ~~One~~ History scarcely mentions her.
Consult Professor Trevelyan again ~~Look~~ . . . .
Glance through the headings of his chapters.
We shall not find her, unless she is a ~~great~~ Queen, like
Elizabeth or Mary in history. Nor shall we find
her, ~~where we find so many of her so much~~ the men
in any collection of anecdotes. Aubrey ~~never~~ has
nothing to say about her. She never <~~scarcely~~> wrote
a word of criticism, autobiography, diary; ~~& true~~
~~there were~~ the scarcely a letter. True there are
the Pastons, & later, in Stuart times, the Verneys -
the Hutchinsons. But What one wants, & ~~who~~
why does not some brilliant student at Girton or Newnham

supply it? - in a ~~masterly & exact account~~, mass of facts;
when she married; how many children she bore; what her house
was
like; had she water laid on? Did she do the cooking?
Would she have a servant? ~~What we want~~
all those ~~obscure~~ facts that lie in parish registers -
account books. That is where the life of the average
Elisa woman is to be found. It would be ambitious
beyond my daring, I thought, looking about the shelves for
books that were not there, lives of obscure women, <written
by women about themselves>
to suggest to the students of Girton & Newnham that
they should re-write history, though I own it seems often
a little queer as it is, lacking in something; but why
should they not add a supplement, <[besides?]> the lives of the
obscure it might be called, & <like> women might
figure there without impropriety? One often finds
them in the lives of great men, vanishing away into the
background, just <in> a flash of an eye, a wink: they are
~~often~~ After all we have lives enough of Jane Austen;
it scarcely seems necessary to consider again what influence the
tragedies of Joanna Baillie had upon Walter Scott; nor
should I personally mind if the homes & haunts of
Mary Russell Mitford were <closed> left unvisited for a
century or so - ~~But~~ <For> what <is so deplorable> I cannot
stand, I ~~said~~, <thought>
~~addressing myself~~ <speaking> in the character ~~of an ill used
journalist called upon to write an article in a~~
upon women one who must read a paper at Newnham in a
& fiction weeks time ~~& cannot find a single fact she~~ <~~that is~~> needed,
is that ~~when one has to talk~~ <is> there are no facts to go
upon. ~~Women left nothing whatever behind them when
they died.~~ when I Here am I asking
why they did not write poetry in the Elizabethan age
& I do not know whether they ~~could she~~ were

taught to write, let alone whether they had sitting rooms to themselves,
~~Money~~ apparently they ~~had no~~t had no money, & according to
Professor Trevelyan they ~~had~~ were married, & whether they
wished or not, before they out of the nursery - say at 15 or 16.
<After that> Then, they were entirely in their husbands power. It
would have been extremely odd, even on this showing, had one
of them written the plays of Shakespeare, I concluded.
~~Indeed, without entirely agreeing with that deceased~~
~~gentlemen, a Bishop, who I think who said~~ & I
thought ~~with pleasure~~ of that old gentlemen, he is dead now,
but he was a Bishop, I think, who had said <~~had it [ ]~~> that it was
<impossible> unthinkable <for> ~~that~~ any woman, past, present or to come, ~~should~~
~~have~~ to have the brain of Shakespeare. He also told a
lady who wrote to him for information on the subject
that cats do not <as a matter of fact> go to Heaven, though they have, he added
stooping ~~to~~ no doubt to stroke the episcopal cat,
wh. was a very fine animal, souls of a sort.
How much thinking those old gentlemen used to save
one! Cats do not go to Heaven. Women can not
write Shakespeare. <What a pity that they are> But they are rapidly dying out,
the Bishops <alas; & the> who knew these facts.
~~Still~~ Be that as it may, I could not help
thinking as I looked at Shakespeares works on the shelf
that it would have been utterly, entirely out of the
question for a woman <then> to have written then. <in> Let me
imagine - since facts are so scarce - what would have
happened had Shakespeare had a wonderfully gifted
sister called, shall we say Judith. Shakespeare we
know, may have been at a grammar school; ~~learnt~~
anyhow he ran rather wild

All this may be moonshine; but what is true in it, so it
seemed to me reviewing the story of Shakespeare's sister as I had
~~conceived it, made~~ <told> it, & ~~seems to me undeniable~~ &
the others, is that any woman born with a great gift then
would certainly have gone crazed, shot herself or ended her
days in some lonely cottage ~~on the hill I~~ outside the
village, ~~alone the~~ in solitude, ~~the sport of boys, but the~~
half witch half wizard, feared & mocked at. For it
needs little skill in psychology to ~~know~~ be sure
that a ~~gifted girl~~ highly gifted girl, who had tried to use
her gifts, would have been so thwarted & ~~prevented~~ <hindered> that
so tortured, ~~in~~ & pulled <asunder> ~~this way~~ & that by her own
[~~mothers~~?] contrary instincts that she ~~would~~ could have kept
her <health &> sanity only by a miracle. Judith Shakespeare
would have seen her brothers always put before her. She to begin with
books & the teaching were for them not her. Then,
~~if she~~ as she grew older the negative discouragement would
have become positive. "~~You are to~~ mend the stockings or
mind the stew, <dust> not moon about with books & papers - "
~~She would be [enforced?] or he by~~ Her father & mother would have
<told her thus charged her> ~~ordered~~ her thus, sharply enough; & being wise people,
~~with~~ who knew the conditions of life for women, &
loved her well - indeed, ~~her~~ she was the apple of her fathers
eye more likely than not, how could she go against them?
The force of her own gift alone drove her to it; but how & she
began to dread hate the force of her own gift! It was
urging her against all that she held dear; ~~it was~~
~~urging her to~~ Her father ceased to scold; he
begged of her instead not to hurt him, not to leave him,
not to do anything that could make him anxious or ashamed.
He would give <buy> her a chain of beads or a fine
petticoat if only &c &c. The force of her gift
broke through that. ~~She ran~~ But at <with> what
pain, with what rending & tearing of instincts

And there were tears in his eyes.

So ~~deep that~~ deeper than any save this cursed love of poetry.
~~Now, we are up against the~~ <Now> ~~At this point~~, when she broke
loose & went to London, ~~we are~~ <she was> up against something
so
deep in herself that <the wonder> she did not board the first cart
she
met going toward home. Perhaps a rough man laughed at
her: ~~Certainly, at the age of 16~~ a pretty girl <of 16> could no
more
~~walk to London without~~ walking along a country road,
standing in the ~~street, alone~~, a London street ~~would~~ <without>
soon have
met with ~~an~~ a violence & a bewilderment which if not
rational - ~~sex, they say~~ <[I say?] it> ~~the idea of~~ chastity
~~may be a~~ <is> fetish, something we invent, in civilised countries
for obscure reasons, ~~that are probably~~ foolish - ~~but~~ still
~~certainly as things are <were> even~~ are, nobody can deny its
profound ~~& intimate connection with every one~~
importance in the ~~mind~~ <life> of woman; or ~~its the~~ dirt
immense nervous stress & dilemma which a
girl would be thrown into who came up to London
~~alone as Judith did to mix~~ & stood alone at a stage
door. Thus, if women had written then,
~~their~~ what they wrote would ~~her~~ have been twisted, &
deformed ~~with all those~~ <with> morbid imaginations; ~~it would~~
~~have been fragmentary~~; & it would have been, undoubtedly
unsigned. ~~Probably that excessive~~ ~~Even now~~ ~~Till~~
~~anonymity is more~~ ~~Even in lately, in the nineteenth~~
~~Century, women were found~~ ~~Till Down to our own time,~~
~~down to George Eliot & Currer Bell & Georges Sand~~
~~anonymity has been~~ Perhaps ~~for from some~~ it is
~~the from some profound sense~~ <the sense> of chastity that dictated
anonymity to women even so late as the nineteenth
Century. Currer Bell, George Eliot, Georges Sand,
all the victims of this strife within them as their
writing shows, sought to ~~disgu~~ veil themselves
~~like it is an the~~ by using a man's name; &
thus did homage to the profound instinct which lay

being
overcome
by a terror
a shame -
for

its religious
significance
the way of her
wrapped itself
round into
nerves &
instincts all
of wh. must be
[brought?]
<out to> the
light of day
[written?] in
anguish; in
protest; in
fear;

unaffectedly
At the last
moment,
vainly,

at the root of womens being, & was certainly encouraged by
the other sex (The glory of a woman is to be unknown, said
Tacitus) for reasons which, ~~since we are not writing~~
when women take to writing books about men, may be explained:
~~to the the task may be bequeathed to As things are,~~
~~or perhaps here we are up against the other fact, which~~
~~is that women, who have possessed so little, are not~~
~~anxious to claim naturally~~ So And the fact that

but that must wait a century or so.

women have never ~~been~~ <until this last hundred years> possessed things, of their own,
<absolutely> for ever (as I hold my £500 from my Aunt)
has its effect; ~~&~~ <for> they are not so anxious for fame as
men are; are content to ~~let~~ do things without
being named or knighted; &, speaking generally, will
pass by ~~an~~ a tombstone or a sign post without
having any irresistible desire to cut their names on its
~~It is always~~ Alf or Bert or Chas. ~~I believe~~ do
~~saying to themse~~ in obedience to that profound
instinct which murmurs, when it sees a fine woman, or even a
dog go by, Cet chien est a moi; & of
course it may not be a dog; it may be a woman, or a
piece of land belonging to a man ~~who is black instead of~~
~~speaks French or German~~. with curly black hair.

The woman ~~of~~ <with an> imaginative gift <that> in the
sixteenth century would <it seemed to me,> have been an unhappy woman,
~~perhaps she would~~ a woman in strife against herself.
~~For The act of making~~ <creation of> a book ~~is~~ - here I opened
~~the volume which contains the Tragedies of Shakespeare - is~~
~~demands~~ All her instincts <conditions> & traditions <all her instincts> were
hostile to the state of mind which seems to be
needed in order to write a book. Here I
opened the volume containing the tragedies of Shakespeare.

What state of mind was Shakespeare in when he wrote Lear &
Antony & Cleopatra? <We only know that he never blotted a line.> ~~So far as I know,~~ Nothing was ever
said about the artists state of mind until the eighteenth century;
<& 19th century> when self consciousness ~~became~~ developed & it became the
habit for men of letters to write autobiographies; Thus
we do not know what Shakespeare felt when he wrote
King Lear; but we do know what Carlyle felt when he
wrote the French Revolution; ~~or~~ what Flaubert felt when
he wrote Madame Bovary. ~~We have the letters~~ of <what> Keats ~~&~~
the ~~letters of Byron, & the letters of~~ felt about his poetry;
~~we know a great deal, thanks to letters & memoirs, about the~~
~~way in which~~ what one gathers from ~~the~~ all this
literature of confession & self analysis is that to write a book is
~~a feat of~~ prodigious<ly> difficulty. Everything is against the writer.
Generally material circumstances are against him. The
[-----] dog will bark; people will interrupt; there is no <money,>
money <must be made> to pay the butcher. ~~Worse~~ On the top of all this,
there is the ~~hostility of the world~~ <worlds hostility> indifference ~~of the world~~
to works of art; it ~~desire comple~~ does not need poems & novels
& histories. It does not care ~~a jot~~ whether Flaubert
finds the right word or whether Carlyle scrupulously
verifies this or that fact. It pays very little for that
~~kind of~~ work; that it does not need. ~~& &~~ And so,
what with hardship on one hand & indifference on the other,
the writer, to judge from his own account, suffers,
especially in ~~youth~~ the creative years of youth, every
form of torture & discouragement. He is
like a man carrying ~~an~~ a precious jar through a crowded
street, ~~with knowing~~ <afraid> that it may be broken at any moment, -
can scarcely fail to be cracked & damaged in transit. Yet
carry it safe he must.

& to ~~be~~ have ~~written about~~ their lives written & have their letters edited <printed> after their death.

~~as~~ wholly, entirely in all its splendour.
~~But such discourage~~ ~~For~~ <But for> women ~~such diffi~~
had to ~~to struggle with~~ <such> difficulties ~~infinitely~~
were infinitely ~~greater~~ more formidable. In the
first place her circumstances were such that to
have a room of her own, let alone a quiet room, or a sound proof
room, was out of the question, unless she was born of
such rich or noble parents that there were rooms & to spare.
That ~~this was so~~, ~~She had no sitting room <of her own> was one of the~~
~~one of the chief causes that led to the womens~~
<Even up to the> ~~revolution~~ in the 19th Century. ~~Miss Davies was~~
<it seems she was without this>
help to ~~That is~~ sufficiently evident from the life of Miss Emily
Davies; <who> ~~&~~ women must have rooms to themselves she
a sitting room said, before anything else; & so ~~built~~ built Girton ~~wh~~ &
was quite ~~incurred a~~ ran it <Girton> deep into debt, for the sake ~~of the~~
beyond her ~~sitting rooms~~, in the sacred cause of sitting rooms, not
means, bed-sitting rooms, for women. ~~How could That was the~~
as is How could one write at all in the common sitting room,
with people going in & out ? one may ask. ~~But~~
And without money, her pin money only keeping
kept her in clothes & ~~was bestowed paid~~ depend<ing>ed on
the good ~~temper,~~ <will> ~~the~~ of her father, she was debarred
from such alleviations ~~& inspirations~~ as came
even to Keats, ~~or~~ to Tennyson or to Carlyle from
~~little~~ a walking tour, a little journey to Paris or
Scotland; ~~all~~ ~~freedom~~ from the ~~lodging or~~
~~College which would give~~ separate lodgings, which,
even if it were miserable enough, sheltered her from the
assaults of family life upon the time & temper. ~~A~~
were nothing Such <material> difficulties would <~~weigh on~~> ~~beset~~ her far more
to the tyrannously
immaterial ~~up~~ than upon men. ~~But~~ The indifference of
the world <which Keats & Flaubert found so hard to bear> was not
in her case indifference; it was

hostility. Here the psychologists of Newnham & Girton, I
thought, might come to our help. For surely it is time ~~now to~~
~~measure~~ that the effect of discouragement upon the
mind of an artist ~~were~~ <was ~~estimated~~> worked out; ~~as, in the~~
~~window of the~~
~~milk a milk shop~~ I have ~~seen the~~ as I have seen
the Diary Company work <[estimate?]> out the effect of ordinary
milk & Grade A milk upon the ~~health~~ <body> of a rat.
The two rats ~~are~~ <sat> in cages side by side; one ~~is~~ furtive,
small & timid; the other is strong bold & self confident.
~~The rats are the same. Both were the same at birth; one~~
~~was fed on richer milk, that is all. From the very beginning,~~
~~the woman was told that she could not write.~~
~~The world~~ Now I have only to open ~~any~~ the evening paper to
read that Lord Birkenhead is of opinion --- but
really I am not going to trouble myself ~~with~~ <to> copy~~ing~~ out
the opinion of Lord Birkenhead upon women's writing.
What Dean Inge says I will leave in peace. The Harley
Street specialist may be allowed to vociferate to the [limits?]
<of his>
without rousing an echo. <in my mind> Mr Oscar Browning may
~~be~~ I will quote "~~Mr.~~ {Mr. O B " was [not?]
because I like to think ~~that~~ <about> Mr. Browning I like to
~~found~~ after examining the students at Girton & Newnham
found ~~consolation in~~ Arthur, the stable boy, ~~so~~
~~superior~~. "Most high-minded". It ~~somehow~~
fills in the portrait of a most interesting man &
~~provides~~ ~~But~~ ~~All~~ <But many of the opinion, tho' they still
rebut [and such?]> They do not
rouse any great annoyance, in me, I thought;
<because> ~~but~~ then my aunt fell from her horse & left me
£500 a year. But one must remember that
few women are even now so happily unencumbered; [<have> in
their?]

They put

what do we feed women as artists upon, I wonder - prunes & custard.

Mussolini too may fulminate in Rome.

whose "[luck?] was

~~Moreover.~~
~~Whatever~~
~~Wherever one looks, outside the arts, in politics~~
~~for example one finds the same with some bewilderment~~
There is an instinct at work in men, I will not
~~try to~~ bidding them always stand at the gate, not only
of the arts, but of the professions, with a sword
drawn - so that even Lady Bessborough,
who was interested passionately in politics, must
humbly bow herself <and creep under> to Lord Granville [Gower?]
. . . . "notwithstanding.

And so she goes on to lavish all her
enthusiasm upon a more important topic, wh. is quite
Ld Granvilles maiden speech in the
House of Commons.

[87 *verso*]

Such a chorus of detraction, such a body of opinion,
signed by the names of professors & patriarchs, must have
been a formidable weapon in the hands of a father, say,
who from the highest motives, perhaps, did not wish his
daughter to leave home & become artist - writer, painter, or
musician. <See what Mr Oscar Browning says, he would say>
Also, any girl who could read ~~&~~ for
herself, must have received a check a shock a lowering of
her vitality as a writer <from reading such opinions.> which
would tell immensely upon
her work. There would always be that assertion, ~~on the~~ <flying
in her>
~~part of some great or important man~~ face to overcome.
<But> Probably ~~for women writers that the~~ <this particular germ
is ~~so~~ far losing its power over> for women writers ~~there~~
~~is now very little of that particular difficulty~~
~~remaining~~; But for painters, it must still be formidable;
for musicians, I imagine, active & poisonous in the extreme.
The ~~man~~ woman musician <[probably?]> must be now where the
~~woman writer~~ <actress is> was in the time of Elizabeth. Nick
Greene told Judith Shre. that a woman acting put him
in mind of a dog dancing. Johnson repeated the phrase
2 centuries later about women preaching. And here
I said, opening a book about music, we have the very
words. written in this ~~year of~~ very year about
women who try to write music

Jane Austen, Ch Bronte could write after a false one is sick to death

[Most if?]

So it goes on. <history repeats itself> One might say that it is
foolish in the extreme of women to take such
things to heart. One might say that ~~a~~ the woman
~~writer~~ <of> genius should ~~be strong enough to~~
not care what is said ~~or written~~ about her. Still,
~~there~~ Keats minded what a reviewer said. It
is the nature of an artist to be absurdly -
extremely sensitive to the worlds opinion. It is

~~The~~ For the mind of an artist in order ~~to be able~~ to
rise to the prodigious effort of freeing, uncramped &
incandescent; entire, the ~~art~~ work that is in him must be ~~in~~
~~the state~~ Like Shakespeares mind, I concluded,
looking at the book which was open at Antony &
Cleopatra.

~~But have I not just said that we know nothing of the~~
~~state of Shakespeares mind when he wrote his plays?~~
~~I decide reflected.~~
~~It is true~~ <~~[Readers?] say The critics say~~> that we know nothing
about Shakespeares; ~~mind~~ <mind>
~~but it seems to me~~ He never told us that he suffered from
the barking of a dog, or the rattle of wheels on cobble or
his neighbour playing on the lute. ~~Indeed it is a~~
~~curious fact that Sh. And the reason, I thought, why~~
~~people say that we know <we know nothing about> Shakespeare is~~
~~the most~~
~~impression we know so little about Shakespeare's, in one~~
~~likes & dislikes That is one of the chief reasons why we~~
~~know Shakespeare so much less intimately than we~~
~~know even his Ben Jonson, or Donne, or Milton.~~
~~All of these had grudges & prejudices. One feels them~~
~~cramped on this side, jammed on the other.~~
He did not tell in any of those things & ~~therefore~~ <thus> he is
~~in one way,~~ less known to us than any other writer.
for we do not know what annoyed him, what he
grudges he nourished, or envies or how he
One knows more about Milton or Donne or
Ben Johnson than about Shakespeare, because
their dislikes & peevishness appear
in their work. They are not burnt up with
heat. Shakespeare ~~was~~ worked at such

differs from them all in the speed
~~Shak~~ Shakespeares mind had burnt up all these
impediments: <they were [consumed?]> it was like molten metal;
& could
then fling along ~~without~~ hot fluid into any shape;
taking the mould of Cleopatra or Caesar or Antony;
~~always so in such a state of~~ never hardening &
~~cooling~~ into crease & ridge; giving us always the
sense of something so ~~mobile~~, so molten, ~~that~~ red hot;
~~How~~ One can almost see the idea splash into the
pool of his mind & ~~mixture~~ & cast sentences in one
spurt; the meaning seems to be cast at ~~the~~
to the body of his thought. With care one could
find passages where the words had almost been
the thought almost comes through the words, so
being too big for them; & yet we catch it, if we
read at full tilt; To do this, ~~one~~
~~we~~ he must have consumed all barren -
impediments in himself, I conclude: He must
have presented no obstacle to his genius. He
did, as far as human being ever did, ~~in~~ get
his work out of him unhurt.

Perhaps the reason why people say that nothing is known about
Shakespeare is that all his <[peevish?]> dislikes & grudges &
difficulties were consumed in his mind. It was so hot that
like molten metal, <& each shape [its?]> ~~flinging itself into~~ ~~any~~
was
shape. One
can almost see the idea splash into the burning ~~metal~~ [hot?]
the thought fusing the words together, so that
~~water~~ & cast sentences at one spurt, the words so
run together that it is only by reading at full tilt that we
can understand: ~~read word by word much of Shakespeare is~~
unintelligible. ~~We never We know~~ <But> Milton or
~~Donne or Ben Jonson much better than we know~~
~~Shakespeare because so much remains;~~ are full of
impediments, <in their writing> things said because of some
grudge or
angularity; ~~they~~ so that we know them better than
Shakespeare in one sense; & yet Shakespeare so pervades
his writing that in another sense we know no one so
intimately. His at any rate was the perfect state of
mind for a writer; ~~all grievances, all narrowness~~
to unveil himself
all desire to protest against ~~this one~~ injustice to himself,
or to proclaim his own rights, to blow his own trumpet, to
make the world suffer ~~for his~~ acquainted with his
own hardships or limitation, ~~is~~ was fired out of him,
& ~~all foreign bodies~~ <are> consumed. He did, as
far as human being ever did, <put forth> ~~get all~~ his work <put>
out of
him unhurt whole & uncrippled as ~~it~~

~~These things considered~~ <Thinking over all this,> it seemed to
me ~~that one~~
~~could say with~~ some inevitable that no
woman would have <written or> signed ~~a poem~~ <her writing> even
in the age of
Shakespeare. What one would expect would be
that rather later, some ~~one~~ <woman> of high rank would
take advantage of her comparative comfort &
freedom, ~~to~~ especially if she happened to be

childless, ~~& would~~ to publish something with her name to it &
risk being thought a freak. There is Lady Winchilsea for
~~instance, a complete case in point~~ to prove it, I thought,
taking down her poems & finding that she was born in
the year 1661, was childless, & noble by birth & marriage.
Further one would expect to find that her {poetry was
disturbed by ~~two~~ fear & hatred. ~~Far from the~~} Her
makes us think the ideal for a writer
state of mind <as a writer> was far from <that> ~~the~~ ideal that
Shakespeare
~~holds out~~ presents ~~us with~~. It was ~~inevitably~~ disturbed
by fear & hatred. She was conscious of injuries, of
limitation. She had perforce to express them in her
poetry however much against the temper of her mind.
Sure enough, here is she, railing against her fate as a woman,
25 How are we fallen! fallen by
~~Men are at~~ <the hu split> The human race is split up into two
parts. Men are "the opposing faction' Men are the
oppressors, men are hated & feared.
Alas! ~~the~~ a woman

~~She~~ Indeed, she has to make herself belief, in order
to write that what she writes will never be published,
~~for which~~ <& solaces herself> ~~anonymity she & but will be~~
she has to whisper to herself, ~~like an incantation,~~ the
sad chant ~~that she~~ what she writes will be written
only for a few people.
To some few friends, & to thy sorrows

Yet it is quite plain, I think, that could she have freed her mind
hardships from these bitternesses, & forgotten these restriction, <&>
could she
~~have written straightly & freely & zealously she would have written the like a true writer, the words forcing themselves~~
into The fire was in her; for now & then the words
are forced into two or three lines of pure poetry.

> Nor will in fading silks compose
> Faintly the inimitable rose.

It was a thousand pities that the woman who could
write like that should have turned ~~her mind into~~
acid to ~~satiri &~~ strife. & satire. But how could she
possibly have helped it, I thought, imagining the ~~life of the~~
<u>Countess of Winchilsea</u>, laughter & the comment; -
a ~~great lady writing~~ the lack of criticism; the adulation
of toadies; the scepticism of the professional poet.
She must have shut herself up in a room in the country
bitterness to write, I supposed, & been torn asunder <thus> by all kinds of
[scruples?] trouble. Her husband was devoted to her, &
put very proud of her; but it still she ~~had no~~ was always
there coming up against people who tittered. <In the absence;> She
became
diffuse, as Mr Murry justly says. ~~One sees~~ her
gift all covered with weeds & <bound about> strangled with
& might brambles &
have & briars. In our day, it would have been a <had a chance of>
grown to freedom,
be different matter. And so, putting her back on the
called shelf I turned to the other great lady, the Duchess that
Lamb loved, fantastic Newcastle; ~~almost~~
d of b. ~~Lady Winchilseas contemporary, the though~~ though her
1624? 1674 ~~elder~~. They were very different; but alike in this,
both were noble, & childless; both had husbands to their
liking; both lived retired, & wrote with passion. And

~~But the Duchess~~ Open the Duchess, & one will find
the same <cry of> rage, "Women live Bats or Owls, labour
like Beasts, & die like Worms, . . . / The best bred
women are those whose minds are civilest"./
Margaret too, might have been a poet. Milton it is said
owed a line to her. As it was, what could bind or
tame or civilise for human use that wild, generous,
[——] hard intelligence? It poured itself out,
higgledy piggledy in torrents of names wh. stand
congealed in quartos & folios that nobody ever reads.
She should have been a thinker; she should have been
taught to look at the stars through a telescope & reason
about things scientifically. ~~The~~ <At Court they sneered & jeered
at her.> Her wits were turned
with solitude & ~~so~~ freedom - No one checked her. She
wrote & wrote at Welbeck alone. Sometimes she
was coarse.
What a vision of loneliness & riot, as of some giant
cucumber spreading itself unpruned over the flowers &
the vegetables; the thought of Margaret Cavendish
brings to mind! What a waste, what an insanity
our ~~life is that allows these minds to grow~~
& yet how inevitable it was; Yet she wrote "The
best bred women are those whose minds are
civilest!" & there she frittered her time away,
inevitably, as it seems to me, plunging into solitude,
~~to~~ railing & ranting, ~~escaping~~ making a figure of
fun of herself. Evidently, the crazy
Duchess became a stock figure, a bogey to

frighten clever girls with. Here, ~~next door~~, ~~was~~ <is> Dorothy
37, 41, 138. Osborne, ~~who lived~~ for example, ~~commenting~~ writing to
227 Temple, about Lady Newcastles new poems,
"Sure the poore woman is a little distracted, she
1624-1674 could never bee soe rediculous else as to
venture writeing book's & in verse too, If
I should not sleep this fortnight I should not come
to that."

~~Indeed, nothing Dorothy Evidently, <Since> a woman's writing~~
~~was ridiculous, one must not & made people stare~~
~~Nothing could~~ And so, since no woman of
sense & modesty could write books, Dorothy, who was
sensible & modest & rather inclined to ~~gloomy &~~
melancholy, wrote nothing. ~~For~~ Letters did not <were permit>
count. A woman might write letters while she was
sitting by her fathers sick bed. She could write
them by the fire while the men talked, without
disturbing them. The strange thing is, I thought
turning over the pages of Dorothy Osbornes letters, what a
gift that girl, untaught, ~~solitary,~~ & solitary had
for the framing of a sentence, for the
fashioning of a scene One could have sworn
she had the making of a novelist in her.
But save this one [~~earl book~~?] casket of letters, <wh.> ~~written to~~
~~her husband~~ <she wrote> before they married ~~nothing~~ & her
husband kept safely treasured, she wrote nothing.
She married him, & they had children. The letters
cease.

~~The fear of ridicule, upon the sensitive & dependent~~
One can measure the <opposition that was in the air> current view of women's writing when one
finds it ~~thus~~ <~~the opin~~> completely accepted by a woman of great gift
that to write a book ~~implied~~ was to be ridiculous, even
distracted. And so we come, I continued, replacing the
single short volume of Dorothy Osbornes letters, to ~~the~~ Mrs.
Behn; She ~~is an interesting figure,~~ And with her we
turn a very important corner; ~~on the road, I thought.~~
We leave behind those solitary great ladies ~~withdrawing~~ <living far away>
<a> ~~to~~ their estates & ~~scribl~~ writing page after page in the
solitude. Mrs. Behn was a middle class woman, a
woman ~~of~~ with all the plebian virtues of
courage ~~&~~ humour & vitality & ~~carelessness; <plain speaking~~ [candour?]> a woman
turned by the death of her husband & some unfortunate
adventures of her own adrift on the world to make her living
[~~ride~~?] by her wits. ~~She was a very passionate woman, I reflected, with a~~ She had ~~to~~ ~~the [cast?] "no great house to withdraw to; no~~
to make money, & she was, it is said, the first woman to make
money by <her> writing. The importance of that fact
~~overt was to me at this stage in my~~ outweighs
anything that she actually wrote, even the splendid
A Thousand Martyrs I have made, or Love in
fantastic triumph sate - I thought, for here begins
~~that enormously important~~ the freedom of the mind,
or rather the possibility that in the course of time
the mind will be free to write what it likes. For,
now that Aphra Behn had done it, girls could
go to their parents & say you need not give me an
allowance; I can earn money by writing. Of
course the answer in the early part of the 18th
century was, By living the life of Aphra Behn! -
Not if I know it; ~~& or~~ Death would be

[Margin: to show oneself]

[Margin: in their own rooms whatever pleased their fancy.]

a change, wh. if I were writing history
I should describe far more fully,
I think of far greater importance
than the agrarian revolt to wh.
Prof. T. devote some space, in the
12th Century.

[97 *verso*]

preferable & soon. That profoundly interesting subject, the
ma~~ns~~<en'>
<the valuing idea of> chastity in women, & its effect upon their
<education;> history here
suggests itself for discussion; ~~but~~ if there were any student
at Girton or Newnham who would go into the matter. Here
it is ~~only necessary to~~ one must pass <it> by, & say merely that
Aphra Behn ~~had a many daughters of the spirit;~~
~~who~~ proved that money could be made by writing, even
at ~~the~~ <a> sacrifice of other qualities; ~~& later, as the 18th~~
~~Century wore on, the middle class woma<e>n improved upon her,~~
[——] & so ~~that~~ by degrees writing ~~as a~~ was
~~tolerated~~ became not merely a sign of folly & a
distracted mind, but ~~possibly the sign of a laudable~~
~~desire to help the family purse;~~ a possible
profession; ~~by degrees~~ a method of helping the family.
Mary Wollstonecraft kept herself by doing translation.
Hundreds of unknown women added to their pin money or
paid a hidden overdue bill with some story or translation.
Money has an immense power of dignifying the
<& making serious what, if it is not paid for, is mere frivolity>
~~trivial~~ The extreme activity of mind which
showed itself as the 18th Century wore on among women -
all that talking & ~~meeting~~ <arguing>, that writing of essays on
Shakespeare, of was founded on <the solid> fact: women could
make money by writing; Therefore ~~it was~~ though it
was well to laugh & sneer at the Blues & their
doings; one could not be ~~quite~~ so ~~drastic as~~
so scathing, nor opposition so rigid as a century
before. Thus at last, towards the end of the
18th Century, a revolution <change> had come to pass.
as important, <as &> perhaps more important, than
those other changes - the change from which
are so solemnly recorded in history. The middle class

[Margin: & might produce an interesting book]

[Margin: serious help in distress, a possible refuge if her father died, or [that?]]

[Margin: ridicule]

woman ~~had~~ began to write. For if Pride & Prejudice matters,
& Middlemarch, & Wuthering Heights, & Villette, then
it matters far more than I can prove in an hours lecture
that women generally, <in the 18th Century> middle class women,
ordinary women
[should?] took to writing. Without these forerunners,
take Jane Austen, & the Brontes & George Eliot could never
have ~~written a word~~ <existed>. ~~For~~ Masterpieces are not ~~born~~
are ~~like the waves of the sea; they~~ solitary births;
they ~~are~~ are the ~~flower~~ <result> of many years of thinking in
common. Shakespeare owes his debt to Marlowe;
the great Chaucer to Gower, & so on. Jane Austen should
writer says certainly have laid a wreath on the tomb of
what has Aphra Behn. & George Eliot done homage to the
been ~~those that fine~~ <shade of the robust> vigorous old lady, Mrs
said [before?] Carter, who
tied a bell to her bedstead in order that she might
wake ~~early~~ <at dawn> & learn Greek.

The Monk's House Manuscript

Here then, one had reached the nineteenth century; & there was, I found, considerably ~~over~~ more than one shelf given up entirely to ~~the~~ standard editions of the works of women. But why, with very few exceptions, were they all novels? The original impulse was to poetry. the supreme head of song ~~was a~~ wrote as a poetess. not ~~novels~~ & [illegible] ~~in France~~, Both in France & in England, the poetess preceded the prose writer. Had it something to do with the middle classes & their lack of sitting rooms? ~~I suppose~~ It must be always difficult to write, I thought, at the common table, in the common sitting room, with people going in & out; but easier to write prose like that & fiction, than poetry or a play. The concentration is less ~~[illegible]~~ intense. Further, people going in & out may be though it sounds impossible, actually a help to a novelist. In his Austen Leigh life of his Aunt Jane he says that she sometimes smiled at things that were said & once was seen to write something down. All the training that ~~the~~ woman in the early nineteenth century ~~got~~ ~~was~~ as a writer was training in the observation of character, in the relations of people. Of course her ~~education~~ training as a woman, which, when one comes to think of it, has been extremely severe & continued through many centuries, has been in ~~lo~~ loving. In that art she is without doubt a master. ~~[illegible]~~ Therefore when the middle class woman took to writing, & not to experimenting [illegible] as they did in the 18th century, she naturally wrote novels. One may even go

Here then, one had reached the nineteenth century;
& there was, I found, considerably ~~over~~ <more than> one shelf
given up entirely to ~~the~~ standard editions of the works of
women. But why, with very few exceptions, were
they all novels? The original impulse was to poetry.
`The supreme head of song' ~~was a~~ <wrote was> poetess. <not
novels [a novelist?]> ~~In France,~~
Both in France & in England, the poetesses precede the
prose writers. Had it something to do with the middle
classes & their lack of sitting rooms? ~~I suppose~~
It must be always difficult to write, I thought, at the
common table, in the common sitting room, with
people going in & out; but easier to write prose like that
& fiction, than poetry or a play. The concentration is
less ~~intense~~ intense. Further, people going in &
out may be, though it sounds impossible, actually a
help to a novelist. In Mr. Austen Leighs life of his
Aunt Jane he says that she sometimes smiled at things
that were said & once was seen to write something
down. All the training that ~~the~~ woman in
the early nineteenth century ~~got was~~ as a writer
was training in the observation of character, in the
relations of people. Of course her ~~education~~ <training> as a
woman, which, when one comes to think of it,
has been extremely severe & continued through many
centuries, has been in living. In that art she
is without doubt a mistress. ~~But~~ Therefore when the
middle class woman took to writing, & not to experimenting
with a pen, as they did in the 18th Century, she
naturally wrote novels. One may even go

further, I said, taking Pride & Prejudice from the shelf, & say
that they wrote masterpieces. One does not of course
wish to give pain ~~or annoyance~~, <or to boast, to the other sex> but
Pride & Prejudice is to my
thinking a good novel. ~~It might of course have been a
better novel if she had not written it in the common
sitting room & hidden it when anyone came in~~
<One wd. not have been ashamed>
There was nothing to be ashamed of, ~~that I can see, in being~~ <if one
were>
caught writing Pride & Prejudice; yet Jane Austen, they say,
was, glad that the hinge of the door creaked so that
she might hide her manuscript if anyone came in.
~~But~~ Would Pride and Prejudice have been a better novel
~~had it been written~~ if Jane Austen had not thought it
necessary to hide ~~it~~? <her manus> I read a page or two & it
seemed to me ~~no, I do not think that Jane Austens <has~~ her> ~~the~~ circumstances
~~in which~~ Jane Austen wrote had done no harm to her
whatsoever. Really, it was a miracle. Here was a
woman writing in 1810 without bitterness without fear;
without protest without preaching. That was how
Shakespeare wrote, I thought, looking at Antony &
Cleopatra; & when people compare Shakespeare & Jane
Austen they may mean that they had both
consumed all impediments; & for that reason we
do not know Jane Austen, as we do not know
Shakespeare; & for that reason, Jane Austen
pervades every word she wrote as Shakespeare
is in every word of his plays. If Jane
Austen suffered in any way it was simply that
~~she had never~~ in those days it was impossible <even> for a
middle class woman to go about alone. She
never even went in an omnibus or had lunch

alone in a shop. Yet perhaps Jane Austen ~~was~~ <was so
perfectly> never
wanted what she had not. But take Charlotte Brontë,
I said, opening Jane Eyre & laying it beside Pride & Prejudice.
<Heavens> ~~Heavens, What~~ power - ~~what indignation!~~
I ~~had~~ opened at Chapter ~~13~~, <12> where Jane Eyre
climb~~ed~~<s> onto the roof ~~& looked out afar~~
& my eye was caught by the phrase "Anybody
may blame me who likes". And what are they
blaming Charlotte Brontë for, I asked. It was
for ~~going now & then for a walk by myself in the~~
~~grounds; it was for this~~ terrible sin; she used to
climb <up> onto the roof ~~& look out over the fields & hills~~
129 ~~& the dim sky line~~ & when Mrs. Fairfax was
making jellies & ~~she used to~~ gaze at the distant view &
long "for a power of vision etc.
~~That she used to long~~ & then that she used to long

who blames me? Many no doubt

So ~~she the~~

One can say, I thought, laying the book down beside
Pride & Prejudice that the woman who wrote those two
passages has more genius than Jane Austen; but, if one
she will never get it out of her whole & entire. She
Her books will be deformed & twisted. She is
at war with herself. Her vision will be distorted.
She will be in a rage where she should be calm;
She will - [be?] - at war with herself. She will die
cramped & thwarted.

One could not but play for a moment with the thought of
what might have happened if Charlotte Brontë had been
given what she longed for, knowledge of the busy world, ~~or~~
& towns & regions full of life; ~~had had~~ <more of> practical
experience,
& intercourse with her kind & acquaintance with ~~a~~
a variety of character. ~~than were possible in those days.~~
~~When Her genius would have benefited enormously.~~
~~She knew exactly what she lacked; & she knew that~~
She puts her finger exactly upon her deficiencies; she knew
better than we do how enormously her genius would have
benefited had ~~it been possible for her to enjoy <these things been possible> these gifts~~
~~happier circumstances been granted her. And again we~~
~~marvel that such books as Villette & Middlemarch &~~
~~Wuthering Heights were written by women from all~~
But ~~they were~~ <it was> not possible, & all these novels were
written by women ~~who lacked~~ without more experience of
life than could ~~pass the [jealous?] authorship of men &~~
enter the highly respectable houses of the <~~to be~~ the sitting rooms
[of the?]> clergy;
~~without exciting~~ <writing> by women ~~writing~~ in the common
sitting room; by women so poor that they could not afford
to buy more than a small quantity of writing paper
at one time George Eliot, it is true, escaped; but only
after all to a secluded villa in St. Johns Wood. "I
never ask anyone to come & see me . . ." she
wrote, in view of the terrible fact that she was living with a
man who was not her husband at the same time
on the other side of Europe Tolstoi was living with
the gipsies & the dancing girls; ~~was at~~ had been a
soldier, had lived the life of a man ~~at~~ of the world,
without ~~any~~ censure, & greatly to advantage of his novels.
~~Make~~ Tolstoi live <[living?]> at the Priory St. John Wood
under a cloud with Mr. Lewes, ~~& we~~ should <could not>

have missed War & Peace, though doubtless the
edifying effect upon us of his submission to ~~a~~ the laws of morality
would have done us more good in the end.

But one could go deeper perhaps. If one shuts ones eyes
& thinks of a novel as a whole it seems <often> to be a creation
modelled ~~in~~ <from> life, though with radical differences ~~which we
cannot enter into here~~; of course, a structure ~~almost~~
leaving a shape on the minds eye; built ~~with~~ in a square block; is
pagoda shaped; with arcades perhaps, or domes; shaped anyhow;
<this shape> it seems to be composed of one emotion ~~an~~ in
relation to
another; mostly of people in relation to people; & the emotion
comes not from our sense of the <general> relationship as ~~much~~
well as from
the particular relationship; <the name in which can> It is in fact an
immensely complex structure, <much of> so heterogeneous that the
wonder is it holds together. What holds it together is something
like integrity. Yet one feels, each of these states of mind,
relationships, facts, ~~maybe~~ vision, is held together by the
writers ~~body~~ <~~aim~~ Authorship> ~~Because he~~ It was like this to
him. <It is a good metaphor.> And
we ~~run over~~ <try him;> hold every word every sentence to the
test;
& if any are fraudulent, <the sentences are wrong> that part of the
structure
wobbles & perhaps falls & only an arch or two is left
standing. A bad novel we say at the end. ~~If everything~~
holds we feel ~~the~~

~~A bad novel is generally bad because~~ The imagination may
fails ~~in its~~ <early> under the immense strain, ~~to see clearly.~~ &
no longer ~~sees~~ distinguishes between true & false. But
sometimes it swerves, sometimes ~~it seems to fumble
as if from their incompetence. It is approximating to
not~~ because the writer seems afraid, or actually cannot
get the thing said as it should be said. For instance
in the last paragraph from Jane Eyre the

[Margin:] ~~to the~~
owing a
certain
looking glass
likeness to
real life;
a structure

[Margin:] to the eye:
& then another
sense,
[however
, is
found was
which is
broken
up?]

[Margin:] Often in
womens
novels
from fear;
[in it?]

imagination swerves aside; because something came between the
writer & her vision. ~~In that instance, it was~~ indignation at the lot of
women. ~~The great~~ Over & over again, women, writing
<imagining> in the past
were ~~weakene~~d swerved from fear, faltered from inexperience.
They
~~could not~~ were deflected by the ~~current that~~ some ~~hostile~~
<adverse>
power — current. Rochester is the portrait of a man by a woman who is
controls — afraid of men. <Often we feel> the whole structure was raised
murder — by a
Fear enters — mind which was slightly distorted by the desire to ~~give~~
[largely — its alter values in deference to some external authority.
into from?] — {We suspect the writers integrity. ~~Either she is~~ {The
commonest forms that such a deference takes are
strength, to imitate men, charm to conciliate them.}
~~But the~~ } ~~Since novels are closely dependent on life~~, <& the
values of life are not a womans values - > ~~the~~
~~question is always~~ And novels are <intricate> honeycombs
<build made up, like> a vast
made of innumerable values. The woman writers
~~often~~ used most frequently to destroy their
She has — integrity by trying to be strong, or again by trying to be
charming For outside pressure was laid on her.
& she responded as her temperament dictated, either by
agression, or by conciliation.[X] She was thinking of
something besides the thing itself, & Thus ~~wrote~~
failed in integrity; down come her books from this
radical fault in their structure. X <I will be strong; I will be
charming.> I will make
this important though I think it trivial, she said; & I
will ~~limit~~ make that trivial though it is important.

But how impossible it must have been not to
fail in — yield, I thought! <&> What genius, what serenity <integrity> it
the — must
way I — have required to hold serenely fast to things as they
[thought?], — seemed to one. <Only> Jane Austen did it & Emily Brontë,
~~but of the thousands of novels written by other~~
~~women, all failed from this swerving aside, or~~
~~some swerving tampering of this fact.~~

It is another feather in their cap

of all the thousand of women who wrote novels entirely ignored this
pressure of opinion. ~~But opinion is What is more~~
~~easily shown, For there~~ Everything was against ~~her~~ <combined to make>
integrity in ~~her heart the most difficult of~~ beyond her reach.
<Not only> ~~There~~ was Sir Egerton Brydges & his descendants enforcing
~~morality~~ a special morality yet women are ~~often~~
sometimes coarse by nature, & to suppress is worse than to
explode; not only did the whole of civilisation say
These things are important & these trivial <often> against her own
~~conception~~; but ~~also~~ She had no Tradition <behind> {(For
we think back through our mothers if we are women;)
<& it is & it is useless to go to the great writers for help,~~though we may~~ however much we may go to them for [pleasure?].>
~~it is useless to~~ & ~~it is~~ the first thing that a woman
would find was that there was no common
sentence ready for her use} ~~Almost entirely~~, literature is
the work of men. <So that on [putting pen page?]> A woman, in the 19th century would find
no sentence fit for her use. ~~It is no~~ was impossible to use
~~the current sentence naturally, & so~~ we find
Charlotte Brontë <herself confined> ~~constantly~~ using it~~unnaturally~~
with all her splendid gift for prose
a ~~sentence which~~ <using it> ~~writing~~ unnaturally, <write> heavily, with a
false emphasis The current sentence, I thought
opening a copy of the Times, runs something like
this
~~That is~~ it is a man's sentence; it derives from Macaulay &
Gibbon. ~~Jane Austen remodelled the current sentence.~~
~~& [wrote?] made it perfectly~~ ~~It~~ Ch Bronte with all
her splendid gift for prose stumbled & fell with that
load on her pen George Eliot committed atrocities
with it that may be left described. Only Jane
Austen devised a perfectly convenient & expressive ~~sentence~~
[woman's?] sentence, & then, with less genius for writing than
C. Bronte, got infinitely more said

[Margin notes:]

with all the power of the press at their command

[barely?]

almost entirely

George Eliot can [~~has been?~~] is said to have written the worst sentence in the [lang?]

Such ~~differences~~ a lack of tradition must have told
enormously upon the writing of women, I thought. All the
older ~~typ~~ forms,like the epic, or the poetic play, has
~~been~~ were already hardened & ~~perfected~~ <set> by the time she
became a writer. The novel alone was young enough to be
moulded at least to some of her
<to her [demands?]> take her mould. Yet who shall say that
even
now the novel is rightly shaped for her, or that
she will not by degrees create ~~another~~ <a> form, <which shall be>
<to be to her> ~~instead of the poetic play or the epic, to~~ what the
epic, & the poetic play were to <her fathers> ~~men in the past~~?

I had now come to a final shelf, (but there are
several standing empty beneath it) where the ~~work~~
books of living women, or of women lately dead ~~ta~~<oo>ke their
stand. It would be discourteous to read the names on the
backs, for one should keep ~~their~~ <ones> preferences <&
[antipathies?]> among the
living to oneself. But the interesting thing was ~~they~~ to
~~be that~~ that `the novel' was by no means
predominant. There were also poems, ~~both~~ long & short;
plays; histories; <biographies;> travels; books of scholarship &
research;
~~there were~~ philosophies, <economics> & scientific manuals.
~~I tried to imagine~~ What <[then?]> had happened to increase the
~~range~~ <scope library>?
What had led them to forsake their station in the
drawing room, beside the tea tray? There was once a
young woman whose father made her an
allowance of £300 pounds a year; I murmured.
Her name was Barbara Leigh Smith - There was once a
young woman called Emily Davies - Well to
cut the matter short, ~~& there is nothing so dull as
the story of a victorious~~ These two women went into

house ~~the~~ it had a flight of steps, a basement, & ferns in the
window, & going into the drawing room found six girls, aged from
15 to 25 moping round a table. ~~Some~~ were <One was>
pressing flowers;
others cutting out underclothes; one tinting a sketch of the
Churchyard in winter; another playing <Mendelson> the piano
All were ~~pale~~; <pasty> all were cross. ~~Why not~~ But ~~why~~
~~dont you go & get~~ how can you work like this? said
the visitors. At that moment in came ~~the father <mother> who~~
~~was terribly overworked, & a clergyman. He wanted dinner.~~
~~In came the mother. she wanted~~ a lady visitor; &
after her, came the mother; & then the father, & it was time for
In short, Miss Davies spent her whole life, <building Girton> & ran
the college ~~to~~ heavily into debt, building <Girton, where these
sitting rooms> sitting rooms for
the daughters of the middle classes. Hence these books.
I ~~laid one or two of them~~ opened one or two of them at
random, ~~laying them down~~ wondering whether if one
took a hasty glance at this & that one could come to any
conclusion, about the subject ~~which~~ that still
weighed on my mind, Women & Fiction. ~~But if I said~~
~~that I thought~~, reading ~~I really cant say that, I thought,~~
~~blushing, though~~ It was now between seven & eight; the
there was nobody else in the room; & the only sound
was the dull hum of omnibuses far away. Why then
should one blush?

another
~~writing~~ doing
[now?] ~~letters~~;
& a third
[~~writing~~?]
with her
fingers
screwed into
ears
write a
[~~book~~?]
presumably
a
novel

No more melancholy task could fall to the ~~lot of~~ <lot of> human
nature <being>
I thought, <entirely> because all ~~such~~ enquiries into one sex
~~sterilise the mind~~
apart from the other sterilise & embitter; but also because
novels, ~~which ever~~ whether written by man or by woman,
provide an anodyne & not an antidote. ~~Here is life~~
~~maundering in still in its with into the novel as on as it does~~
~~about three o'clock in the afternoon~~; glide one into
a torpid dream in which the afternoon seems infinitely
prolonged; instead of a ~~plucking the heart of reality out~~
flaming in our eyes the burning <torch;> brand - ~~for certainly~~ <in
other words>
Shakespeare seems to get more into the minute than Balzac,
~~Still, there were the usual things happening~~. ---
Often it is better to begin six chapters deep in a novel, & if
nothing is ~~going~~ <happening> then, <one may lawfully> to give it
up. Meanwhile I was
~~reading about~~ running my eyes up & down the pages; &
it was obvious that something was not quite in order. This
gliding [prosing?] was interrupted, by a tug here & there; a prick;
some 'word leaping out at one' flashing its little torch light
in ones eyes & waking one up from the afternoon lethargy.
The ~~woman~~ <writer> was trying to get herself free from some
entanglement evi~~dently~~; ~~she was~~ 'unhanding' herself as they say
in old plays, ~~getting a freeing her [book?] from the throbs~~
~~of some old~~ Jane Austen's sentence was not then
appropriate <[any longer?]>? I asked. Alas that it should be so,
for
~~was [therever?] there ever a~~ what could be easier, or more
exact? And <to read> this woman was ~~like a using far too many~~
~~words;~~ to read her was like being at sea in a small boat,
first a plunge then a roll ~~then~~ up ~~we~~ <she> goes, ~~& then~~
~~&~~ down ~~we~~ <she> falls - & all the time she is using too many
~~words; & she~~ she skimps her adjectives & then
she lavishes them; & ~~suddenly~~ probably she
is putting ~~far too many~~ in the wrong things & leaving out

with a
complete
absence
of [merit?],
~~elongated~~

the right ones. For on looking back over that first chapter it seemed
had been given a bucket full of splinters - & if a novelist
expects us ~~makes~~ us do her composing for her, ~~I~~ she is much mistaken
I said, thinking how completely one could trust to Jane Austen
to do that for one. I surrender myself to delight, &
occasional <calms or> boredom, when I read Jane Austen I thought;
she breaks from melody to melody like <~~an opera by~~> Mozart ~~in~~
in Figaro ~~Figaro.~~ ~~This woman~~ However, ~~it could not be denied~~
~~that~~ there was this to be said for the modern; she did not
~~recall 'real~~ life' for which one must be thankful; since
~~anything the call back make one think that it was~~
~~three o'clock~~ She did not persuade one, ~~or rath~~ that all life is
spent <at about 3 pm> winding <in the> why ~~since~~ there is no soap in the soap
dish, & if the gas man comes, the cook is out, & if
4 yards cost 7 11 then 6 yards & a quarter will
cost something ~~more~~ else <money> & it is important ~~to remember~~
to write to the dustman who has forgotten to call,
She did not ~~for over a fortnight.~~ <the> & the smell in the basement is
lower one's ~~awful <in > all life is not that, anyhow She tried to say, in~~
vitality ~~whatever the~~ She was trying <apparently> to say something ~~that~~
in that &c ~~matters to mattered to her~~ <on the only> about a party down the
&c river
way. ~~(but the~~ ~~Here I got~~ Obviously it was
a young womans first book. She might be 27 or 28;
born therefore about 1900, educated at Oxford perhaps,
for the scenes seem<ed> laid there; & earning, so I judged from
perhaps the ~~shape~~ <spirit> of the sentences, about £300 a year. She was
by writing thinking for herself. To decide her [taste?] as a writer - it
In other words would be necessary to follow her along until ~~thinking herself~~
she was ~~unobserved, she got~~ she got herself landed with a
writes a situation - but I will give her every liberty,
I said generously as one does to young writers, to

~~In say~~ choose her situation; she shall make it up of any~~thing~~
any odds & ends she likes; but then <when she has faced herself with it> I shall say to her,
~~now Jump~~. I shall be ~~merciless~~ merciless. I shall say to her
"Jump."

But before that ~~was possible~~, <a chance> happened she used an expression
~~that made me~~ which completely changed the current of my thoughts;
irritatingly too; for it is intolerable, in the middle of one
train of thought, to be switched onto another ~~of a different~~
<I read> ~~She said~~ "Chloe liked Olivia; they shared a ---"
<the words came at> the bottom of the page; the pages had stuck; while
fumbling to open them there flashed into my mind
the inevitable policeman; the summons; the order to attend
the court; the dreary waiting; the Magistrate coming in
with a little bow; the glass of water; the counsel for the
prosecution; for the defense; the verdict; this book is
~~called~~ obscene; & flames rising, perhaps on Tower Hill,
as they consumed <that> masses of ~~print~~ paper. Here the
pages came apart. Heaven be praised! It was only a
laboratory. <Chloe & Olivia> They were engaged in mincing liver which is
apparently a cure for pernicious anaemia. But the
thread by which we hold to a book is so stretched, so
attentive is so intense a process, that one jar like this
breaks it, & away the mind flew, thankful for a rest, on
some other theme. ~~I lit a cigarette, &~~ I
repeated [idly?], out of its context, Chloe liked Olivia" ---
& I ~~persuaded myself that I had here got upon a trail~~
~~of great importance~~. ~~it then~~ & it struck me
~~that this [warning?]~~ how ~~odd it was that~~ immense a
change was there. Chloe like Olivia, but

that was shared

Chloe & Olivia

hence the -
peculiar
nature

Cleopatra did not like Octavia. How completely the whole
situation in Shakespeares play would have been changed if
Cleopatra had shared a laboratory with Octavia!
Shakespeares conception, if one dare say, of the relations of the
two women, is a little conventional. ~~How~~ Is she taller than
I am? How does she do her hair? - Cleopatra is
~~purely & simply jealous~~ has one single ~~relationship~~
emotion about Octavia; it is jealousy.X The play presumably
required no more. But how interesting it would have been if
the ~~simple jealousy had been~~ the relationship between the women
had been ~~more~~ complicated. I tried to remember any case in
the whole of literature where two women have <been described>
shared a
laboratory together. ~~They share~~ In Ibsen they share
laboratories, or the equivalent, <that all> with men. ~~But~~ It was
strange to think ~~that the whole of literature is concerned with~~
all the great women in fiction are, until Jane Austen,
~~describ created by men, & <created> observed~~ by men, ~~in such situations~~
~~as men can see them~~ as men were forced to observe them
in ~~relati~~ their relations to the opposite sex. What a
small section of a woman is known then to men;
~~I could~~ for that was the only relationship in which men ~~could~~
<can>
observe them. Hence the peculiar nature of woman in
fiction; ~~her for~~ her unreality, her ~~extreme~~ beauty, <&> her
~~extreme meanness~~. <vileness>. {X She is ~~always~~ seen by her lover,
never
~~But women~~ have friends; they even have friends of their
own sex; & nowadays, they share laboratories with friends
of their own sex.} Yet what should we know of it
~~This~~ <How> ~~would seem to be~~ a great <a>limitation~~; for~~ how arbitrary a
simplification this has introduced into the portraits of women
by men can be judged by ~~supposing that~~ imagining
what would be the loss to literature if men were
only represented as the lovers of women, never ~~in~~ as the
friends of men, or ~~in their~~ as soldiers, travelers, prophets.
were reduced to that one important, but not unique, relation~~ship~~

All the
relations
are with
men.

were seen
<by the
[other?] sex>
in their
relation
to the other
sex;
~~as men could~~
for ~~since~~
career, or
at any
rate

by her friend;
never by her
fellow workers

~~if the whole was of [their?] being was expressed~~
~~if they were only shown in love. They would~~ be ~~very~~ Only a
very few parts <in the play> could be allotted them.
Now if Chloe likes Olivia <& can write,> something of great importance has
happened, because this liking, especially now that it is
fortified & complicated ~~with~~ <by no> ~~memory of lovers, the~~
sharing laboratories, going into Parliament, making discoveries, <looking at facts> &
will, ~~seeking out the~~ digging in Crete, & soon,
when will serve as a torch ~~in the hands of the younger~~
~~generation~~, to light up that vast dark cave, where nobody
has yet been, I thought; ~~Nobody has~~ Chloe will say
Olivia offers an extraordinary

She can tell us what women are like when they are alone.
If Chloe likes Olivia she will light a torch in that vast
~~dark cave~~, <unlighted chamber> I thought. She will watch ~~it is~~
Olivia (who
had it seemed two small children) putting down the jar in
the shelf & rolling up her apron. <It is a sight that> This
has never been seen
since the world began, she will say, but under her
breath if she will take my advice, for women ~~have never~~
~~are more~~ are so wary, so suspicious of observation
~~that~~ that they are off at the flicker of an eyelid.
The only way to do it would be to talk of something
else, so in the most oblique way possible, gently
& then <no ~~other~~ remark> conclude, but not with a notebook ~~at to~~
& a
that what — pencil in hand - all these observations need to be
to do — taken in the shortest of short hand, almost dispensing
with words, -- ~~how~~ what happens when the
organism (are we not in a laboratory?) that has
under the — been in the dark these million years not only feels
shadow of the — the light ~~coming~~ falling on it, ~~like~~ but behold - there is
rock — actually a piece of food ~~coming my~~ <her> way, -
Knowledge is it? Action? And she reaches out for
it (Olivia was a medical student before she married, &
has now come back to some form of research work)
& has by some entirely new <activity> organisation &
combination to ~~make it~~ absorb it into ~~her life blood~~.
a system already so highly developed for other
purposes, so <u>extraordinarily</u> complex, so sensitive, that
what ~~to do with that new experience is puzzling~~
that ~~one~~ it hardly knows what to ~~make~~ do with
this ~~astonishing~~ addition. Any thing added means
an immense disturbance; ~~sends the most~~
& fresh organisation

The naturalist-novelist, ~~the observer~~ has now an
~~extraordinarily interesting~~ new field ~~laid~~ thrown open to her;
where things are growing, - actually, I suppose, changing the
shape of the petal a little, or sprouting a new leaf -
~~I do not know~~ what<ever> simile <may> commend itself to <the>
botanists,
~~It is rather a perilously~~ ~~But~~ ~~And heaven knows, she~~
need ~~not confine herself to that~~ ~~Nor need she limit~~
~~herself to the actually new~~ <& ~~to watch a~~ what cd. be more
interesting than> ~~an astonishingly interesting~~
~~occupation, to watch~~ <in the> a human organism <in> change; ~~But~~
as it reaches out ~~for the towards something new. Nor~~ is
~~she by any means limited to~~ ~~But~~ as it reaches out
to absorb these new experiences into the old. And
what could be more interesting than to observe it, doing so -
unless indeed, to go with ones little torch -
Chloe has three hundred a year & likes Olivia - ~~back~~
hither & thither in ~~to all those~~ <so> that ~~is how it~~ burns,
whitely, steadily, not flickering <&> like Merediths torch or
Ibsens, with his <[---]> inevitable stumblings, <&> his
inevitable prepossession - <it was [impossible?]> to go into very
small shut
in back streets
rooms. There sits a lady with a lap dog; <& all the [ ];>
women
who do nothing all day; hopeless & embittered women;
But those are the stock phrases, the reach me down
that one buys in any emporium of ready made [~~general~~?] fiction
The hostess
The truth in all these cases, of ~~idle women, hard~~
~~women, cruel, indifferent women, would~~ be
might be worse than ~~we know it but~~ surely
~~more truth less~~ the slip shop falsehood that we
have, but more interesting, <exact> with an edge to it. And
And she must make them fit, every bump every angle -

And there came into my mind whole processions of
ordinary women ~~whom nobody had ever written about without~~
unwritten about, living in the rooms which are ~~not quite~~
~~holding their heads up~~, in the long streets which the
motorist curses driving out of London because ~~they are~~
~~always~~ one must ~~drive~~ pull up suddenly to avoid
a very ~~ancient~~ ancient lady, leaning on the arm of a
middle aged woman, ~~who~~ so respectably booted &
furred that one fancies that dress must be a ritual.
And they cross going somewhere or other; as they <the elder [at aslant?]>
must have done these seventy-six years; she
may well have seen - But one is not satisfied with a list
of the ~~battles & [—]~~ wars & ~~treaties~~ coronations she has
seen; the streets all decorated for some triumph; the
guns firing in Hyde Park. What has she seen, on
Monday & Tuesday, say in April & November, say
1870 & 1875? Thus one tries to clarify &
pin down with date & season, adding even a
clear sky or a cloudy, the moment which is lost for ever;
~~No biography; no history; nothing said about~~
~~herself~~ ; ~~cups~~ <The> dinners all cooked; cups & saucers
washed; children got up on time for school & now gone
out into the world. All has vanished; &
~~no Chloe coming now with her white steady~~
all has vanished. No biography, no history has
a word to say about it. ~~Chloe, coming with~~
~~her light this year of grace 1928 could hardly~~
~~light up more than an inch or two of that~~

neither dark or light -- sometimes customers own material is made up -

the clothes laid [ ] with camphor - [just?] to keep the moth out

on the 10 or 25th of

~~profound darkness. because they do not think of themselves~~,
Chloe's torch could show us a great many things never
seen in the light of day before; once she gets it firmly in her
hand.

And thinking idly that the old woman ~~in her furs had~~

(~~to~~ as a way out of reading a novel)

had now escaped the motor & ~~crossed the road, I~~
turned the corner out of sight I went my way & with the
rapid step of the [new generation?], over the Bridge, back into
London, still thinking of this dumbness; this intolerable
accumulation of unwritten life; <how> ~~for one knows~~ how
women stand at street corners, arms akimbo, often
with rings embedded in their fat swollen hands, talking
with a gesticulation that seems like the fling of
Shakespeares words, could one catch them; past the
violet seller, ~~the match~~ the vagrants, match girls,

but no [phrases?] to fit them, no exact [kind?]

seeing everywhere, like the light ~~in the~~ & shadow on the
sea that curious change in the face, as a man comes,
or as a woman comes, as if the nerves were
signalling a whole wordless but expressive message; &
so to ~~decorative~~ <the> shops, where it is said to be
wrong to loiter, life being what it is; For ~~life~~

[thinking to say of this?] is awful: or it shd. be

while life will approve ~~of~~ you for playing golf, as for
shooting pheasants, ~~life will be very severe~~
~~critical & sarcastic & draw unpleasant conclusions~~
if I go or Chloe, the authoress of this novel
goes, wandering among shops.

Still the hierarchy of what is important &
what is not important persists, I thought,
If she describes Marshall & Freebodys she will be

approved by the anonymous gentleman in Art & Letters. She will be "~~courageously~~ aspiring to excellence by courageously acknowledging the limitations of her sex"; from which I infer that the description of a shop is not a ~~difficult~~ proper to engage the attention of the other sex.

Which is not right, I said to myself~~;~~ laughing at the thought ~~that~~ of the Bishop who knew that cats did not go to Heaven. The Bishop ~~I said~~ would ~~be able were he in the flesh to say it is better to~~ say it is not right to go to shops. He would say it is better to play golf. It is better to shoot pheasants than to buy clothes. & I wondered
<She will have to go in there, & describe all that>
And so they will tell this young novelist that she must not describe a woman's shop for the subject is unimportant. The emotions ~~<felt by> roused by it are~~ trivial, they But will say - but I was doing them an injustice, I ~~suddenly~~ for ~~the~~ was there not a review somewhere an article somewhere among the litter - somebody who said, < - > ~~oh~~ here it was "female novelists should only aspire to excellence by courageously acknowledging the limitations of their sex" - ~~there seems~~ to be ~~which ever~~ way it is a ~~great deal~~ ~~It looks then as if she ought to Perhaps then she ought to do nothing else. Between the Bishop & the reviewer what is a female novelist aspiring to excellence to do? To go in, or~~ to the shop or to stay out of the shop? If the ought they to describe shops, or ought they not to describe shops? The Bishop says dont; the [also?] ~~But I differ~~ why was not the

~~When~~ Why there had been ~~no~~ good description of a womens shop. with its flashy stuffs & [trumpery & its smells?]; & the

certainly life that goes on -

& her own vanities & again

	the reviewer not more precise? Why did he not tell us
	as in common kindness he might, these are your limitations.
& between the	They are perfectly obvious to me; May one describe a
two	shop? or may one not describe a shop?
we have to	The only way out is to pretend that there is nothing easier
plunge &	~~nothing more simple & limited pretty & first rate,~~
risk it	~~light and airy, graceful & conciliatory. Then~~
	What are the limitations of the aspiring female novelist
	I demanded; & was then driven to [~~turn~~?] read my book.
But are shops	What did she feel about the limitations of her sex?
easy to	She had done her boating party & her laboratory;
describe?	She had looked up many more facts than she needed;
But a	she had broken the back of the old sequences
pox on all	so completely that one could not guess what
[these	was going to happen next. ~~And~~ But what
questions?]	appeared to be the conclusion of the whole affair
	was ~~a~~ this <then -> She left them sitting there & went into
	into the garden. ~~without quoting the whole passage~~
	~~I cannot of course~~ There they all were
	sitting talking - all sorts of people: all sorts of
	people against a large window of some sort,
	She opened it. ~~The~~ It was an extraordinary effect,
as an	The mens noses, the womens shoulders, seen suddenly
aspiring	like that With an embroidery [of this sky?]
female	Then there were vast spaces without a star:
novelist	darkness itself. I saw what her endeavour was
	We were to feel they have their relation to
	this to <us.> We were to feel ~~the magnitude of things~~ ~~Exist~~
	in themselves. We were to feel something very
	tremendous about the immensity of the soul.
	<I dont think it occurred to her that sex had much to do with it.>

The Fitzwilliam Manuscript

Chapter 4 Cont.

Women & Fiction

22nd March 1929

To my regret I had slipped unthinkingly into praise of my own sex. "Highly developed" — "infinitely intricate" — such are undeniably terms of praise & when by praise of one's own sex is always suspect, but in this case how could one justify it? For nobody can be a prophet always sayeth [illegible] that women are under, [illegible] advanced than they are. But nor is there anything like the mark on the wall, no mark on the wall measuring their precise height; even now only a very small proportion have been [illegible] first second or third Class at the universities; while in the great tests of the professions of the army & navy, of trade, finance, politics, diplomacy they have not even been entered, & have remain almost entirely unlabelled even at the present day. Whereas one has only to open Debrett or Whitaker almanac to add up the various honours [illegible] Sir Hawley Butts has reached to know all that one has any right to know about him.

When then I say "highly developed, infinitely intricate", I am unable to verify my words either by Whitaker or Debrett or the University Calendar. In this emergency the best I can do is to appeal to Keats Voltaire, Heine, Goethe, Cowper, Shelley, Johnson, — to those great men in short who have for one reason or another [illegible] on, lived with, confided in, made love to, written of, admired, [illegible] & shown what can only

Look up, but [illegible] for Sawley Butts [illegible] K.C.B. F. & [illegible] [illegible] [illegible] [illegible] [illegible] [illegible] in the almanack [illegible] columns

form

[illegible]

[illegible]

Chapter 4. Cont.

Women & Fiction

22nd March To my vexation, I had slipped unthinkingly into praise of my own
1929 sex. "Highly developed" - "infinitely intricate" -
such are ~~undoubtedly~~ undeniably terms of praise; &
not only is praise of ones' own sex ~~always~~ suspect, but
in this case how could one ~~possibly~~ justify it? For not only are
~~not only are~~ the professors <~~as~~> always ~~saying~~ <convinced> that
women are
far cruder, <&> simpler ~~far less advanced in~~ than they are; ~~but~~
nor ~~have they ever~~ <but> ~~is there anything, like a <the>~~ mark ~~on~~
there is ~~the wall,~~ no mark on the wall, measuring their precise
height; <to go by.> ~~no~~ Even now only a very small proportion have
been ~~labelled~~ <classified> first second or third class at the
universities; while in the great trials of the ~~bar or the~~
professions, ~~or the~~ of the army & navy, of trade, finance,
politics, diplomacy they have not even been entered,
look up the & they remain almost entirely unlabelled even ~~to this~~ <at the>
Rt.Hon. Sir present
Hawley Butts, ~~moment~~. <day.> Whereas one has only to ~~refer~~ <open> to
~~O.B.E.~~ M. P. Debrett or
K.C B. a Whitakers almanac to ~~add up~~ the ~~various~~
member of ~~see what grade of distinction the least <look up> Sir Hawley~~
to know ~~Butts~~ <he>
precisely ~~has reached thanks to his~~ to know all that we have
where any right to know about him.
~~in the~~ When then I say "highly developed, infinitely intricate',
~~sight of~~ I am unable to verify my words, either ~~by~~ <in> Whitaker or
~~God & man~~ Debrett. or <in> the University ~~records~~ Calendar. In
he stands. this emergency the best I can do is to ~~call to my~~ refer to
in the ~~help~~ Voltaire, <Heine> Goethe, <Cowper & Shelley, Browning,
estimate Keats> Dr. Johnson; -
of his to those great men in short who have
fellow man for one reason or another sought out, ~~depended on,~~
~~written to~~ lived with, confided in, made love
to, <written on,> admired, trusted, & shown what can only

be described ~~as a need of~~ <some need of a dependence upon>
certain women. That <all> these
relationships were ~~always~~ absolutely Platonic, <I will not affirm,
&> Sir
William Joynson Hicks will probably deny.

got nothing
from these

But ~~what reason kept them attached~~, we should wrong these
illustrious men very greatly if we ~~insisted~~ insisted
that ~~all~~ they ~~got out of these alliances was~~

only in the gift
of the sex
which is the
opposite
of ones own

bodily pleasure, & comfort, & flattery ~~& a~~ <from these>
alliances.
What they got, it is obvious, <was> something that their
own sex was unable to offer; & it would not be rash
perhaps to define it further as some stimulus, some
<renewal> increase of creative power. <only provided by the
~~opposite~~ sex> ~~There they were,~~ the door <opened,>
<& there she was> ~~these different women~~ in ~~their~~ <her>
drawing rooms among
their children perhaps, or with a piece of embroidery on

or ~~sweeping~~
~~the~~ washing
up dishes
in the
scullery;
but ask

their lap; at any rate the centre of some different order &
system of life altogether. ~~First, it would be a great~~ rest,
the contrast between this world & his own - whether his
were the lawcourt or the study or the House of Commons;
& then, more ~~subtly,~~ would at once refresh &
invigorate; & then would ~~arise,~~ follow, even in
the simplest talk, such a natural difference of
opinion or feeling that ~~his own reasoning would be~~
~~made flexible~~ the familiar ~~of her~~ furniture of his

restored

own mind would be ~~refreshed~~ <renewed>; & then, ~~the~~
~~exhaustion the depression~~ { ~~if he had left some argument~~ or
~~chapter unfinished, exhausted by the effort of imagination~~
~~reason or imagination,~~ the sight of her creating in a

find the
word or
seize the
argument

different medium would so fertilise his own creative his
mind that ~~without~~ while watching her at work,
~~his own~~ he would ~~begin again to~~ < insensibly solve> create the
argument or ~~the~~ <finish his> poem left ~~behind~~ in exhaustion at
home
when he set out to visit her. Every Johnson
has his Thrale for some such reasons as these;

& when the Thrale marries her Italian ~~singing~~ <singing master>
musician
<feels not> not merely that his evenings at Streatham are over but
that
the fountain of his being is ~~sealed, forever~~ sealed up.
And without being either Dr. Johnson <Voltaire> or Goethe
one ~~may~~ can feel, though very differently, ~~the sort of~~
the power at work; ~~&~~ I thought, ~~thinking~~ but ~~realising~~
~~at the same time that~~ the resources of the English language
would be very much put to the stretch & while flights of
words brought illegitimately into existence by any one who
should <try to express it;> take her torch in her hand & go into the
ordinary
nursery; <& our creative woman> ~~Moreover~~ she does not sit there
forever,
but comes down stairs & goes into the drawing room.
~~So simple as it seems~~, <& the reason> why should language have
to be
~~stretched or & new flights of imagery devised to describe~~
~~her would be that if I come into the room I am~~
~~aware of not of anything being made in words or~~
~~stone, but of~~ For if I come into her room - &
~~at once my mind was flooded with a variety of ideas -~~
~~sensations; beyond count, emanating from~~
~~rooms, but only when some character of my own sex~~
~~sat pouring out tea.~~ But theis room is always different.
hideous, disagreeable, repulsive, stimulating
deadening, romantic prosaic, full of the
light of seas, thunderous, opening on magic
seas, on the contrary looking into a prison yard,
with hard cane chairs, soft & luxurious, full of
[ ], dour as a granite wall --
if a woman, I have only to open her door -
go into her room, I thought, to How

the nature
of this
intricacy this
highly ~~stage~~
of ~~education~~
developed &
educate
<u>sensibility</u>
diversity in
words, not
obliquely
as it
influences the
poem or the
law.

should it not be so? For have not women sat in the common sitting room for a million years or so; & has it not collected ~~received~~ stored up her spirit, & is it not by this time so permeated with her creative power that the power must needs ~~put~~ ~~get~~ reach out & seize a pen or a paint brush or even write music for the piano ~~for~~ instead of forever playing on it -- This creative power, which is so different from any that a man has, ~~must~~ has by now overcharged the walls of the ordinary sitting room, & must for the safety of the house itself, find other expression.
~~But it would be a thousand pities, I thought,~~
Yet how different it is from the creative spirit of a man, I thought - And I concluded that it would be terrible waste if they ~~chased it away~~ frightened it away, or wasted it (for it was won only by centuries & centuries of culture) A thousand pities if they wrote like men, or lived like men, or looked like men; & I thought how inadequate two sexes are to the understanding of the world; ~~how necessary~~ it would be so that the endeavour of the universities should be to increase the difference, not ~~to make them like each other~~.
& if an explorer should come back & bring us word of other sexes looking at the world with other eyes, nothing would please me more, though ~~the~~ Professor X ~~would at~~ once ~~try~~ to <getting out his measuring rods to> prove that he was 'superior'.

And how delightful it would be to watch

The naturalist novelist has now a new field thrown open to
her~~;~~ new specimens <of her own sex> to observe; for what could
be
more interesting than to watch human nature
breaking into a bud there, ~~taking~~ changing a colour
there, as it reaches out in ~~directions where it was severely~~
to regions where it has never been before?

for there is no mistaking the preliminary signs: the pricking, the

Mary Carmichael, I thought, will have her work cut out
for her merely as an observer; & then she will not be
<forced> ~~allowed~~ to limit herself any longer to the respectable
houses
of the upper middle classes. She will go, ~~frankly~~,
without a trace of kindness, curiosity, or condescension;
but in the spirit of fellowship, into the small obscure
rooms where sit the courtesan, the harlot, & the
lady with the pug dog. There they still sit in the

into sunlight & air <from> which ~~has been withheld~~ it has been curtained up till now.

rough ready made clothes which the male writer has had
perforce to clap upon their shoulders. Mary Carmichael
will make these old garments ~~fit;~~ ~~they will come to~~
get close as a grape skin to every angle & hollow.
& there <~~if~~ it> will be a ~~most~~ curious excitement ~~in reading her~~ to see the old ready made figures as they really <are at last>
marvellously renewed. However the majority of
women, I thought, are neither harlots nor courtesans;
nor do they sit clasping pug dogs to dusty
velvet throughout the afternoon. They come out,
~~of an afternoon~~, & cross the street - here I
thought of one of those long streets somewhere
south of the river whose infinite rows are
innumerably populated; ~~so that often the motorist~~

taking out her measure & scissors;

A very ancient lady, I thought, ~~comes~~ crosses the road leaning on the arm of a middle aged woman, both so respectably booted & furred that dress must be a ritual, & the clothes put away in cupboards with camphor throughout the long summer months. They cross the road when the lamps are being lit, as they must have done year after year. The elder, <who is close on eighty> if one asked her would say that she has seen the streets decorated for the battle of Balaclava; or that she heard the guns fire in Hyde Park for the birth of Edward the 7th. But what did she do on April the 11th 1863 or November the 2nd 1875? for then one tries to clarify & pin down with day & season the moment which is lost forever. ~~For~~ All the dinners are cooked; the plates & cups are washed; the children sent to school & gone out into the world. All has vanished. No biography or history has a word to say about it. And the novels without meaning to must lie.

to fetch something
to visit someone

Mary Carmichael must go into all that too, I thought; & went on in thought through the streets of London, feeling the pressure of dumbness, the accumulation of unrecorded life all round me; whether from the women at street corners with their arms akimbo & the rings embedded in their fat swollen talking with a gesticulation like the swing of Shakespeares words; ~~or~~ <or> from violet sellers & match sellers, <&> old crones stationed under doorways, ~~with~~, or from drifting girls whose faces lighten &

darken with signals, like the waves in sun & cloud, at the
coming of man or woman; all that she would have to
~~explore~~ explore <Above all, its profundities; its instincts;> her
own soul ~~too~~, & its vanities & its
desires; & what her beauty is to her, or her plainness, &
her relation to this forever changing &
turning world of gloves & shoes ~~with inlaid insteps; of~~
& ~~coloured~~ stuffs ~~that hang~~ sway up & down among
the fain~~test~~ scents & an air that comes <[out?] through chemists
bottles> down
arcades of marble. For in imagination I had ~~come~~ to
~~some vast shop; where~~ gone into a shop <it was laid with marble &
hung with ribbons> & it
seemed to me that Mary Carmichael might
have a look at that ~~in passing~~. too in passing.

~~But perhaps~~ But it was time to bring these
random reflections to the test of fact; ~~the~~ Mary
Carmichael's book lay open before me; &
it would be interesting to see ~~what she had~~
whether she had done any~~thing~~ of ~~all~~ the things that ~~to me~~
~~as~~ <to> a reader seemed possible. ~~It was clear that~~
One's first impression had been unfavourable
~~because~~ <for> she refused to allow ~~the~~ one to slip along saying
what a good taste in style I have. ~~Also she had~~
because ~~though this is no~~ I can ~~tell~~ <see> that Jane Austen
Jane Austen wd. never have
would have written like this only infinitely better.
The old comparisons never came to mind. Then the
sequence was broken which was annoying, because it
disturbed one's old complacent certainty
that the depths of the human heart ~~are always the same~~.
~~the same in all ages; &~~ lie displayed before one,
to the credit of ones own heart, always & forever the
same. But beyond this, I noted that though

she had nothing like the imagination <~~has~~ love of nature> of
Charlotte Brontë ~~or the~~ <or the healer of>
~~breadth of~~ George Eliot She enjoyed, advantages through
no <through no merit of her own> her predecessors, Lady
Winchilsea, & Charlotte
Brontë & George Eliot, she had, ~~thanks~~ escaped their
obsessions. She ~~was~~ had not to spend her time railing
against "the opposing faction"; nor need she climb on to the
roof & ruin her peace of mind longing ~~for~~ that she might
<for> travel, & ~~see the world & know different sorts of
people,~~ experience & knowledge of the world & character.
Fear & hatred were ~~almost~~ entirely gone, or the traces
showed only in a slight exaggeration of <her sense of> freedom;
in a
slight tendency to the satiric rather than the romantic
in the treatment of the other sex. There could be no
doubt that as a novelist she enjoyed some astonishing
advantages. She had a sensibility that was ~~far
from~~ very wide and very free. It responded to ~~the~~ an
almost imperceptible~~. It was~~ touches upon it. It
<feasted> ~~revelled~~, like a ~~thing~~ plant newly stood in the air,
in every sound & sight. <that came its way> It was too, ~~extremely~~
very subtle, <in> ~~very~~ & ~~would insensibly make one
hold one's breath now & then with~~ ranged <placed> among
almost unknown, or unrecorded things, which had
coming to the surface after all these years. ~~Nobody~~
Awkward though she was & ~~tongue~~ without ~~the~~
<bearing> ~~incompar~~ ~~ease~~, the ~~incomparable~~ unconscious
nobility of long descent, which makes ~~or~~ the least
<gesture of a> Thackeray or a Lamb ~~good~~ easy & delightful,

~~one could not doubt that~~ she had mastered the first great
lessons she wrote as a woman, but as a woman who has
forgotten that she is a woman so that her sentences
were full of that curious <sexual> quality ~~of sex, which~~ is <which
comes ~~when~~ to either sex when>
unconscious of itself. None of this would avail
her however, in the supreme crisis, in what one calls
'a situation', were she not possessed of the building
power~~;~~ ~~the~~ which comes it may be from profound
conviction; ~~No~~ No abundance or fineness of
sensibility would avail unless she could ~~so~~
~~order her trophies that~~ & ~~see in them some thing~~
~~beneath the beyond the sensation its trophies were~~
somehow related by a logic which she herself had
forged won; so that she could build up out of the fleeting
<&> the personal, the ~~thing which is not thrown~~
lasting edifice. which remaining, ~~when~~ unknown. So I
read on till she faced herself with a situation as she was
bound to do. She ~~was coming to it now, for~~
there are no mistaking the ~~preliminary signs~~, the
quickening, the coming together, if not ~~visibly~~
& came to ~~on the spot, behind the scenes~~, ~~of~~ all the forces ~~she~~
a [murky?] had ~~summoned~~; <round> already wakened. ~~It was to~~
place would ~~happen when she~~ And I watched her
~~making ready for the crisis, &~~ saw ranged about to
prevent her Bishops & reviewers, Deans & Doctors,
professors & patriarchs, all ~~who sit~~
~~with their clamour,~~ ready with warning &
advice. Do this because you are a woman;
dont do this because you are a woman; you

cant do this & you shant do this, you never have done this
and you never will do this; ~~keep off this grass; dont
venture here without a permit~~; only scholars &
fellows are allowed on the grass; ladies are not

aspiring
but graceful
female
novelists
this way,

admitted without a letter of introduction from the Dean ---
So they kept at it, like the crowd at a fence on a
racecourse; & it was her trial to take her fence without
looking to right or to left. If you curse you are
lost, I said to her; equally if you laugh. Think of the
jump only, I implored her, as if I had put the whole
of my money on her; & she went over; like a bird.
But there was a fence beyond that, & a fence beyond
that. Whether she had the staying power I was
doubtful, because the <course was long> clapping & the roaring ~~of
the~~
fray the nerves. But she did her best.
Considering that she was not of the blood royal, that
she was unknown girl, writing her first novel,
in rather a bare room, without perhaps quite
enough of ~~those~~ desirable things, <~~like~~> wine & good cigars,
<time & money>
she did not do so badly, I thought.

~~But in order to bring off the last scene,
which was the most ambitious, she needed another
hundred years of contemplation~~. It was a ~~curious~~
scene, Give her another hundred years of
~~doing nothing~~ & she will write that last scene
quite remarkably well. ~~All the people are sitting in
a room together; suddenly she opens the draws the
curtain & you see them with their noses & their
naked shoulders against the sky.~~ If only
she could no nothing for a hundred years or so, & forget a
few ~~facts~~ & not be in such a hurry, & get things
into proportion, & leave out half & so on,
she would be a poet
I said.

Give her
another
hundred years
to [look about
her?] &
she will [be?]
herself, I said
shutting
the book.

The Fitzwilliam Manuscript

Chapter Five

Chapter Five

26th March
1929.

Next ~~morning~~ day the ~~[illegible]~~ light of an October morning was ~~falling on their backs, &~~ coming softly into the room falling in dusty shafts ~~into the room~~ through the uncurtained window. London was winding itself up, again presumably — at any rate one might look out of the window & see, ~~what~~ what London was doing. ... that takes one to the window to look at London is a good one; one can spend hours looking at London; ~~especially~~ [illegible] ~~when one has spent hours looking at books.~~ ~~Nobody~~ seemed at the moment to be thinking about ~~[illegible]~~. [illegible] ~~It~~ seemed to be wholly indifferent to Antony & Cleopatra. Nobody was thinking about Shakespeare. — They did not care a straw whether ~~one~~ wrote like this or whether one wrote like ~~that~~. Nobody was reading or had read or would ever read Antony & Cleopatra. They did not care a straw for the future of fiction or the death of poetry or the development by the average woman of ~~[illegible]~~ style completely expressive of her mind. They were ~~hurrying to work~~ ... all such questions had one ... Their indifference was ... If such questions had been chalked on the pavement, ... nobody would have stopped to read. ~~They were~~ And one felt more stimulated than depressed by their indifference, because ~~[illegible]~~ there was surely a truth ~~[illegible]~~, because they were engaged in hurrying to work & their indifference ... the ... hurrying feet which would ... whatever one wrote ... They were all hurrying to work. ~~[illegible]~~ carrying little cases ... They were hardly distinguishable from ... in this crowd. ... ...

[illegible margin notes: "... at same rate"; "standing at the window"; "on the 26th of ... 1928"; "wished to read them"]

Chapter Five

26th March 1929. Next ~~morning~~ <day> the ~~soft~~ light of an October morning was
~~falling on these books, & coming softly into the room~~
falling in dusty shafts ~~into the room~~ through the
ego-centricity uncurtained window. London was winding itself up again
presumably - at any rate one might look out of the
without window & see, ~~what~~ <what London was doing.> ~~Any excuse that~~
any excuse ~~takes one to the~~
at all ~~indow to look at London is a good one; one can spend~~
~~hours looking at London; especially, I thought, when one has~~
standing ~~spent hours looking at books. Nobody seemed~~
at the ~~wat the moment to be thinking about Antony & Cleopatra.~~
window ~~It~~ <London> seemed to be wholly indifferent to <the play. ~~It~~>
Antony & Cleopatra.
Nobody was thinking about Shakespeare. ~~They~~
On the 26th ~~did not care a straw whether one wrote like this or~~
of October ~~whether one wrote like that~~. Nobody was reading or
1928 had read or would ever read Antony & Cleopatra. They
did not care a straw for the future of fiction or the death of
~~poetry or the~~ development by the average woman of a
style completely expressive of her needs. ~~They were~~
~~hurrying to work, all such questions, had one~~
~~Their indifference was~~ If such questions had been
stooped to chalked on the pavement, <wd. have been rubbed out in a> nobody
read would have stopped to
them. read. ~~They were~~ And one felt more stimulated
than depressed by this indifference, because ~~it was so~~
<And> there was sanity & truth ~~in it, because they were~~
~~engaged in hurrying to work,~~ & this indifference; in
the nonchalance of the hurrying feet which would
rub out whatever one wrote <was written> so soon. They were all
hurrying to work; ~~they were~~ carrying little cases &
bags. They were scarcely distinguishable, their
in their browns, their
purples, their
navy blues; their
[—] felt helmets
their felt hats.

clothes were so much alike; & yet ~~if one thought to oneself~~
~~There are only~~ very soon
Even from a window on the top floor <one was able to
distinguish> enough to fire
one with curiosity, to make one ask a thousand
questions. Nor did they all hurry. In every London
street there is always somebody who is completely idle.
~~He will presumably be some where~~ some extraordinary
spectator, ~~apparition, who has no kinship with this~~ without business or
attachment. Also there are drifters; to whom the streets
serve as club rooms. <who> They hail men in carts;
they ~~talk~~ pass the time of day. Also
there ~~are very~~ are funerals, to which, that man who has
no belief whatever in the immortality of the soul,
takes off his hat; ~~there are~~ errand boys, &
~~now & again a very~~ distinguished figure; a lot of
with the paper ~~living & thinking has been done by that man, to judge~~
under his ~~by the way he~~ comes down the steps. ~~Nor can there be~~
arm ~~anything more deplorable than the~~ Soon the first
carefully impression of a common object, which is work, is
avoid destroyed. On the contrary there is no common
to whom object; ~~unless the negative one, that they do not care for~~
a lady ~~& hence~~ the futility of going down to Cambridge -
(she has pretending that 'we' care for whatever it may be:
someh when, as a matter of fact. . . At this moment
collected a as so often happens in London, there was a complete lull in the
set of fur) traffic;
cessation of all life; the street was empty; no
~~car or cart~~ nothing came past; & ~~the~~ a single
leaf fell from the plane tree which stands at corner; as
So the leaves would ~~be falling at Oxbridge;~~ & the
fell at Oxbridge, gold into the many-coloured river.

~~& the reflection in the river should be more~~ With that curious
And then,~~though nothing whatever happened, it became clear,~~ <with
that descent of the leaf>
it seemed as if ~~from the demeanour of the~~ &
one were on the trail of some~~thing curious~~ force,
as instinctive ~~as that of the falling leaf; the street~~
~~undoubtedly the~~ as its fall; <&> as incessant; <inevitable> as
observing eternal. The common object; I thought, is that; <~~all~~> when the
the taxidriver: ~~who would get the same fare from the~~
~~middle aged man as from the young lady with the~~
open the ~~pretty coat, open his door. He would be paid the same;~~
door, ~~but <for> she was pretty, & he was a man. That is the common~~
~~force that goes up & down this street all day long.~~
~~And it then became~~ more ceremoniously There was
~~And~~ At once the street became ~~lit up~~ <full> with signals, &
~~it had its current, washing up & down ceaselessly; &~~ one could
feel the current washing up & down; & everybody seemed
to be eddying in its power to an end <the [run?]> of their own; so
that even the taximan, opening his door with some
compelling civility to the young woman in patent leather
shoes was being given half a twirl by the current; &
she was being borne off by it - for it was Saturday
morning, I remembered, & very fine; ~~the light~~
~~at held up in the finest cloth~~ Perhaps it would
be the last fine half holiday before the winter.
That is where they are all going, I thought, watching
the traffic which now seemed fuller & busier than
usual; There had fallen a splendid tear
From the passion flower at the
gate.
She is coming my dove my dear
She is coming my life my fate.

And the answer, I said, drawing back into the room,
  My heart is like a singing bird
    Whose nest is in a water'd shoot;

  My heart is gladder than all these,
    Because my love is come to me.

What poets, ~~oh~~ what poets they were, I exclaimed, & picking up Shakespeare I could not help capping ~~Tenny~~ their verses with ~~his,~~ what Tennyson & Christina Rossetti had said with Antony;

had said to his Emily & ~~Chr~~ Rossetti to her Mr Cayley with Antony an.

It fell <intuitively, inevitably> & made me think of the river into
which leaves were now
falling. And the thought of the river, perhaps, ~~brought~~
made me perceive, ~~stealing~~ some~~thing~~ <current> ~~of the same sort~~
eddying ~~round~~ round the corner, down the street, a
~~fine current which was drawing the people who had~~
~~seemed without common object together. at any rate~~
~~it appeared the as if the people were being drawn~~
~~together, in some sort by some kind of influence,~~
~~as if the taxi gliding slowly past were in the current,~~
gliding people together, ~~making them brush close to~~
~~each other, & then~~ The taxi came ~~along~~ down the
~~current & stopped~~ ~~stopped,~~ for example, & the
a coming together, a drawing close; ~~thick as~~ <of figures;>
some~~thing that~~ impression of attraction derived
from nothing more definite than ~~looks~~ <a glance> & hesitations;
from ~~the courtesy~~ <[even?]> of the cab driver <open in> to the
girl in
patent leather shoes; ~~from the consciousness~~
~~which was~~ from her ~~gesture~~ <look> as she ~~step~~
was swept off ~~into what had this likeness to a current.~~
round the corner. ~~Difficult~~ No detective could
have said that anything had actually happened; ~~but~~ yet
yet enough had happened to make it ~~seem~~
~~very~~ perfectly certain that it was a
Saturday morning, & that in an hour or two all
~~these people who now seemed~~ <these> detached <now> would be
instinctively & ~~inevitably~~ attracted together;
have given way to unity. One gains these impressions

the thought of the river & the of the inevitable & instinctive fall of the leaf made me perceive something of the same sort in [her the?] gliding the cab with it (for now a cab [came) & stops?] there helpless her burden attached across the street,

from almost intangible things; ~~even~~ from light coloured stockings,
as from ~~the~~ <white> paper that florists pin round flowers. One
gets the impression of people stirred by some festivity, <yielding
to some natural attract>
& the thought, evanescent as it was, had the strange
effect of ~~making~~ communicating, even to an observer
remote in an upper room, something ~~foolish too~~,
~~that~~ resembl~~ed~~ing ~~that approach of the the~~ their instinctive
~~desire to~~ ~~contentment, as if~~ One ~~can could only expl~~
~~come together~~ Perhaps, I thought, returning to the page on which I had
& satisfaction; written so boldly <u>Women & Fiction</u>, the mind ~~has~~
also has the ~~power~~ <desire> to ~~be~~ unify itself; & I
recalled how ~~often~~, in making the notes ~~which are here
strung together~~ I had been ~~more & more~~ conscious of
effort; as if the tension of thinking always of one
sex alone had been fatiguing <straining> some muscle; &
the sight of the girl ~~getting~~ greeting the young man at the
corner had worked, & it was a profound relief to
~~be made think~~ when the strain was relaxed; as it was,
so ~~suddenly, when I saw the stopped thinking & let
lost~~ <by> seeing even that ordinary sight ~~had been relieved
the strain~~, for instead of making my mind ~~isolate
some fact~~ separate, it became single. {In other words,
I thought, sitting down to my talk again, the
we have it in our power to use many different
consciousnesses; ~~I~~ <one> can think ~~back~~ through ~~my~~ ones
mothers, as through ~~my~~ <ones> fathers; ~~I can
think~~ one can think of ~~civilisation~~ creating as
the ~~inheritors of~~ <as a part> civilisation; or as an alien.
Even in ~~this~~ making these notes I had}

But what do I mean by the unity of the mind, I thought,
remembering my own statement that a woman
thinks back as a writer through her mothers; remembering
too, how, when I walked down Whitehall, <there had been> a
distinct
break in my consciousness; ~~had~~ From being the
natural inheritor of civilisation, its statues, its
government buildings, its triumphal arches, I had
suddenly become an alien, a critic: & <as if I had thought back
through a different universe to a woman in a tree; who had
denied that this civilisation was any of her doing> ~~And~~ <For>
now I
must in honesty register the fact that the sight of a
couple meeting by appointment at a street corner has the
power to ~~make my mind~~ reduce these ~~fractures~~ <[divide?] to a
whole;> to make
my mind easy & not strained & to give me the full &
use of my faculties; <&> to ~~render me~~ plunge me into that
layer of unconsciousness which is, at any rate physically,
the most comfortable of all. ~~For~~ One should
conclude then ~~that any~~ on the evidence of ones own
~~comfort~~ <body> that ~~to think~~ there ~~is some~~ are ~~the same~~
~~in the~~ two sexes also in the brain; & I went on,
amateurishly to devise a scheme <of the soul> by which
~~one has two~~ in each of us there preside two powers,
one male one female; ~~&~~ & <in> the man's brain
~~embodies~~<the man predominates over> the woman ~~to the man, the~~
~~woman's brain~~
& in the womans brain the woman predominates
over the man. And sometimes, for a
special purpose one can wilfully accentuate
whichever side one wishes to be dominant.
~~all this time,~~ I thought, ~~I have been~~ as I had
been doing, so that I ~~thought I~~ was always

Clearly the mind has a great many scarcely discovered possibility.

thinking back through my mothers, & splitting my consciousness
apart instead of letting it flow~~, as~~ undivided.
~~But~~ ~~To explore~~ any further ~~into this~~ It would doubtless be possible to explore much further into this matter & to trace the exact point at which a woman becomes conscious of thinking through her mothers; at which she sees the the primeval woman in a tree; lamenting so it seems the course that human destiny must take. For if I had not got the task before me of peopling every jungle, every forest, every swamp, I should go swinging through the sun, she says - but these thoughts are manifestly fantastic. One must leave them, & concentrate only upon

But this splitting up is painful. The coming together is pleasant. Shall one then conclude that the ~~right~~ <proper> state of mind for a writer of fiction (For it ~~wd. take too long to explore the~~ one must limit the enquiry) is a state in which

man side of the brain think

both sexes in the brain co-operate: a woman thinks <in which the woman side & the>
as a woman & as a man simultaneously, though if she is ~~right~~ an intelligent & gifted woman, the woman <side> ~~predom~~ preponderates over the man?
Let me now advance a little more amateur psychology, & suppose that this union of the two sexes in one brain can only take place at hush of midnight.
Not a light must burn; not a wheel grate on the cobbles. In fact the writer must be profoundly

steeped in oblivion that ~~he does not~~ his faculties,
are unaware of the least supervision & bring
& go about their task like conspirators ~~confident~~
at dead of night. <at> The least help or advice. ~~from being~~ would
they will start - ~~make them at once~~ drop their booty; ~~So that if~~ a
~~woman says~~, ~~the most fatal thing of all is to interfere~~.
Let us then add to all these injunctions to women,
(who are after all used to advise) Draw the curtain,
& let the marriage take place, & never presume for a
moment to say, now I am a woman, now I am a man; they
have to be allowed to do that job for themselves. And
the only way to attain this oblivion is to exercise
day after day, night after night, every faculty freely;
so that when the marriage night comes you, the writer,
can sink into oblivion; & ~~let them~~ do their ~~work~~
~~unfettered.~~ he can be & look at the stars; he can take a
rose & pull its petals apart; he can float down the
stream & watch the swans sailing the other way proudly

Concentrate
one is able to
concentrate
one's mind,
<one's whole
ones con-
sciousness>
to stand
being at
any point
one wishes.

if one is
a woman,

~~when~~ in
writing

For clearly the mind is able to divide itself, infinitely, to
<take any angle attitude point of view it wishes;>
~~separate itself from It can take this atti~~ can
separate itself from the people on the street for example, &
~~observe them as a sight. Or it can~~ think of them as outside
oneself. Or ~~it~~ <one> can become part of them, as happens ~~in any~~
~~omnibus, when there is an~~ for instance going along a
~~crowded street~~ in an omnibus when there is a block.
~~Or Also I remembered~~ Then, ~~when one is in the~~
~~attitude of a writer if one is writing, the a woman~~
~~so I have as I~~ if one is writing one thinks back
[unconsciously?]
through one's mothers; & if one is a woman, one ~~cannot~~
~~we~~ is often surprised, say in walking down Whitehall,
to find oneself splitting off from civilisation, &
from being the ~~unconsci~~ natural inheritor of all
~~these~~ <the> ~~streets triumphs of~~ electric light & locomotion to
becoming on the contrary outside government
buildings & triumphal arches, ~~their~~ an alien, a critic.
Clearly the mind is always altering its focus, &
~~arranging its~~ bringing the world into different
perspectives. But some of these states of mind ~~are~~
seem, I thought even ~~though there are~~ <if> adopted spontaneously,
to be less comfortable ~~physically~~ than others. ~~Here Now~~
~~for example, looking at the~~ They ~~seem to involve~~
some ~~distortion~~, <effort> ~~as if one were holding~~
~~forcing ones mind to hold itself out in an~~
~~doing ones mind a violence;~~ In order to ~~hold~~ <keep in> them
one is, unconsciously, ~~holding~~ ~~sup~~pressing <holding something
back>
Gradually the repression becomes ~~an effort,~~ <a strain> & one
welcomes the There may be some state of

mind ~~which~~ in which one could continue for <a> longer
time without any effort; & this perhaps, I thought,
coming in from the window, is one of them. For
certainly when I saw the couple get into the taxi ~~the~~
~~strain had vanished,~~ my mind felt as if ~~two sides~~ <after being
divided>
~~from being two~~ it had ~~been~~ <also had> come together again ~~after~~
~~being~~ & ~~the its powers in unity~~ <after being divided> in a natural
fusion. ~~That is to say, one~~ seemed to recover ease & to
lose consciousness; ~~& to be~~ <It is perhaps not fantastic to> One
might conclude
then, I thought, turning to the page on which was written
Women & Fiction,} that ~~there the brain also~~
~~has two sexes.~~ ~~There is are forces <parts>~~ in the brain which
~~correspond~~ there is something corresponding to the
sexes in the brain also. And I went on
amateurishly to devise a plan of the soul, ~~in~~
~~which~~ so that in each of us two powers
preside, one male, one female; & in the man's
brain the man predominates over the woman, &
in the woman's brain the woman predominates over
the man. The normal, <&> ~~the~~ comfortable state of
being is that when the two are living in harmony
together, spiritually co-operating. If one is a
man, one should ~~be letting~~ the woman part of the brain
~~take action,~~ <has> effect; & a woman <also> must ~~also~~ have
intercourse with the man in her. <Only> Then <do> we get a
mind that is fully fertilised, ~~that~~ <&> is using all its
faculties, It was something of this sort
that one meant ~~by~~ when one spoke of the unity of
the mind.

One must conclude then I thought turning to the page on
which was written Women & Fiction, that any ~~divorce~~
stress laid upon the sex of the writer means sterility.
A mind that is purely masculine cannot create,
any more than a mind that is purely feminine.
But clearly it would be well to try these theories on a
fact or two before one appeared on a platform with a
roll of paper in ones hand & ~~that desperate~~ ~~desperate~~
<a look of>
a~~n~~ conviction on ones face.

looking up & down the shelves devoted to the living.

The purely masculine writer is ~~too~~ commoner today
than he has ever been, I thought; whatever the reason.
Presumably the suffrage campaign has much to do
with it. For many years an enormous emphasis
was laid on sex; nobody could grow up without thinking
I am a man, or I am a woman; ~~&~~ nobody could
escape argument & theory. No age can ever have
shown a more strident self-consciousness on the part
of men, I thought, remembering the long list of
books about women which are ~~sign~~ written by men,
yearly monthly, almost weekly one would think.
Obviously <some men write> some profound instinct of self-
assertion
is here expressing itself; one which it would be extremely
interesting, & ~~further~~ amusing into the bargain to
investigate. A history of ~~the mind~~ of man in ~~its~~ his
relation to women would be one of the most
amusing books in the language if some young
woman, with ~~an income~~ <a capital> of not less than thirty
thousand pounds in her own control would write it.
But here I am only concerned with fiction, I reminded
myself; with Mr A. & Mr B & Mr C. & Mr D.

~~For I am going to be a coward, I thought, & call it courtesy. I am not going to say aloud what I think of all this fiction & poetry & criticism,~~

And what does one find when one looks at the ~~fiction~~ - ~~that is the poetry, the fict novels, the at the imaginative work of the men? an extraordinary~~ at their books? - they are all alive, so that I dare not mention them by name. Pure masculinity is <in> certainly ~~in the~~ in the ascendent. {Whatever I read, poetry, fiction, criticism, I find myself saying, ~~oh b~~But ~~this man~~ <he has> has no power of suggestion. ~~He is as clever as he can be, I say, he has a~~ <his> intellect <is> ~~so highly~~ developed that one might think ~~that it was taken out at night & polished~~ & to the I add of course, making my deferential ~~courtesy~~ curtsey to the many generations of culture & good feeding that have ~~so~~ polished that particular faculty so brightly, his intellect is ~~splendid~~. <magnificent> He is ~~accomplished~~,
<competent he is> muscular,
~~up to Every sort of~~ he is efficient beyond any doubt or proof that I can apply. He is experienced He has had the run of the world these centuries. He has been in every part of the globe, ~~often~~ often with a flag in his hand. ~~He has~~ But [~~still~~?] <still> he has no power of suggestion". ~~What a futile & feminine~~
~~It must of course be obvious that~~
This foolish notion kept popping into my head & spoiling the ~~splendour~~ fervour of the peroration. What did one mean by it, I wondered, taking down this novel & that book of criticism, & that poem beginning to dip about among the pages:

of course a young man, is very much obsessed by himself. No
wonder. <Lady Bessborough ->
This is written by a man who has never forgotten the fact of
his sex. Somehow, before one has read three pages one is
~~up against~~ the letter I. 'I' stands in the foreground
of the novel; a stalwart figure, ~~doubtless, very well
made & dressed~~ well proportioned, but dominating the
view. Behind him one may catch a glimpse of a tree or a
town; but not for long. He returns methodically
persistently, with a devotion which is impressive to the
fact of himself. But that is excusable. I mean something.
<deeper; by the lack of [suggestive power.?]>
But these are the books of young men, It may
be that it is impossible for them not, in this age, to
lay so great a stress upon [the?] sex that it becomes
so out of all proportion that it bores one. It crushes the
It may be that they are consciously using only one side of the
brain. It may be that we have reached a state of
disillusionment when we no longer sing . . . . .
~~The~~ Seeing the manx cat in the quadrangle. Thus it is
It may be that in a hundred years or so the
marriage of the mind of man will be impossible.
At any rate, I said, taking down books of such
illustrious fame & wide [world?] circulation that
no body can now add an atom or detract
the works of Mr Kipling, & Mr Galsworthy. Here are
two masters who affect me with the most
dismal forebodings! People used to write
books wh. were comprehensible by men & women
equally. Here are books that only men can
understand. And I remembered

one is under
the shadow
of the
the letter
which is
cut in
one
rigid
I think.

Otherwise one might find oneself hopelessly at sea.
Coleridge certainly did not mean by an androgynous <mind>, I
thought going to the book case & pausing before the many
books there, a mind that ~~has~~ has any ~~particular~~ special
sympathy with women: a mind that takes up their cause, or
~~anything~~ devotes itself to their interpretation.
The androgynous mind is less apt to ~~make~~
make these distinctions than another. It is a mind
that is resonant; <&> porous; that transmits emotion
~~from one perpetually~~ without impediment; that is
ceaselessly creative; ~~& will~~ incandescent; undivided.
In fact one goes back to Shakespeares mind as the
type of the androgynous, the man-womanly mind;
though it would be impossible to say what Shakespeare
thought of the other sex. <That> ~~The It~~ may indeed be one of
that it does not think of sex separately - ~~condition of~~ the characteristics <condition> of the ~~mind~~ fully
developed mind - a condition ~~which~~ now so much
harder to attain than it was then, I thought, ~~proceeding~~
to the ~~modern~~ coming to books by living men; &
there pausing, uncertain which to open. <Nobody could grow up
now without thinking I am a man or I am a woman> ~~For here
under my hand, the~~ No age can have been so
stridently ~~self~~ sex-conscious as ours~~,~~ is I thought;
~~putting my hand upon one of the~~ remembering those
innumerable books by men about women in the
British Museum;X the Suffrage Campaign no
doubt was the cause of it. ~~Nobody could
grow up without thinking I am a man, or I am a
woman; &~~ It ~~bred in~~ must have roused
in men an extraordinary desire for self assertion;
it must have made them lay an emphasis

upon their own sex & its merits which they would not have
troubled to think about had it not been challenged, ~~by~~
~~For really the opposition to womens <education> must have been~~
~~largely self asser largely And that~~ That perhaps
accounts for some of the characteristics that I find here, I
continued, opening ~~book~~ <a novel or two & ~~laying them in~~> ~~books~~
~~of poetry, of criticism,~~
~~novels & biographies~~: a novel by a Mr A. ~~It is~~ They
~~written~~ <wrote> under the shadow of the letter I. One
can only just catch a glimpse of ~~the~~ <a> landscape, ~~behind~~.
~~Back we come~~ of a church, of a tower perhaps behind.
~~I. I. I.~~ No doubt he is a <u>good</u> fellow; ~~a~~ earnest &
indefatigable & ardent; {but what a drought is in his
soul! What a parched pea he makes of the human
race!} ~~For here, having argued very ably his own~~
~~<His> state of mind on every conceivable~~ ~~Himself, his own~~
~~state of~~ ~~He will argue us all blue in the face; that~~
<that> can I deny the muscularity, the energy of his mind.
~~But~~ the splendid ~~development~~ <polish> of that particular
knob which we call intellect. ~~Certainly~~ But -
after all, he has not been fed & taught for centuries
without putting a polish on that which I respect from the
bottom of my heart. But - & here I turned
two or three chapters over rapidly seeking I knew not
what. ~~But I kept repeating as if what~~
~~I read~~ ~~what~~ a drought is in his soul! But,
~~& I turned another chapter or two what parched~~
~~peas he makes of the human race!~~ but of the
shadow of the letter I all is shapeless as mist.
There is not a bone in these womens bodies, I
continued, reading how he had met a girl on a
beach. His is <It is not> ~~very~~ not hostile to her - not at

[Margin: written by men ~~who are still~~ now living, indeed in the prime of life]

all: he is indifferent; & it is <from> his indifference that is so &
blind; <you cannot know that>

turning a few more pages;

dull for the reader; ~~but~~ & now~~, here, we are in for it,~~
I thought, knowing by unmistakable signs that
~~we were to go through a scene~~ of the moment approached
~~when decency was going to be violated, &~~

It is on the brink. He ---

~~when the [usual?] crisis was to be~~ of the inevitable
crisis. It was ~~very conscientiously~~ done ~~very~~ It was
~~horribly perfectly frank.~~ Everything <It was> was done ~~in~~
openly ~~that used to be done privately.~~ Everything was said
plainly. ~~But that used to be unsai said not at all.~~
~~Indecency~~ Nothing could have been more indecent.
But - But I cannot go on saying "But" &
not finishing the sentences, I remarked. that <[writing it has
been?]> But I am bored.
~~In spite of the majestic intellect? I enquired~~
But why was I bored? Partly because of the dominance
of the letter I. & the aridity which <like the giant beech tree> it
casts ~~all~~
~~round it~~; in the

so that when he comes to write of women unfortunately he forms the letter I

neighbourhood. ~~It is~~ <But in> all Lady Bessboroughs fault I said;
She would always, pretending that Lord Granvilles
maiden speech was so important; ~~how can they~~
~~Lord Granville help thinking back, if I choose to~~
~~write a novel, I. I. I when he~~ so that he thinks
too much about himself altogether. And then, I
continued, ~~it is the fact, for which for whatever reason~~
remembering ~~incongruously perhaps~~ that lunch party at
Oxbridge, & the cigarette ash, & the manx cat, & ~~my~~
Tennyson & Christina Rossetti, ~~he no longer~~
All in a tangle together, they no longer hum
under their breath, She is coming my dove, my dear,
& my love, my love, is come to me. So that when
They meet on a beach what can he do? She is

Naturally only one thing. <And> {Imagine, romance, dream,
rhapsodise he cannot, ~~being much to his credit,~~
as honest as the day & logical in the extreme. ~~So he~~
does the one thing he can do; & And that he does,
to do him justice, very valiantly, ~~in the full light of day~~,
~~But~~ ~~He does it again, & he does it again~~, <over & over> I continued
~~turning over page after page; for anything I knew he may be~~
~~doing it on every page <which, I added a> But I am bored. once is enough~~
~~Is that not~~ <this is> an awful confession, <[I made?]> does it not prove me
~~hopelessly~~ cold ~~as~~ ice ~~& as remote~~ old as the hills?
an ~~implacable unworthy of the confidence~~ unworthy to
read, incapable of <understanding> ~~criticising~~ this novel? - I remain
~~bored~~. Seems to me ~~dull~~ monotonous.

The ~~fact may~~ be <truth is> I thought, that while one must
humour Mr A. for not pretending ~~to feelings which he has~~
~~not, one cannot but <but wish> if one is a woman, but~~
~~attach quite the same importance to this <an> act~~
~~obviously of the highest importance to Mr. A. Once~~
~~would have been enough.~~ That Mr A, had a
greater range of emotional experience.
Nor is it interesting, once it has been said, I continued;
Shakespeare's <[indecency?]> ~~indecency is quite a different matter, for~~
it uproots a thousand queer things; ~~but this~~
in me, which I recognise & find of interest I do not know.
But it is not Mr. A's fault; ~~for what has happened~~
to ~~[poor?] Mr. A. is again~~ The fault of Miss
Clough & Lady Stanley of Alderley. When they
remarked in their quiet way that girls have
some character & brain, Mr A: ~~encouraged in~~
said, & one cannot blame him, I can do this; &
it is half in protest ~~against this~~ against any

[Margin:] over & over & over (I said turning the pages) again.

[Margin:] as

[Margin:] Why Mr A.s indecency is dull, or perhaps it is a question of contrivance. Mr A. does it as the nurses say on purpose

possible diminishing of his importance that he goes on doing
it. that he attaches such importance to a physical
act which Shakespeare lumped in with a thousand
other states of mind & made poetical. poetry of.
~~However~~
~~Really~~ What it amounts to, I thought, ~~putting~~
glancing at a critic, a highly able, a very honest critic
& finding there a whiff of the same unmistakable
fervour is that <perhaps> men are now <for many more reasons
than I can stop to investigate> writing ~~for men, & it is~~
solely for men, & it is a mistake for a woman to read them,
for she ~~will expect~~ will inevitably look for something
that ~~they cannot give her~~. <she will not find> ~~They have lost the~~
It is the — power of suggestion I thought; I read what Mr. B. has to
~~say of Swift poetry the art of poetry; & it~~
that for my ~~own~~ part I miss; & I read, very dutifully,
Mr. B. on the art of poetry {The knob of intellect has
been developed to such an extent that it ~~has~~ now occupies a
little compartment all by itself.} The mind, from being
porous & transparent has become a honeycomb of
separate chambers; ~~so densely~~ walled with steel
so that not a sound carries from one to the other; I
& very — thought, reading Mr. B. all that he says is sensible,
liberal — acute learned in the highest ~~degree~~; but his feelings no
longer communicate, ~~so that when I~~ & so his
learning & his acuteness remain unfertilised, & when I
it [pales?] like — ~~put an~~ <apply what Mr. B> lay what Mr B. says <into my mind>
a parched — about poetry
pea to the — to Shakespeare nothing happened. Whereas I have only to
[former?] — take a ~~little~~ sentence of Coleridge into my mind for all
sorts of things to happen.
But of course I went on, it is not Mr. B's

fault, for he is a fellow of this college, & a professor <at> some
university; the fault is mine, ~~&~~ And it is my fault,
my feelings too that when I read Mr. Churchills eloquence I cannot
are too make it fit any feeling of my own. I can only think
small for that huge leather arm chairs & vast mahogany tables &
his words: turkey carpets so thick that the foot sinks in them
~~some~~how write like this when they are alone
after dark in an office. The size of the sentence is
far off getting too big for me, I thought; & when I see these
[rather metaphors approaching I feel that I am going to be
nearby?] I crushed to death And ~~all this preaching; I went on,~~
then the weary gesture of the burdened soul, I thought;
~~& then But this how exaggerated, how~~
~~surely it is not necessary to groan like that, in public.~~
coming to the preachers & the prophets. In the old days
They used to lead one to church by another way; less
vociferatingly. ~~Still, I concluded, there are reasons~~
~~doubtless for these~~ ~~But~~ And by that time I
had reached the complete works of Mr Kipling & Mr
Galsworthy; ~~which needed~~ where I paused, not
merely because one could not run a finger quickly over
that <vast> bulk, but because it is often said that these two are
~~so great that~~ unsurpassed.

Critics often say, I thought, that the Forsyte Saga will never be
surpassed in our day. ~~At any rate,~~ <&> in view of the
of their books enormous celebrity of these writers, & the~~ir~~ prodigious
circulations, there could be no discourtesy in naming them, &
if one ~~did not agree with the estimate of the~~
found oneself dissentient, <&> puzzled, out of it, in reading them,
~~the fault~~ one merely proclaimed ones own folly
~~ones own~~ <&> lack of the critical sense. For I cannot
deny that Mr Kiplings books puzzle me. There is a man of
genius undoubtedly. Nothing can surpass ~~his force~~,
his vividness, his power of bringing the object before the
eye. But - 'but' <were> 'buts' beginning again? What
~~was~~ <did> I mean by it this time I demanded, hastily glancing
through ~~the~~ Plain Tales from the Hills & ~~the~~
Many Inventions & Wee Willie Winkie: <But> ~~It was~~
[makes me the emotion <is wrong> perhaps. It <~~The~~ At least it> made me so
un ?] uncomfortable. The
officers were always turning & looking the other way. The
The male was always alone with his work. The
Empire was always being saluted by solitary men who had
sown the seed. One blushed, as if one had been
caught eavesdropping at ~~a~~ some masculine orgy
It was highly uncomfortable; ~~& in~~ &
I noted, as a proof of my own incapacity, that when
I had read a story or two, ~~nothing remained~~ in my mind;
it was as if the surface had been vigorously scrubbed or
hailed upon with hard dry sharp pellets; nothing
got beneath the skin: Of Mr. Gals
Mr. Galsworthy has nothing like Mr Kiplings
genius, but he is of course a man of
commanding ability & ~~his~~ the Forstye Saga is

often said to typify, to sum up a whole side of English life. There is old Jolyon, & there is June & there is young ~~It is a vast family,~~ They are typical, <just such> representative, extraordinarily like some ~~British~~ well to do British family ~~but which~~ one has ~~known~~ met, or even stayed with, but - ~~Again the But referred to these something~~ Another but. This time it was more decided. <But England is not like a Christmas number of the Graphic I think.> This wont do at all, I added. Nobody was ever in the least like this. Old Jolyon ~~is merely a~~ has nothing to him. The country is like cardboard. The motor car is not a real one. And yet, how admirably everything [looked?]; the butler, the hat, the plate the glass; the nice bit of mahogany; & this old mans leather shoes. The Forsytes are undoubtedly the best got up family in the whole of fiction I thought, going back almost with physical pleasure to the thought of their baths & their dogs & their nice clean lavatories & linen with lavender pressed between the sheets. ~~Oh~~ But - ~~well when the picture fell on Jolyon &~~ Precisely the same thing happened as with Kipling, when they began to have scenes, & situation, I ~~had to leave the room.~~ ~~I saw it coming~~ It is bound to happen, I said long before the end. The picture will come down on the old man's head. He will die in a upper room; & perhaps the old clerk will die too. <Anyh> All the swans will burst out singing, & I shall be overcome with laughter & <[have?]> rush into the gooseberry bushes to hide my ~~idiotic~~ <[there?]> merriment. To avoid that catastrophe I shut the book.

If I [poke this field or park?] it would crumple up like thin paper. One could tear them across as one tears a house party in the Tatler

It is in the emotional values that we differ, I thought. Their
sentiment seems to me sentimentality. Their reality is to me
unreal. Obviously, they are right, ~~or they would not~~
because hundreds & thousands of people agree with them
But I cannot help thinking I concluded that their
appeal is almost entirely to their own sex. They are
~~writing about~~ <It is> the world of men; ~~they are~~ that they are
describing; they are celebrating male values; & applying
male standards. Their sense of what is tragic -
what is funny is purely masculine: There is not a
touch of the woman anywhere in either of them.
Therefore they are entirely without suggestive power to a
woman, & it is no more possible for me to ~~understand~~
them than it is for me to sit down & write a column
about the Boat race when I ~~do not~~ <scarcely> know bow from
stern, or cox from stroke. All I know is that I am
horribly bored.

write good criticism of criticism

All this is ~~not only~~ extremely unfortunate for me,
since ~~it limits my reading. &~~ makes me ~~unappreciative~~
unable to appreciate the finest work of our greatest
living writers. Moreover, the trouble (for it is to me a
trouble whatever it may be to the world at large) is
likely to increase, I thought. ~~Self conscious virility is
in the ascendent~~. ~~Literature will become more & more
purely masculine~~; One has only to travel in Italy to
see that it is perfectly possible ~~of~~ for ~~one~~ sex <which has all
this in its hand.> to suppress the
other completely <The male is completely dominant in Italy.> one
must not put ones feet on the seat of the
railway carriage. One must not take off one's
coat in the dining car. On every little chemists shop ~~in~~ a
back alley ~~is~~ <are> stamped the swarthy features of the Duce.
And ~~in the main streets~~ wherever there is a blank wall
large enough <for a> to display ~~a poster,~~ some vast sheet
proclaims <[there?] some> the triumphs of the aviator ~~or the
general~~
& incites the sons of the state to heroism. It is all
very <sterile> airless & ~~dry~~ (I mean to a woman) ~~& apparently~~
I thought, remembering Rome; but ~~while all this~~ <what> street
drumming & trampling ~~makes the body harder~~ & more
~~athletic~~ what effect does it have upon <poetry,> the mind? I shall
Well, ~~it seems doubtful;~~ <apparently there are answers at least>
there has been a
meeting in Rome <I remember reading in> (according to the
Times) of the Academy of
Ten, whose object is to develop the Italian novel;
"The speeches were marked by a Fascist tone", <I read> & a
telegram was sent to the Duce expressing the hope
that the Fascist era would soon give birth to a
poet worthy of it." Perhaps it will:
But I shall not like poetry ~~when it is~~ that comes out of an
incubator, I thought. ~~I shall~~ not be able to read a word
~~of the literature which has only~~ no mother, but only a
father. Poetry needs a mother as well as a father -

They have the guns, & they have the

One feels as if one's mind had been tied up in [string & stamped upon & one corner a pliant court & was for the little?] boys strutting about in black shirts

I shall find not [like?]

Poetry ought to have

Shakespeare was
androgynous:
so was Keats, so
were Sterne, Cowper,
Lamb, - ~~in our time~~ all were
androgynous.

Milton & Ben Jonson had too
much of the male in them; so
had Wordsworth, & ~~But~~ Tolstoi
Proust In our time, ~~Proust was~~ <Proust on the other hand
~~a~~ was wholly androgynous; ~~& Hardy~~
but ~~I~~ alas the greater It is>
number of living writers - with
some most valuable & important
& exception - ~~seem~~ <write like> me pure men.

it has to do with the ~~manx~~
manx cat I saw in the quadrangle;

[160 *verso*]

However, ~~that is all my own~~ <the> fault, ~~I concluded,~~ rests with us,
I concluded, thinking back through my mothers again;
for if only ~~women~~ <we> had ~~remained~~ <stayed> shut up in the sitting rooms
~~men would not have been virile,~~ embroidering a bag,
~~men~~ the ~~other sex would not have had to assert its~~
virility; or at most taking a walk on the leads,
~~so that~~ The ~~blame for all~~ <It is a strange thought> this Cock-a-doodling,
is to be laid to the charge of a very small, but
resolute woman, the daughter of a clergyman, by name
Miss Emily Davies: ~~And~~ It is entirely ~~due to her~~
that our literature ~~is also infected with~~ <is infect> Cock-a-doodledum; ~~&~~
~~to escape wh~~ & it is she who drives me when I
want to enjoy a ~~good~~ book <use all myself with a> to seek it in that happy age <among [the kind for example?]>
when the mind <of the writer who [was?]> was using both ~~its sides sexes~~. <sides of the mind>~~*~~ But, I
reminded myself, this is perhaps a temporary state of
affairs; & much of what I am saying will already
seem out of date to an audience composed entirely of
young women who have not yet come of age.
<~~Even so~~ But even so I would advise young women>
To them however I would say, I thought,
taking up that sheet of paper which was still headed
"Women & Fiction", ~~that it is of the utmost importance to use both~~ ~~on no ac~~ who wish to be writers <if they are going to be writers> on no
account to think of their sex. <stress the fact of [this?]> It is fatal to ~~lay stress~~ <lay stress upon>
~~upon the <any> feminine qualities of the mind; fatal It is~~ if
~~you begin to say~~ [I?] am a woman & I want to
avenge some grievance or plead some cause of my sex.
It is fatal to say ~~I have inherited from~~ <my sex has [endowed?]> ~~the~~ possess
my sex an astonishingly complex & sensitive
organism, & so lay stress upon that complexity &
sensibility. It is fatal to accentuate ~~in~~
~~for any reason~~ the in any way or for any reason the

[of this
say,
virility in
hers ?]
& looking
at the view
by taking

her fault

to [turn
from the
writer - ?]
with some
very happy
exceptions
however -
to to seen

be gunandros
not single

to be
woman-manly
& not pure
woman from

~~gifts of that are~~ disposition which the mind has received ~~by~~
from its sex. And ~~this~~ <'fatal'> is no figure of speech; for
cut off from fertility. anything written with that conscious bias is somehow
infertile; ~~&~~ it has no ~~roots~~. Brilliant &
effective & powerful it may appear for a day to two; but
it can not grow in the minds of others; ~~to live &
grow in the minds other minds it must have the
fertility The power of living & growing~~ ~~It What is~~ The
purely feminine is sterile <&> uncreative. Some
collaboration <of both [sides?]> has to take place in the mind ~~of~~
between
both sexes.

How this is to be done, how in the past it has been done,
no critic, ~~no~~ psychologist can tell us. One might
hazard a guess ~~that~~ from reading Shakespeare, or
that the mind cannot grasp it that the prelude to ~~this art is~~ <[in?] the> creation is a state of
awareness, ~~so~~ <~~so~~ [incandescent?]> wide as the sky, <so>
sensitive as the sea.
And clearly, without his saying it, often ~~his~~ <Shaks'> mind <this
awareness> was in
violently ~~tempest~~ <against> tossed - ~~strewn on~~ ~~thrown~~ hurled on
the
cliff in fragments <&>: broken; severed to atoms. <A [world?] of>
Experience <of> must
have gone before. But to communicate that experience to
~~us~~, - there the imagination boggles: it is impossible to
conceive the speed & the control, the violence & the calm,
that were needed to write a scene say in Antony &
Cleopatra; ~~always to~~ be flying before the break of that
gale; & ~~never~~ here & there & in & out; now to be
nobody now to be Caesar, to be some old soldier
next & then a girl singer: & all in time; ~~to some other
something; which we do not see~~ all done to the beat ~~of a~~
of an invisible drum. ~~Is it it the freedom of it
that most amazes us?~~ ~~One is left with a sense of~~ nothing
<is left> unsaid that can be said; ~~indeed reading~~ it is the freedom
of it

that remains overwhelming. One has been liberated; set free -
one finishes Antony & Cleopatra feeling that. It must have been
~~And from~~ written like that one feels; like mind
without fetters.
~~This then would seem~~ Let us then suppose that the
first ~~the~~ must come experience, as varied as can be; & that this
is ~~communicated in without a single~~ but that to
communicate experience needs above ~~all things freedom~~. <must be
done in ~~peace~~ freedom> If
Shakespeare had said ~~"I am this sort of man"~~
~~"I" had interfered with the marriage of his own ideas,~~
~~we they would~~ They [ ] will marry only if we let them
alone. ~~One~~ ~~Interf~~ If Shakespeare had kept popping his
head in, ~~saying~~ surely ~~not a all~~ The thought of these
vast [sentences?] wd. have been checked; the amazing
melting together of words to form a meaning almost
~~beyond~~ our reach would have been hardened: separate
Why "Daffodils that come before the
swallow dares". <wd not have been> To ~~write like, surely~~ one
<writes if he> must have given up thinking of each word by itself
~~So~~ So ~~then one must~~ The right state of mind then is
peace; The marriage night comes at last, when
experience has been won. And then one must pull the
curtains; & blow out the candles. Communication
must be done at dead of night, without a mouse
stirring. The writer must lie back in perfect
quiet & let ~~the~~ ideas marry each other, without -
hurt, or a movement ~~as~~ to impede them.
One may lie back when one is writing & pick the petals
from a rose, or watch the swan sailing past one
down the river.

The Fitzwilliam Manuscript

Conclusion

Conclusion

More than one ~~such that~~ thought that led me to the conclusion that everything ~~depends, if you are a woman~~ — ~~want to write fiction, upon money, a room of your own.~~ ~~promised to offer to you~~ that I said I would lay before you in order that you might see for yourselves how I reached my conclusion that everything depends (if you are a woman) upon ready money & a room of your ~~your own~~ own.

Perhaps you will object that I have made too much of the importance of ~~purely~~ material things — like food & drink, & quiet, & travel, & the ability to be idle. You may say that great poets have done without them. But have they? Let me quote to you the words of ~~Sir~~ the Professor of English Literature at Cambridge —

No one could put my point more plainly. "~~Intellectual freedom~~ — the poor poet has not in these days, nor has had for two hundred years, a dog's chance . . . . . . a poor child in England has little more hope than had the son of an Athenian slave to be emancipated into that intellectual freedom of which great writings are born." Women have always been poor, not for two hundred years merely but from the beginning of time. They have not had a dog's chance of writing poetry. They have had less intellectual freedom than the sons of Athenian slaves.

Conclusion

~~These then are the notes that thoughts that led me to the conclusion that everthing depends, if you are a woman & want to write fiction, upon money & a room of your own.~~ ~~I promised to offer for your~~ that I said I would lay before you in order that you might see for yourselves how I reached my conclusion that everything depends (if you are a woman) upon <having> money <of one's own> & a room of ~~your~~ <your> own.

Perhaps you will object that I have made too much of the importance of ~~purely~~ material things - like food & drink, & quiet, & travel, & the ability to be idle. You may say that great poets have done without them. But have they? Let me quote to you the words of ~~Sir~~ the Professor of English Literature at Cambridge -

No one could put my point more plainly. "~~Intellectual freedom~~ The poor poet has not in these days, nor has had for two hundred years, a dogs chance . . . . ~~&~~ . . . a poor child in England has little more hope than had the son of an Athenian slave to be emancipated into that intellectual freedom of which great writings are born." Women have always been poor, not for two hundred years merely, but from the beginning of time. <Women> They have not had a dog's chance of writing poetry. They have had less intellectual freedom than the sons of Athenian slaves.

However, thanks to the ~~obscure~~ toils of those obscure women
of the nineteenth century of whom I wish we knew more;
thanks, curiously enough, <to two wars> to the Crimean War,
which

which freed the ordinary woman

~~opened lit Florence Nightingale out of the drawing room~~
~~which she loathed almost to~~ & to the European War,
~~There which~~ these evils are on the way to being
bettered. Otherwise you would not be here tonight, &
your chance of earning five hundred <pounds> a year by your own
hands <precarious as I am afraid it is> would be considerably
more precarious ~~than it is~~
even than it is.

But, you may object, why ~~do you~~ attach so much
importance to this writing of books by women, ~~when it~~
~~can only~~ <when it> ~~which~~ requires so much effort, so much
unpleasantness, ~~which will~~ <when it> leading <often> to the
murder of our
Aunts, & ~~the~~ certain very grave altercations with
very certain very good fellows, ~~who want us~~ I admit
that my motives are largely selfish. I like reading;
~~I like reading~~ <&> ~~books of all sorts; books about women as~~
~~well as books about men~~. Hitherto my diet, I consider,
speaking as a member of that large class the
common readers of England, has been a trifle monotonous.
History is too much about wars; biography too much about
great men; poetry has shown I think a tendency to
sterility, & fiction - I have ~~already~~ sufficiently
exposed my grave disabilities as a critic of modern
fiction <& will say no more about it>. All this leads me ~~to~~ quite
selfishly, to
ask you {to murder an Aunt or two;} by hook or
by crook to possess ~~yourselves of~~ yourselves,
even if it comes to murdering an Aunt or two, of

sufficient money to ~~sit down look at the~~ <explore> world ~~for~~ a
room of <your own so that>
~~with your own eyes, & to say~~ for yourselves; and to say
without fear of furour what you think of it.
I am not confining you to fiction. If you would please me
(& there are thousands of people ~~in~~ who are of the same
way of thinking) you would write ~~travels~~ books of travel &
~~history~~ & adventure, of research & scholarship, of
history & biography, ~~of~~ criticism ~~too;~~ ~~But this is~~
& science. ~~When I look at~~ ~~One~~ ~~b~~Books ~~has~~ <have> a way of
influencing ~~another~~ each other. ~~When I find Jane~~
~~Harrison's~~ Fiction & poetry will be much the better for
standing cheek by jowl with <all> the <rest> others. philosophy
<& [critic?]>

But when I come to glance through the notes I have
made I find that my real motive is not purely &
solely selfish - There ~~Does~~ run through these notes,
scattered & fragmentary <discursive> as they are, the conviction
that
a good book is a good thing, that a good writer is a good
person. {If you ask me to justify this belief, I
cannot do it, because it rests upon something so}
so that when I am urging you to do what pleases me,
I am also urging you to do what is good for you, for the
world at large. How to justify this belief I do
not know, because it depends upon ~~the something~~ an
~~so~~ <as> intuitive ~~that~~ & unrecognised conviction,
as simple ~~almost~~ as the desire for bread when one is
hungry; & that is ~~that we live~~ in ~~a world which~~
that we are which is <assures one> that we live in a world
which is wholly real, but very largely muffled up. <for some
reason almost entirely covered up.>
wh. is half covered up. & from wh. the cloak must be torn

Reality ~~<Moreover> is a most curious thing, because it is never the same for t.~~
(Forgive me for my clumsy use of language) is the thing that
leaps out on us ~~in~~ unexpectedly at some corner. It is the
strangest thing, because one can never foretell when it will
come - {why, for example, a paper drifting along a dirty

that strikes <off> a moment for ever

street is suddenly real & all the} & it is always different
for different people. Yet it is the quality that ~~gives~~ <alone has power>
~~importance to~~ to give importance, & lastingness; <leap upon the moment & endow it with immediacy> which is
all the stranger, considering what trifles sometimes seem

but what is strange is that it will make

real, & what mountains mere sawdust. However
this may be, the writer is ~~the expert~~ ~~in touch with reality:~~ <a> the lightning conductor ~~whose gift it is~~ to
attract ~~the lasting, the real out of the great mountain of that mass of~~ a person whose has ~~the astonishing~~
good fortune to live, more than other people, in the heart of

on this manner

~~reality~~. So at least I assume from reading
~~the~~ what are called masterpieces. ~~So~~ ~~It is indeed a perpetual source of amazement, as one to find, how~~

There,

whether it is ~~An~~ Lear or Emma or ~~War &~~ Lycidas or
La Recherche one finds, ~~often in the most unex~~
growing one are the sense of a world miraculously
uncover. Now it is a heath; now ~~only~~ a tea cup in a drawing
room; but they burn, made vivid, lasting; & that
enemy, which is the muffled the unreal, shrinks for
the time to nothing. ~~And I go on~~, to
[~~So~~?] And ~~further I~~ & I assert, - for there is
no proof to be had - that this freeing, Next I

go on to say that as nothing is more ~~depres~~ dismal,
than the feeling, so common, perhaps inevitable, of the
being swaddled, drugged, knocked senseless, &
numbed all over ~~by~~ & finally knocked into
torpor by unreality -- it ~~may be having to~~
~~catch a train, to see a~~ which the world views alas,
unreality as it goes round - there is no escaping it -
& many forces conspire to hold ones head in it -
civilisation in many ways requires it - one must be
civil - one must be tolerant & so on -- So
on the contrary those who ~~have the right to~~ live at
enmity with unreality, whether they fight it with the
pen or the paint brush, or by thumping on the piano,
or by sitting up till three o'clock talking about -
anything under the sun, ~~those~~ are the enviable
people; ~~because they get are constantly in touch with~~
~~those are the people who get most from~~ <meaning> out of life,
~~not~~ to
~~be solemn & die with~~ - & give meaning to other peoples
lives. So that when I ask you to kill your
Aunt & write a book I am only asking you to ~~let~~
~~do a little~~ work ~~in the cause of for your own good for all~~
~~of our Good~~ to ~~uncover~~ <[then?] uncloak> a little of the world that
is dying <suffocating>
under ~~its~~ <a> blanket of unreality.

[Margin: One must be something then one is not]

[Margin: or in any other way, but the pen & the brush seem to me the sharpest weapons]

~~And~~ It is high time, if I may say so, ~~that~~ speaking as
you ~~should do this get to work,~~ who are ~~women not~~
~~over yet come~~ young women should get to work. You may
say <object> pointing to the habitable globe, that for
swarming with black & brown & coffee coloured & white
inhabitants, all busily engaged in traffic & commerce
& love making, <we have had other things to> surely we have
done <something as it is> a good
deal. Without us those seas would be [unsailed?]& those
deserts ~~without~~ uninhabited. There would not be a

[Margin: one of the vast clan of common readers,]

[Margin: you are a little late in sitting down to your desk.]

picture on the walls or a paving stone in the streets.
~~And I accept your~~ Certainly your excuse holds some
truth in it; but may I remind you that in 1880 a <1856 a college was
founded for>
married woman had a right to her own property; that in
~~1900~~ she was . . . that in ~~189~~ 1900 she -
& that in 19~~20~~<19> she was given a vote. ~~Is it not
high time then that you~~ <And> In 1928 the bankrate was
the lowest on record? All this being so, surely it is
~~time that~~ <time> ~~possible~~ that you should enter on another
stage of your immensely long, highly obscure, <terribly
~~undistinguishable~~ laborious> but not
I think, <altogether> discreditable career. ~~There [runs?] is to my
mind~~ ~~Take a room act; kill your kill~~
~~Unless I am gravely mistaken an act of very great
brutality Proceed then to the rescue of that~~
<It will not be the easiest:>
I am not asking you simply to write 'the book of the year'
& have your photograph in the evening paper. I am
~~asking you~~ not asking you to cut a dash & figure in papers as
the well known Mrs Smith whose latest book
entirely eclipses everything she had ever written
No: I ~~literature in my~~ view ~~is no~~ does not
~~consist of a~~ I am asking you to undertake a far
more difficult & ~~yet~~ I think <more> important enterprise
~~Years ago,~~ ~~When I was making the [notes?]~~ & that is to
conspire together ~~to~~, anonymously perhaps, without
very much reward perhaps, to free that great
poetess who was Shakespeare's sister. ~~Do not~~
look for her name in the poets biography by
Sir Sidney Lee. She <[died?]> ~~came~~, poor girl, to a
bad end, & was burried where the omnibuses
stop at the Elephant & Castle. But

in fact, poets have no bodies; <& are not buried;> they are
continuing
presences; they are in ~~us~~ you & they are in me, as
we ourselves ~~may be unknown~~ shall ~~be in the~~ live
<in her> writers who shall come after us. Shakespeare's sister,
~~in spite of the Bishop who~~, ~~is impr in prison~~; she is
locked up in ~~all~~ of us who are here tonight, & in many
others who ~~have still not~~ are ~~work~~ washing up the
dishes & putting <in [drawers?]> babies to bed. ~~But~~ And my
belief is, that if ~~the habit of freedom, of so~~
<[you?]> ~~we~~ had say five hundred a year <say> each, ~~& a~~ rooms to
ourselves, ~~we should begin to free this immensely~~
if ~~we~~ had the habit of freedom, said ~~always~~
precisely what ~~we~~ <you> thought, (~~disagreable as it sounds)~~
if ~~we rummaged the mind, &~~ if ~~we~~ sat down &
looked out of the window & saw human beings not merely
in their relation to each other, but in themselves;
& the sky too & the trees; ~~not merely in relation to~~
~~our~~ & if we looked past Miltons Bogey which is
~~unfortunately~~ a who may be a very charming man, ~~but~~
at reality; if we faced the fact that ~~we~~ <there is> do not
<no arm to> cling to arms; but go alone & cannot be
protected; & thus stand <up solely in> alone against fate
then there ~~would follow, slowly, difficulty~~,
~~the spirit of poetry in us~~ then the spirit of
~~For~~ poetry would be freed; &
Shakespeares sister, drawing her life from
the lives of <the> ~~the~~ unknown forerunners, as her
brother did, would be born. ~~For~~
~~it is plain I think that wherever there has been a~~
~~woman who could write she has been preceded~~

[Margin: if you have time to dream,]

[Margin: need not shut out the whole mind;]

As for her coming without that ~~work~~ cut
~~freedom~~, that effort, that determination to explain &
dream & make the language fit for a woman to
~~write~~ <make> poetry of it, ~~it is~~ <that is> not <im>possible. ~~But~~
~~to be~~
~~condemned to~~ ~~But~~ But I maintain that ~~this~~ the
effort ~~which is needed~~, even if it is a great one,
is worth while.

2nd April
1929

Appendices

Introduction to Appendices

Two undated fragments of manuscript apparently written after Virginia Woolf completed the draft of *Women & Fiction* are transcribed in the first two appendices. Excerpts from a complete typescript of *A Room of One's Own* that Virginia Woolf typed and then corrected and altered are presented in the third appendix. In the fourth, the text of the original article "Women and Fiction" is given. The significance of the appendices for the composition of *A Room of One's Own* is discussed in the introduction to the transcript.

Appendix One This undated two-page variant opening appears in one of the ringed notebooks that Virginia Woolf used for drafts of "Phases of Fiction", and which is now preserved at the University of Sussex (Monks House Papers B.6.d).

Appendix Two This page of notes for the final section of *A Room of One's Own* is to be found on the last page of a reading notebook Virginia Woolf started keeping around 1923 (Monks House Papers B.2.o).

Appendix Three Virginia Woolf's typescript for *A Room of One's Own* was sent to Harcourt Brace in May or June 1929, and returned to the Monks House Papers in 1970. The typescript varies from the first editions in a number of revealing ways, and it contains some overlapping pages which may indicate there was more than one typed draft. The most important differences between the typescript and the first editions - differences that sometimes correspond to the manuscript of *Women & Fiction* and sometimes do not - are given here. Page numbers of the typescript have been given along with a chapter indication in square brackets before each excerpt, but the line and page arrangement of the typescript have not been followed. Cancels and insertions in Virginia Woolf's hand are represented in italics and then marked with angle brackets or lined out as in the transcription of the manuscript. The mainly illegible typed cancels have been omitted, as have minor mistypings and Woolf's typographical corrections of her typing.

Appendix Four The text of the article Virginia Woolf wrote between her Cambridge papers and *Women & Fiction* is taken from the American *Forum*, March 1929. Leonard Woolf included it in *Granite and Rainbow* in 1958.

[Appendix 1: Variant Opening, Monk's House Papers]

A Room of ones Own

But, you may say, we asked you to speak about
women & fiction: What has that got to do with
a room of one's own? I will explain: When you asked
me to speak about women & fiction ~~it seemed simple
enough. A few . . . .~~
~~But that in thinking it over, the subject but at <on> second
sight the words seem not so simple:~~
I sat down on the banks of a river & began to think

which seemed the most interesting

what the words meant. They might mean simply . .
And when I began to consider them in ~~this~~ <that> last way - I
~~saw at once that I should if I considered women &
fiction in that way I should never come to any
Conclusion except a~~
saw that I should never come to any conclusion.

And that is ~~not what you asked me.~~ Only an opinion, ~~& not by any means~~ as a practical matter: it is not the whole truth about

I should only ~~come~~ express an opinion - that one <she> must
have money & a room of ones own: ~~And~~ <that she must have
500 a year & a room with a lock on the door.>
But why did I come to hold that opinion? ~~That is~~
That is what I propose to tell you; & since
I am only giving you an opinion, & not a conclusion,
I am going to let you see for yourselves how I came by it.
I am going to develop in your presence as fully &
freely as I can the train of thought which led me to
think this. ~~The only way when a subject is as
controversial & as complicated as this one appears is not~~

~~is to write fiction~~.

For it is useless to pretend that one can tell the truth about a
subject that is as complicated & controversial as this <one> is.
~~One can only write~~ ~~Here~~ ~~I think Fiction is likely to~~
~~be more truer than truth: if you see how I came to~~
~~Often it is only to~~ One can only show what went on in
one's own mind; one can only give one's audience the
chance of drawing their own conclusions, as they
~~notice the~~ observe the limitations, the idiosyncracies,
of the speaker.
Therefore I propose, making use of all the liberties &
licenses of a novelist to tell you the story of the three days

As you will see at
once, that is only an
opinion, an irrelevant

& given you very much less
than you asked. But
In order to make what reparation I can I
am going to lay bare the train of
thought that ~~But my excuse is that~~
~~on a~~ ~~the subject is too complic.~~

But in order to
make what
reparation I can
I have
evaded the truth.
Instead I am
going to give you
fiction. I am going to
develop

[Appendix 2: Notes for Conclusion, Monk's House Papers]

<u>Conclusion</u>

These are my notes.
Add. destroy. Conclusion - money & a room of <your own.>
But I will my only qualify
You may accuse me of laying too much stress on
Money.
The reason is that bars are necessary.
Firstly
I hope not anger: often laughter: but always
astonishment That this is an instinct
wh. is wrapped up with all kind of things.
But when
~~Fiction does~~ You can only have [intellectual?] freedom
if you have money. &
And you can only write if you have unbroken freedom
What is the importance of writing?
Reality. The rest of life is humbug.
You have achieved at N. & G. part of this
already. More than is had by [women?] in
[Cbr?].
But more is needed. Aunts must be killed.
If you look literature can only be kept going
by many people.

[Appendix 3: Typescript, Monks House Papers]

A ROOM OF ONES OWN

[Ch. 1, p. 1:]

But, you may say, we asked you to speak about women and fiction - what has that got to do with a room of one's own? I will try to explain. When you asked me to speak about women and fiction I was not sure what the words meant. I sat down upon the banks of a river and pondered them.

. . . . .

[Ch. 1, pp. 2-3:]

All I could do was to offer an opinion upon one minor point - to say that a woman must have money and a room of her own if she is to write fiction; and that as you will see leaves the great problem of the true nature of woman and the true nature of fiction unsolved. I have shirked the duty of coming to a conclusion upon these two questions - women and fiction remain so far as I am concerned unsolved, unknown. But in order to make some amends I am going to do what I can to show you how I arrived at my opinion upon the other point, that a woman must have money and a room if she is to write at all. I am going to develop in your presence as fully and freely as I can, with all its irrelevancies and ~~accidents, the~~ <*redundancies the*> train of thought that led me to think this. Perhaps if I lay bare the ideas that lie behind it you will find that some bear upon women and some bear upon fiction. At any rate when a subject is highly controversial - and any question about sex is that - one cannot hope to tell the truth. One can only show how one came to hold ~~whatever~~ <*ones*> opinions. ~~one does hold.~~ One can only give one's audience the chance of drawing their own conclusions as they observe the limitations, the prejudices, the idiosyncrasies of the speaker. ~~Here~~ Fiction <*here*> is likely to be truer than fact.

Therefore I propose, making use of all the liberties and licenses of a novelist to tell you the story of the three days that preceded my coming here - how, bowed down by the weight of the subject which you have laid upon my shoulders, I pondered it, and made it work in and out of my daily life. I need not say that what I am about to describe has no existence; Oxbridge is an invention; as ~~so are St. Miriams and~~ <*is*> Fernham; "I" is only a convenient term for somebody who has no real being.

. . . . .

[Ch. 1, p. 4:]

I will not trouble you with that thought now, though if you look carefully you may find it for yourselves in the course of what I am going to say. ~~It is merely this Money and a room to yourself, if you want to write. The future of women and fiction depends on it; money and rooms to themselves~~.

. . . . .

[Ch. 2, p. 44:]

~~It may be too,~~ <*Perhaps*> I thought, as I opened my purse, the looking glass theory <*also serves to*> explain~~s~~ what otherwise <seems> irrational and against human interest - the strong wish on the part of one sex that the other shall not bring trophies to the common store surpassing those which he brings himself. Were a tribe of women discovered in Central Asia, say, one of whom had written plays better than Lear, another made a discovery of greater importance than Einstein<*s*>, the news would be received in London at first with incredulity; later, if it were confirmed, such a rage, such a jealousy would seize upon the rivals, that they would steal off at dead of night and make away with these divine works, or write over the Anne or Jane on the title page an emphatic George or John.

. . . . .

[Chs. 4-5, pp. 92-101:]

All the great novelists like Thackeray and Dickens and Balzac have written a natural prose, swift but not slovenly, expressive but not precious. They based it on the sentence that <*was*> current at the time. The sentence that <*that was*> current at the beginning of the nineteenth century ran something like this, I thought,

"The grandeur of their works was an argument with them, not to stop short, but to proceed. They could have no higher excitement or satisfaction than in the exercise of their art & endless generation of truth & beauty. Success prompts to exertion; & habit facilitates success."

That is a man's sentence; behind it one can see Addison, Gibbon and the rest. It was <*a sentence that was*> unsuitable for a woman's use. Charlotte Brontë with all her splendid gift for prose stumbled and fell with that clumsy weapon in her hands. George Eliot committed atrocities with it that beggar description. Jane Austen looked at it and laughed at it and devised a perfectly natural shapely sentence proper for her own use and never departed from it.

"She examined into their employments, looked at their work, & advised them to do it differently; found fault with the arrangement of the furniture, or detected the housemaid in negligence; & if she accepted any refreshment, seemed to do it only for the sake of finding out that Mrs. Collins's joints of meat were too large for her family.

Thus with less genius for writing than Charlotte Brontë she got infinitely more said. Indeed such a lack of tradition such a scarcity of tools must have told enormously upon the writing of women, I thought. Moreover, a book is not made of sentences laid end to end but of sentences built, as I have already said, into arcades or domes. And this shape too is also largely traditional, <*&*> handed down to men by the men who made them. *The form is no more suited to a woman than the sentence.* ~~Thus~~ <*But*> all the old forms, like the epic and the poetic play were ~~already~~ hardened and set ~~into forms which could not have suited her~~ by the time she became a writer. The novel alone was young enough to be soft in her hands -<*another reason perhaps why she wrote novels.*> Yet who shall say that even now 'the novel' (I give it inverted comma to mark my sense of the word's inadequacy) who shall say that even this commonest of all forms is rightly shaped for her use? No doubt we shall find her knocking that into shape for herself when she has the free use of her limbs; and also providing some new vehicle - not necessarily in verse - for the poetry in her. <*For it is the poetry in her that is denied outlet.*> ~~How would~~ <*And I went on to ponder how would*> a woman write a poetic tragedy in five acts? Not in verse, I think.

But these are difficult questions ~~lying~~ <*which lie*> in the twilight of the future. I must leave them if only because they stimulate me to wander from my subject into trackless forests where I shall be lost and, very likely, devoured by wild beasts. And I do not want, and I am sure that you do not want me, to broach that very dismal subject, the future of fiction so that I will only pause here one moment to draw your attention to the great part which must be played in that future so far as women are concerned by physical conditions. The book has somehow to be adapted to the body, and at a venture I would say that women's books should be shorter, more concentrated, than those of men, and framed so that they do not need long hours of steady and ~~continuous~~ <*uninterrupted*> work < *- for interruptions there will always be. Nor are they always harmful, for most people of course, write too much. Moreover*> ~~For~~ the nerves that feed the brain would seem to differ in men and women, so that if you are going to make them work their best and hardest you must find out what treatment suits them - whether these hours of lectures for instance which the Monks devised, presumably, hundreds of years ago suit them - what alternations of work and rest they need, interpreting rest not as doing nothing but as doing something, but <*what that*> something ~~different~~ <*is*> and what that difference ~~is~~ <*should be. All this should be discovered.*> *And* Here quite inevitably the advice must come from one's own sex; the experiments must be made by them and on them. And yet I continued approaching the book case again, where shall I find that elaborate study of the psychology of women by a woman? If they are not going to be allowed to practise medicine ----

Happily my thoughts were here given another turn.

----- 5. ------

I had come at last in the course of this rambling, to the shelves which hold books by the living; by women and by men; for there are almost as many books written by women now as by men. Or if that is not yet quite true, it is certainly true that women no longer write novels solely. There, I thought, is Jane Harrison's book on Greek archaeology; there is Gertrude Bell's book on Persia. There are books on all sorts of subjects which a generation ago no woman could have touched. There are poems and plays and criticism; there are histories and biographies, travels and books of scholarship and research; there are even a few philosophies and books about science and economics. But what had happened, I asked, thus to increase the range of women's writing? What led them somewhere about the middle of the last century to forsake their station in the drawing room beside the tea pot, to come down off the roof and actually go on foot alone ~~to the towns, the~~ <*those*> regions of busy life which Charlotte Brontë dreamt of with such passion but was never to see? <*What was that great revolution?*> All definite statements about such complex events have an element of falsehood; one has come to dislike the superficial flash of the picturesque phrase. Still, if I were a historian, I should here begin my next paragraph with a splash. "The guns roared in the Crimea. Earth works and bastions were destroyed; the limbs of living men were torn asunder. Into the valley of death rode the six hundred. Meanwhile, a single shell crossed the seas; passed the power and pageantry of Westminster; penetrated into peaceful villages where for generations the caw of rooks had mingled with the sound of church bells; swept unseen over meek heads bent in prayer and praise; sought out a peaceful manor house among old trees; and crashed through the drawing room door. The mahogany panels were shivered for ever. The key was but a mass of molten and disfigured metal. Out stepped a single figure - a ~~frail and~~ solitary woman. In one hand she bore a roll of lint; in the other a lamp. Her name was Florence Nightingale. The reign of women's servitude was over. Doors were flung wide. Out poured etc. etc. "

There would be some truth in that gaudy picture perhaps, though that last sentence, I am afraid, still ~~has~~ <*~~had~~ waits*> to be <*~~re~~*> written. Doors there still are <*& doors that are locked*>. But perhaps it would be more to the point if I discovered with Florence Nightingale's help what was going on in that drawing room before the shell from the Crimean battlefield crashed into it. Just before that event, in the year 1852, Florence Nightingale as it happened sat down one day and wrote an account of her feelings as a woman in a drawing room which she calls Cassandra. <*One must remember that*> in many ways she was better off~~, one must remember,~~ than ninety-nine women out of a hundred. Her father was an enlightened man, little affected by that "whimsical despotism" of his time; and they were rich; and she was better educated than most women. Yet wrote Florence Nightingale - but it is hardly writing, it is more like screaming - "Look at the poor lives we lead . . . <*It is a wonder that we are so good as we are, not that we so bad"*> Life for a woman meant "ordering the dinner, hunting for a governess for your children, and sending pheasants and apples to your poorer relations". Nor were these occupations dignified enough to secure privacy or consideration. "Women are never supposed to have any occupation of sufficient importance not to be interrupted." Yet, if she despised such occupation, or tried to work at anything more congenial, "feelings", - and "feelings" are often much more binding than facts, were hurt. "Women never have an half hour in all their lives (excepting before or after anybody is up in the house) that they can call their own, without fear of offending or of hurting some one". <*Indeed, "A married woman was heard to wish that she could break a limb ~~in~~ that she might have a little time to herself"*> (And here, I thought, that gallant old woman Harriet Martineau who lived at about the same time, corroborates Miss Nightingale. She used always to do her work before breakfast, she said. And she welcomed her family's loss of fortune, because it brought her freedom to use her wits, almost as Florence Nightingale must have welcomed the Crimean War for the same reason, a proof that men and women may take different views of the same subject.) <*But to return to Florence Nightingale in the drawing room.*> This way of life, Florence Nightingale goes on, was fraught with the utmost danger. Listless day dreaming became inevitable. The hours were spent thinking - not passionately as Charlotte Brontë thought, but despondently and foolishly, of things that could never be. "The system doomed some minds to incurable infancy, others to silent misery." And she goes on - but I advise you to read the document yourselves if you want to know to what a pitch of hysteria, to what a shriek of nervous agony those conditions could bring a woman of fine nature, of high intellectual powers. Had the shell not crashed through the door, Miss Nightingale, I think, would have gone mad, as I think so many women must have gone ~~crazy, silly,~~ <*mad,*> distracted, before her time, without even a pen to express their agony on paper. It was partly the thought of the frittered energies, of the great gifts ruined and run to seed, that haunted her and maddened her. What a choice that was - that she had seen and had almost had to make - <*between*> incurable infancy, or silent misery!

But Florence Nightingale felt with exceptional violence; ~~she had unusual gifts,~~ and her exceptional career would have been of little benefit to the average perhaps, had it not been for the labours of more ordinary women, like Emily Davies, and Miss Clough, and Barbara Leigh Smith. Miss Smith's father <*it appears*> was an eccentric man and had the extraordinary idea of allowing his daughter three hundred pounds a year. A man, I thought, ought to have known better. That was the start of the mischief, I ~~thought~~, <*reflected*> looking at a life of Miss Davies which tells the story. That was how the business began for then Miss Leigh Smith with her three hundred pounds ~~could do as she liked,~~ could start a society of some sort for the discussion of all these iniquities; marriage laws, property laws; the ~~lack~~ <*need*> of a vote; the ~~lack~~ <*need*> of education and all the other needs and iniquities which make it hard to read of women in the nineteenth century without rushing to the window to get a breath of fresh air. And so these two young women, I thought, making up the story as I glanced from book to book, became friends and conspirators, <*&*> went on one day in the fifties after the Crimean war in <*to*> a house like many of its kind with a flight of steps, a basement, and a couple of ferns in the window. They went into the drawing room and there they found six young women aged between fifteen and twenty five moping round a table. One was knitting a stocking; one was cutting out underclothes; one was dreaming listlessly with her feet on the fender; one was embroidering a bag; one was playing Mendelssohn on the piano; one with her fingers screwed in her ears was writing a novel. All were cross and ~~dependent~~ <*despondent*> and had their nerves on edge. In came Miss Davies. In came Miss Smith. But how, said Miss Davies, can you work like that? Where's your sitting room? How can you paint like that when you aren't allowed to study the nude, said Miss Smith (I) How can you compose music when you have only one piano between the four of you and no teaching in the art of composition? How - At that moment (as I told myself the story) the door opened for the tenth time that morning, and in came an elderly lady, asking for arnica - Tommy had fallen and cut himself.

Also the Bishop was coming to lunch. Were the flowers arranged - what about another course after the beef? The Bishop was coming to lunch ---- In short Miss Davies devoted her life to the building of Girton. Miss Davies ran the college heavily into debt; Miss Davies protested that the students must have sitting rooms even if they went without arm chairs. Hence, I said, turning to the shelves these books

----

(I) The Slade was opened to women in 1872 on condition that they did not study from the nude.

. . . . .

[Chapter 6, p. 125:]

Perhaps a mind that is purely masculine cannot create, any more than a mind that is purely feminine, I thought. But it would be well to test what one means by an androgynous, conversely by a gunandros mind by looking at a book or two.

. . . . .

[Ch.6, pp. 127-141:]

It took place on the beach under the hard, hot sun. It was done very openly. It was done very vigorously. Nothing could have been more indecent. But.....I had said "but" too often. One cannot go on saying "but". One must finish the sentence somehow *<I rebuked myself.>* Shall I finish it, "But I am bored!" But why was I bored? Partly because of the dominance of the letter "I" and the aridity, which, like the giant beech tree, it casts within its shade. Nothing will grow there. That however, I said, is all Lady Bessborough's fault. Lady Bessborough with her passion for politics, always pretended that the Napoleonic wars were not half so important as Lord Granville's maiden speech. Naturally he believed her, and when he comes to write (for Mr. A. is the spiritual descendant of Lord Granville, just as Mary Carmichael descends from lady Winchelsea) his pen forms the letter "I" by instinct. And then, I continued, he descends too from Oscar Browning, who found the stupidest man more intelligent than the cleverest woman; so that when he comes to write about women he does not say anything very interesting about them; but simplifies them and cannot put a bone in their bodies. They are jelly fish adapted to his lust. And then I continued, remembering the lunch party at Oxbridge, and the cigarette ash and the manx cat and Tennyson and Christina Rossetti all in a bunch, as he no longer hums under his breath, "There has fallen a splendid tear from the passion flower at the gate", when Phoebe crosses the beach, ~~"She is coming my dove, my dear, she is coming~~

~~my life, my fate,"~~ <*& she no longer replies "My heart is like a singing bird, whose nest is in a water'd shoot"*> what can he do? Being honest as the day and logical as the sun, there is only one thing he can do. And that he does, to do him justice, over and over (I said turning the pages) and over again. And that I added, aware of the awful nature of the confession, ~~and that~~ <~~*which*~~ *while*> it proved me cold as ice and old as the hills, seems somehow dull. Shakespeare's indecency uproots a thousand other things in one's mind, and is far from being dull. But Shakespeare does it for pleasure, and Mr. A., as the nurses say, does it on purpose. But it is not Mr. A's. fault, I said, skipping through the rest of the book; it is the fault of Miss Clough and Miss Emily Davies. When Miss Clough and Miss Emily Davies said that girls had brains and must be allowed to use them, Mr. A's. grandfather, the anonymous gentleman who wrote for the Saturday Review, said on the contrary, they have but two desires, to serve men and to minister to their needs; and Mr. A. (who descends of course from his grandfather) says in much the same manner "And they can't do this!" And it is in protest against Miss Clough and Miss Davies that he does it, again and again, and attaches what would otherwise seem to be a disproportionate importance to the physical act which Shakespeare who had not know Miss Clough and Miss Davies lumps up together with a thousand other states of mind and makes poetry or comedy of.

What, then, I begin to fear I thought, <*shutting Mr. A. &*> glancing at a critic, and then at a biographer and then at a poet, all well known, and young and brilliant, is that virility has now become self conscious - that is to say that men are <now> writing only with the ~~masculine~~ <*male*> side of their brain. It is a mistake for a woman to read them, for she will inevitably look for something that she will not find. I do my best to read them, I added, looking at the brilliant poets and critics and biographers sorrowfully and wondering what was wrong with them, or perhaps with me. It is the power of suggestion that I most miss, I thought, taking Mr. B. the critic in my hand and reading, very carefully and very dutifully, his remarks upon the art of poetry. Very able they were, acute and full of learning; but the trouble is, I thought, that his feelings no longer communicate; his mind is separated into different chambers; not a sound carries from one to the other. Thus when I take a sentence of Mr. B. in to my mind it falls plump to the ground - dead; but when I take a sentence of Coleridge into my mind, it explodes and gives birth to all kinds of other ideas, ~~which~~ <*& that*> is the only sort of writing ~~that has~~ <*of which one can say that it has the secret of*> perpetual life. ~~in it.~~

But of course, I continued, putting the admirable Mr. B. back on the shelf, this is a purely subjective test and may well prove only my limitations as a reader, not his as a critic. It is also my fault, I cannot doubt, that when I read those eloquent passages by Mr. C. which seem to blossom in purple and red, I feel as if the gilt arm chair were spouting to the mahogany side board in the dusk. And when I see his metaphors approaching slowly over the horizon they look like the stuffed ravens in the Götterdämmerung, and one is anxious lest they should topple over <*in mid-career*> and fly out again up side down among the laughter of the audience. Everything seems <*to be*> at least ten sizes too big for a living person, I thought, the sentence surely is getting bigger and bigger; rhetoric is getting nobler and nobler; one can almost see the poor little ideas going off to the powder closet to be rigged up in~~to~~ brocade and have rouge dabbed on their cheeks. And then the weary gesture of the burdened soul, I thought, coming to the preachers and the prophets, which sounds like the sighing of the grampus in the midland sea - surely they used to lead us to church less vociferatingly. But it is all the fault of women, I concluded, who held up magnifying glass instead of ordinary glass when men looked at them for so many years; and thus indirectly led to the foundation of the Indian Empire, ~~and~~ <*the establishment of*> the British ~~Dominions~~ <*Colonies*> ~~beyond the seas~~ and the eloquence of Mr. C.

<*~~That~~*> All these books are written by men and for men I reminded myself, sorrowfully replacing them, and I am as much out of place when I read them as I should be at that city banquet to which I listened in the other night. ~~And~~ <*For*> when I heard them clinking their knives and forks and praising the prowess of their fathers and the Prince of Wales told them exactly how many million sprats had been caught in the North Sea - it was an astonishing number, certainly - I could hardly keep myself from shouting into the loud speaker, Let us now praise unknown women, and demanding that Princess Mary should celebrate <*the labours of the*> charwomen and tell us how many steps ~~they~~ had <*been*> cleaned <*by them*> every year; ~~but it~~ <*which*> would have been useless. I am just as much out of my place here as there, I murmured. But by this time I had reached the complete works of Mr. Kipling and Mr. Galsworthy, where I paused not merely because one could not run a finger quickly over that vast bulk, but because it is often said that these two are unsurpassed by any other writers of our time. Critics often say, I thought that the Forsyte Saga is one undoubted masterpiece of the twentieth century. In view of the enormous celebrity of these two writers and their prodigious circulations one might well pause and ask the reason why one disagreed, if one did disagree, why one was puzzled, if one was puzzled, for such bewilderment and disagreement must point <*when the sales of a book run into six or seven figures*> to some defect in taste and critical ~~insight~~. <*judgment.*> Whatever the reason, I cannot deny, I thought,

that Mr. Kipling's books puzzle me. Here is a man of undoubted genius. Nothing can surpass his vividness, his power of bringing the fact before the eyes. But - were "buts" beginning again? What did I mean by "but" this time? I demanded, hastily glancing through Plain Tales and Many Inventions and Soldiers Three. But - it was the emotion perhaps that made me so uncomfortable. Officers turned their backs and looked the other way. The Man was alone with his work. The Sower sowed the seed. The Flag - one blushed as if one had been caught eavesdropping at some purely masculine orgy. And I noticed as proof of my own incapacity to understand that when I had read a story or two ~~- and I could not stop once I had begun~~ - it was as if the surface of the mind had been vigorously scrubbed and pelted with hard dry pellets but not a word, not a scene got beneath the skin.

Mr. Galsworthy of course has nothing of Mr Kipling's genius. But he is undoubtedly a man of commanding ability, and his books are often said to sum up a whole side of English life. There are generations of them - Jolyons and Junes and Bosinneys - they are symbolical, typical, significant of the well to do British families that one has met riding up the Alps or staying in good hotels. But - another "but". This time there could be no doubt to what it referred. But it is all as thin, as papery, as glossy as the pictures that are given away with the Christmas numbers of the illustrated papers. If one gave those fields a poke with the point of an umbrella they would crumble in. One could tear the whole of that family party across as one tears the photograph of a country house party sitting on the steps of a ducal mansion in the Tatler. But the Forsytes are undoubtedly the best got up family in the whole of British fiction, I thought, going back almost with physical pleasure over the memory of their good dinners and good cigars and padded arm chairs and the crisp terse speech and their highly polished boots and their well bred dogs and their clean pocket handkerchiefs and their sheets nicely scented with lavender. But - it was precisely the same "but" that had interposed itself between me and Mr. Kipling. It was the emotion that was uncomfortable. It is coming; it is brewing; it is about to burst upon my head, I began saying long before the end. That picture, I am sure, will fall upon the old man's head; he will die of the shock; and the old clerk will speak over him two or three obituary words; and all the swans on the Thames will simultaneously burst out singing. But I shall rush away before that happens, I said to myself, and hide among the gooseberry bushes, for to be witness of that *<tense, that symbolical, that>* masculine emotion would be intolerable. To avoid that catastrophe I shut the book.

I was saying "but" then to the emotional values. The sentiment of these famous writers seemed to me sentimentality; their reality to me was unreal.

When they made that gesture which summons and makes significant, nothing happened. Nothing could happen, because there was nothing to come together; the values were all on the surface. To me therefore, nothing memorable, nothing substantial remained over when I had read these books. But obviously this is my eccentricity and not theirs. Obviously they are right, for hundreds and thousands of people buy their books and laugh and cry at their bidding. It may be, I conjectured, that they are bought by men and read by men; that their appeal is almost entirely <to> their own sex. It is not only that they are celebrating male virtues, and describing the ~~man's~~ world *<of men>*; it is that there is not a touch of the woman in either of them. Therefore they are entirely lacking in suggestive power to a woman and it is no more possible for me to write an intelligent criticism of their books than to write intelligently of the Boat race, when I do not know bow from stern or cox from stroke. All I know is that the scene in my mind is so brightly but crudely painted that when I have skimmed it once I can ever look at it again. The sketch is undeveloped.

All this is very unfortunate for me, I concluded, because it makes me unable to appreciate the finest work of our greatest living writers. And the trouble is likely to increase, I thought, putting Forsyte Saga back on the book case, for self conscious virility is probably in the ascendant. One has only to travel in Italy at least to see that it is perfectly possible for one sex to suppress the other completely. And I remembered the network of regulations in Italy, the dining cars and the railways carriages, and how one must not put one's foot here and one must not take off one's coat there. On every little grocer's shop there was stamped the head of a swarthy man whom one was invited to wish to live for ever. And wherever there was a blank wall large enough to display a poster, vast black letters celebrated the flight of some aviator, or the triumph of some General. Flags and banners urged all the little boys to march under them and wherever there was a court yard large enough to receive them grown men in black shirts wheeled and turned in response to the shouts of officers. It was all very military and masculine and dry (I mean to a woman), I thought, remembering Rome, but the military side of it is beyond my purview; what effect has all this drumming and trampling upon poetry, I wondered? Well, apparently, there is a certain anxiety about fiction in Italy. For according to a newspaper that lay upon the table there has been a meeting of Academicians, whose object is to "develop the Italian novel". Men famous by birth, or a finance, industry or the Fascist corporations" came together and discussed the matter, and "a telegram was sent to the Duce expressing the hope that the Fascist era would soon give birth to a poet worthy of it". We may all hope that, I said, but I doubt that I shall like poetry that comes out of an incubator. Poetry ought to have a mother as well as a father. The Fascist poem will be a horrid little abortion such as one sees in a glass jar in the museum of some county town. ~~They do not~~ <*Such monsters never*> live long, it is said; one has never seen a prodigy of that sort cropping grass in a field.

However the fault for all this rests with us I thought, thinking back through my mothers again, for had we stayed shut up in our sitting rooms embroidering bags or now and again taking a walk on the leads and looking at the view, the other sex would not have had to assert its virility. The blame for all this cock-a-doodling is to be laid to the charge of a certain very small demure wom~~a~~<*e*>n, who issued sometime about 1850 from an obscure parsonages and middle class homes in the North of England; Miss Clough Miss Leigh Smith, Miss Emily Davies. It is entirely their fault that English literature is infected with cock-a-doodledum; and it is they who drive me, when I want to stretch all my faculties on a book, to seek it in that happy age, before Miss Davies and Miss Clough were born, when the writer used both sides of his mind equally. One must turn back to Shakespeare then; for Shakespeare was androgynous; and so was Keats and Sterne, and Cowper, and Lamb and Coleridge. Milton and Ben Jonson had a dash too much of the male in them. So had Wordsworth and Tolstoi. In our time Proust was wholly androgynous, if not perhaps a little too much of a woman. But that failing is too rare for me to complain, since without that quality books are airless and sterile. However, I consoled myself with the reflection that this perhaps a passing phase; ~~and~~ that much of what I have said in obedience to my promise to give you the course of my thoughts will seem out of date; ~~and~~ <*that much of what flames in my eyes will be*> unrecognisable to young women who have not yet come of age.

Even so, the very first sentence that I would write here, I said crossing over to the writing table, and taking up the page headed Women and Fiction is that it is fatal for anyone who writes to think of their sex. <It is fatal to accentuate by any pride or humility the disposition which the mind has received from its sex.> It is fatal to remember that one is a woman. It is fatal to be a woman pure and simple; one must be woman-manly. It is fatal to lay the least stress on any grievance; to plead even with justice any cause; in any way to speak consciously as a woman. And fatal is no figure of speech; for anything written with that conscious bias is doomed to death. It ceases to be fertilised. Brilliant and effective, powerful and masterly, as it may appear for a day or two it must wither at nightfall; it cannot grow in the minds of others. Some collaboration has to take place in the mind between the woman and the man before the art of creation can be accomplished.

What this collaboration is, how it takes place or has in the past taken place, no critic or psychologist can tell us. One might hazard a guess from reading Antony and Cleopatra that the prelude to creation is an experience of such width and variety that one must take the sea and sky for likeness if one seeks one. And the experience was agitated, broken, tempestuous; the mind was taken and thrown against the rocks and shattered in a thousand fragments. But there must have been some reconciliation; some marriage of opposites <*must have taken place*> to produce that sense of freedom that remains with one when one has read the play. One would not have had that feeling if Shakespeare had been interfering and checking and forcing his mind back. Any such consciousness would have chilled the flow of the words that are all melted together and made them harden and fall off separately one by one. "Daffodils that come before the swallow dares" must have been written at a stroke; whole scenes have that molten uniformity. It is presumptuous, it may be, even to make an image of what went on in that particular brain. But whatever was Shakespeare's state of mind, one might perhaps arrive at the general statement that the whole of the mind must lie wide open if it is to work freely, if this marriage is to take place between opposites, if we are to get the sense that the writer is communicating his experience with perfect fullness. There must be freedom and there must be peace. Not a wheel must grate, not a light glimmer. The curtains must be close drawn. The writer, I thought, once his experience is over must lie back and let his mind celebrate its nuptials in darkness. He must not look or question what is being done. Rather he must pluck the petals from a rose or watch the swans float calmly down the river. And I saw again the current which took the boat and the undergraduate and the dead leaves; and the taxi took the man and the woman, I thought, seeing them come together across the street, and the current swept them away, I thought, hearing far off the roar of London's traffic~~.~~ *into that tremendous stream.*

~~These are some of the thought, some of the experiences, both true and fictitious, that I said I would lay before you in order that you might see for yourselves how I reached that prosaic conclusion that everything depends, if you are a woman, upon having five hundred pounds a year of your own and a room with a lock on the door. Perhaps you may object that I have made too much of the importance of material things. Even allowing a generous margin for symbolism allowing that money stands for the power to contemplate, and that a lock on the door means the power to think for~~

~~oneself, still you may say that the mind should rise above such things; and that poets have often been poor men. Let me then quote to you the words of your own Cambridge Professor of Literature, who should know better than most of us what goes to the making of a poet. Sir Arthur Quiller Couch then writes:—~~

Here then I have reached the conclusion - the prosaic conclusion - with which I set out, that it is necessary to have five hundred a year and a room with a lock on the door. I have tried to lay bare the thoughts and impressions <by which I have come to it. *I have asked you to follow me*> whether they sent me <*flying*> into the arms of a Beadle, or to <*take*> book<*s*> ~~shelves~~ <*from their shelves,*> or to look out of the window. While I have been talking I hope that you have been contradicting - making whatever additions and inferences <seemed good to you.> Many things are visible to you that are not visible to me and much that I think plain will seem to you questionable. That is all as it should be, ~~where~~ <*since*> truth is only to be ~~got at~~ <*had*> by comparing a great many different opinions. I will only now anticipate two criticisms which are so obvious that you can hardly fail to make them.

I have not expressed any opinion, you may say, upon the comparative merits of the sexes even as writers. That was done purposely not from cowardice or evasiveness but because I do not believe that gifts whether of mind or character can be weighed like sugar and butter, not even in Cambridge where they so adept at putting people into classes and fixing <*caps*> ~~labels and rosettes upo~~n their foreheads. I do not believe that even the Table of Precedency which you will find in Whitakers Almanac represents a final order of values, or that there is any sound reason to suppose that a Commander of the Bath will ultimately walk into dinner behind a Master in Lunacy. All this pitting of sex against sex, of quality against quality, all this claiming of superiority and inferiority, ~~seems to me to~~ belong to the private school stage of human existence when there are "sides", and it is necessary for one side to beat another <*side*>, and of the utmost importance ~~for~~ <*to*> walk up to a platform and receive from the hands of the headmaster himself a highly ornamental pot. As people mature they cease to believe in "sides" or headmasters, or ornamental pots. At any rate where books are concerned it is notoriously difficult to fix these labels of merit in such a way that they do not come off. Even if I could fix them, and could say to you with all the infallibility of that Bishop who is dead now that women are debarred by the inscrutable decrees of Providence from ever writing a book of the highest merit, that would seem to me an ~~irrelevant and~~ uninteresting statement, because even ~~if it true and~~ Providence with his long white beard has so arranged it, ~~that does not alter~~ the fact that any piece of writing done with integrity, any thing seen with fidelity has an absolute importance which is immeasurable. Indeed, this measuring ~~seems to me the~~ <*is the*> most futile of all occupations, and to submit to the decrees of the measurers the most servile of attitudes. As long as you write what you wish to write, whether you are man or woman, that is all that matters; and whether it matters for ages or only for hours ~~seems to me a matt~~ it is impossible to say.

. . . . .

Appendix 4: 'Women and Fiction', *The Forum*, March 1929

The title of this article can be read in two ways: it may allude to women and the fiction that they write, or to women and the fiction that is written about them. The ambiguity is intentional, for, in dealing with women as writers, as much elasticity as possible is desirable; it is necessary to leave oneself room to deal with other things besides their work, so much has that work been influenced by conditions that have nothing whatever to do with art.

The most superficial inquiry into women's writing instantly raises a host of questions. Why, we ask at once, was there no continuous writing done by women before the eighteenth century? Why did they then write almost as habitually as men, and in the course of that writing produce, one after another, some of the classics of English fiction? And why did their art then, and why to some extent does their art still, take the form of fiction?

A little thought will show us that we are asking questions to which we shall get, as answer, only further fiction. The answer lies at present locked in old diaries, stuffed away in old drawers, half-obliterated in the memories of the aged. It is to be found in the lives of the obscure - in those almost unlit corridors of history where the figures of generations of women are so dimly, so fitfully perceived. For very little is known about women. The history of England is the history of the male line, not of the female. Of our fathers we know always some fact, some distinction. They were soldiers or they were sailors; they filled that office or they made that law. But of our mothers, our grandmothers, our great-grandmothers, what remains? Nothing but a tradition. One was beautiful; one was red-haired; one was kissed by a Queen. We know nothing of them except their names and the dates of their marriages and the number of children they bore.

Thus, if we wish to know why at any particular time women did this or that, why they wrote nothing, why on the other hand they wrote masterpieces, it is extremely difficult to tell. Anyone who should seek among those old papers, who should turn history wrong side out and so construct a faithful picture of the daily life of the ordinary woman in Shakespeare's time, in Milton's time, in Johnson's time, would not only write a book of astonishing interest, but would furnish the critic with a weapon which he now lacks. The extraordinary woman depends on the ordinary woman. It is only when we know what were the conditions of the average woman's life - the number of her children, whether she had money of her own, if she had a room to herself, whether she had help in bringing up her family, if she had servants, whether part of the housework was her task - it is only when we can measure the way of life and the experience of life made possible to the ordinary woman that we can account for the success or failure of the extraordinary woman as a writer.

Strange spaces of silence seem to separate one period of activity from another. There was Sappho and a little group of women all writing poetry on a Greek island six hundred years before the birth of Christ. They fall silent. Then about the year 1000 we find a certain court lady, the Lady Murasaki, writing a very long and beautiful novel in Japan. But in England in the sixteenth century, when the dramatists and poets were most active, the women were dumb. Elizabethan literature is exclusively masculine. Then, at the end of the eighteenth century and in the beginning of the nineteenth, we find women again writing - this time in England - with extraordinary frequency and success.

Law and custom were of course largely responsible for these strange intermissions of silence and speech. When a woman was liable, as she was in the fifteenth century, to be beaten and flung about the room if she did not marry the man of her parents' choice, the spiritual atmosphere was not favorable to the production of works of art. When she was married without her own consent to a man who thereupon became her lord and master, "so far at least as law and custom could make him," as she was in the time of the Stuarts, it is likely she had little time for writing, and less encouragement. The immense effect of environment and suggestion upon the mind, we in our psychoanalytical age are beginning to realize. Again, with memoirs and letters to help us, we are beginning to understand how abnormal is the effort needed to produce a work of art, and what shelter and what support the mind of the artist requires. Of those facts the lives and letters of men like Keats and Carlyle and Flaubert assure us.

Thus it is clear that the extraordinary outburst of fiction in the beginning of the nineteenth century in England was heralded by innumerable slight changes in law and customs and manners. And women of the nineteenth century had some leisure; they had some education. It was no longer the exception for women of the middle and upper classes to choose their own husbands. And it is significant that of the four great women novelists - Jane Austen, Emily Brontë, Charlotte Brontë, and George Eliot - not one had a child and two were unmarried.

Yet, though it is clear that the ban upon writing had been removed, there was still, it would seem, considerable pressure upon women to write novels. No four women can have been more unlike in genius and character than these four. Jane Austen can have had nothing in common with George Eliot;

George Eliot was the direct opposite of Emily Brontë. Yet all were trained for the same profession; all, when they wrote, wrote novels.

Fiction was, as fiction still is, the easiest thing for a woman to write. Nor is it difficult to find the reason. A novel is the least concentrated form of art. A novel can be taken up or put down more easily than a play or a poem. George Eliot left her work to nurse her father. Charlotte Brontë put down her pen to pick the eyes out of potatoes. And living as she did in the common sitting room, surrounded by people, a woman was trained to use her mind in observation and upon the analysis of character. She was trained to be a novelist and not to be a poet.

Even in the nineteenth century, a woman lived almost solely in her home and her emotions. And those nineteenth century novels, remarkable as they were, were profoundly influenced the by the fact that the women who wrote them were excluded by their sex from certain kinds of experience. That experience has a great influence upon fiction is indisputable. The best part of Conrad's novels, for instance, would be destroyed if it had been impossible for him to be a sailor. Take away all that Tolstoi knew of war as a soldier, of life and society as a rich young man whose education admitted him to all sorts of experience, and *War and Peace* would be incredibly impoverished.

Yet *Pride and Prejudice*, *Wuthering Heights*, *Villette*, and *Middlemarch* were written by women from whom was forcibly withheld all experience save that which could be met with in a middle class drawing-room. No first-hand experience of war or seafaring or politics or business was possible for them. Even their emotional life was strictly regulated by law and custom. When George Eliot ventured to live with Mr. Lewes without being his wife, public opinion was scandalized. Under its pressure she withdrew into a suburban seclusion which, inevitably, had the worst possible effects upon her work. She wrote that unless people asked of their own accord to come and see her, she never invited them. At the same time, on the other side of Europe, Tolstoi was living a free life as a soldier, with men and women of all classes, for which nobody censured him and from which his novels drew much of their astonishing breadth and vigor.

But the novels of women were not affected only by the necessarily narrow range of the writer's experience. They showed, at least in the nineteenth century, another characteristic which may be traced to the writer's sex. In *Middlemarch* and in *Jane Eyre* we are conscious not merely of the writer's character, as we are conscious of the character of Charles Dickens, but we are conscious of a woman's presence - of someone resenting the treatment of her sex and pleading for its rights. This brings into women's writing an element which is entirely absent from a man's, unless, indeed, he happens to be a working man, a Negro, or one who for some other reason is conscious of disability. It introduces a distortion and is frequently the cause of weakness. The desire to plead some personal cause or to make a character the mouthpiece of some personal discontent or grievance always has a distracting effect, as if the spot at which the reader's attention is directed were suddenly twofold instead of single.

The genius of Jane Austen and Emily Brontë is never more convincing than in their power to ignore such claims and solicitations and to hold on their way unperturbed by scorn or censure. But it needed a very serene or a very powerful mind to resist the temptation to anger. The ridicule, the censure, the assurance of inferiority in one form or another which were lavished upon women who practised an art, provoked such reactions naturally enough. One sees the effect in Charlotte Brontë's indignation, in George Eliot's resignation. Again and again one finds it in the work of the lesser women writers - in their choice of a subject, in their unnatural self-assertiveness, in their unnatural docility. Moreover, insincerity leaks in almost unconsciously. They adopt a view in deference to authority. The vision becomes too masculine or it becomes too feminine; it loses its perfect integrity and, with that, its most essential quality as a work of art.

The great change that has crept into women's writing is, it would seem, a change of attitude. The woman writer is no longer bitter. She is no longer angry. She is no longer pleading and protesting as she writes. We are approaching, if we have not yet reached, the time when her writing will have little or no foreign influence to disturb it. She will be able to concentrate upon her vision without distraction from outside. The aloofness that was once within the reach of genius and originality is only now coming within the reach of ordinary women. Therefore the average novel by a woman is far more genuine and far more interesting to-day than it was a hundred or even fifty years ago.

But it is still true that before a woman can write exactly as she wishes to write, she has many difficulties to face. To begin with, there is the technical difficulty - so simple, apparently; in reality, so baffling - that the very form of the sentence does not fit her. It is a sentence made by men; it is too loose, too heavy, too pompous for a woman's use. Yet in a novel, which covers so wide a stretch of ground, an ordinary and usual type of sentence has to be found to carry the reader on easily and naturally from one end of the book to the other. And this a woman must make for herself, altering and adapting the current sentence until she writes one that takes the natural shape of her thought without crushing or distorting it.

But that, after all, is only a means to an end, and the end is still to be reached only when a woman has the courage to surmount opposition and the determination to be true to herself. For a novel, after all, is a statement about a thousand different objects - human, natural, divine; it is an attempt to relate them to each other. In every novel of merit these different elements are held in place by the force of the writer's vision. But they have another order also, which is the order imposed upon them by convention. And as men are the arbiters of that convention, as they have established an order of values in life, so too, since fiction is largely based on life, these values prevail there also to a very great extent.

It is probable, however, that both in life and in art the values of a woman are not the values of a man. Thus, when a woman comes to write a novel, she will find that she is perpetually wishing to alter the established values - to make serious what appears insignificant to a man, and trivial what is to him important. And for that, of course, she will be criticized; for the critic of the opposite sex will be genuinely puzzled and surprised by an attempt to alter the current scale of values, and will see in it not merely a difference of view, but a view that is weak, or trivial, or sentimental, because it differs from his own.

But here, too, women are coming to be more independent of opinion. They are beginning to respect their own sense of values. And for this reason the subject matter of their novels begins to show certain changes. They are less interested, it would seem, in themselves; on the other hand, they are more interested other women. In the early nineteenth century, women's novels were largely autobiographical. One of the motives that led them to write was the desire to expose their own suffering, to plead their own cause. Now that this desire is no longer so urgent, women are beginning to explore their own sex, to write of women as women have never been written of before; for of course, until very lately, women in literature were the creation of men.

Here again there are difficulties to overcome, for, if one may generalize, not only do women submit less readily to observation than men, but their lives are far less tested and examined by the ordinary processes of life. Often nothing tangible remains of a woman's day. The food that has been cooked is eaten; the children that have been nursed have gone out into the world. Where does the accent fall? What is the salient point for the novelist to seize upon? It is difficult to say. Her life has an anonymous character which is baffling and puzzling in the extreme. For the first time, this dark country is beginning to be explored in fiction; and at the same moment a woman has also to record the changes in women's minds and habits which the opening of the professions has introduced. She has to observe how their lives are ceasing to run underground; she has to discover what new colors and shadows are showing in them now that they are exposed to the outer world.

If, then, one should try to sum up the character of women's fiction at the present moment, one would say that it is courageous; it is sincere; it keeps closely to what women feel. It is not bitter. It does not insist upon its femininity. But at the same time, a woman's book is not written as a man would write it. These qualities are much commoner than they were, and they give even to second and third-rate work the value of truth and the interest of sincerity.

But in addition to these good qualities, there are two that call for a word more of discussion. The change which has turned the English woman from a nondescript influence, fluctuating and vague, to a voter, a wage earner, a responsible citizen, has given her both in her life and in her art a turn toward the impersonal. Her relations now are not only emotional; they are intellectual, they are political. The old system which condemned her to squint askance at things through the eyes or through the interests of husband or brother, has given place to the direct and practical interests of one who must act for herself, and not merely influence the acts of others. Hence her attention is being directed away from the personal centre which engaged it exclusively in the past to the impersonal, and her novels naturally become more critical of society, and less analytical of individual lives.

We may expect that the office of gadfly to the state, which has been so far a male prerogative, will now be discharged by women also. Their novels will deal with social evils and remedies. Their men and women will not be observed wholly in relation to each other emotionally, but as they cohere and clash in groups and classes and races. That is one change of some importance. But there is another more interesting to those who prefer the butterfly to the gadfly - that is to say, the artist to the reformer. The greater impersonality of women's lives will encourage the poetic spirit, and it is in poetry that women's fiction is still weakest. It will lead them to be less absorbed in facts and no longer content to record with astonishing acuteness the minute details which fall under their own observation. They will look beyond the personal and political relationships to the wider questions which the poet tries to solve - of our destiny and the meaning of life.

The basis of the poetic attitude is of course largely founded upon material things. It depends upon leisure, and a little money, and the chance which money and leisure give to observe impersonally and dispassionately. With money and leisure at their service, women will naturally occupy themselves more than has hitherto been possible with the craft of letters. They will make a fuller and a more subtle use of the instrument of writing. Their technique will become bolder and richer.

In the past, the virtue of women's writing often lay in its divine spontaneity, like that of the blackbird's song or the thrush's. It was untaught; it was from the heart. But it was also, and much more often, chattering and garrulous - mere talk spilt over paper and left to dry in pools and blots. In future, granted time and books and a little space in the house for herself, literature will become for women, as for men, an art to be studied. Women's gift will be trained and strengthened. The novel will cease to be the dumping ground for the personal emotions. It will become, more than at present, a work of art like any other, and its resources and its limitations will be explored.

From this it is a short step to the practice of the sophisticated arts, hitherto so little practised by women - to the writing of essays and criticism, of history and biography. And that, too, if we are considering the novel, will be of advantage; for besides improving the quality of the novel itself, it will draw off the aliens who have been attracted to fiction by its accessibility while their hearts lay elsewhere. Thus will the novel be rid of those excrescences of history and fact which, in our time, have made it so shapeless.

So, if we may prophesy, women in time to come will write fewer novels, but better novels; and not novels only, but poetry and criticism and history. But in this, to be sure, one is looking ahead to that golden, that perhaps fabulous age when women will have what has so long been denied them - leisure, and money, and a room to themselves.

Notes

The following selective notes explain allusions in the text and provide additional information on the manuscript. Well known persons, places, characters and works have not usually been identified, nor in most cases have further descriptions been provided of writers discussed by Woolf. The following works and their short titles have been used in the notes:

Common Reader 1 and *2* - Virginia Woolf, *The Common Reader, First Series* and *Second Series*, ed. Andrew McNeillie (Hogarth Press, 1984, 1986).

Diary - *The Diary of Virginia Woolf*, ed. Anne Olivier Bell and Andrew McNeillie, 5 vols (Hogarth Press, 1977–84).

DNB - *The Dictionary of National Biography*, ed. Leslie Stephen and Sidney Lee, et al. 22 vols (Oxford University Press, 1912, Supplements, 1901–).

Essays - *The Essays of Virginia Woolf*, ed. Andrew McNeillie (Hogarth Press, 1986–).

Room - Virginia Woolf, *A Room of One's Own* (Hogarth Press, 1929).

page 1 *Fitzwilliam Manuscript* *See* Introduction, pp. xiii–xiv. The Fitzwilliam manuscript is written in purple ink and consists of 135 leaves of punched two-hole paper. It is paginated throughout in pencil (except for the page between 110 and 111) but not in Woolf's hand. The first 90 leaves (pp. 3–100 in the transcript) measure 20.5×26.5 centimetres, have a printed margin line, and bear the watermark name "Chariot *page* 1 Fine Laid" and a winged figure in a chariot. The next 45 leaves of the Fitzwilliam Manuscript (pp. 125–74 of the transcript) measure 21× 26.5 centimetres, have a margin line drawn in black, and bear the watermark name "Cambrian" with a dragon figure. The punched holes of the manuscript cannot be aligned; some of the leaves have been punched twice in different places. (See note to p. 101 for a description of the Monks House Manuscript.)

3 *Based on a paper . . . some alterations* *See* Introduction, pp. xv–xix.

4 *Mary Beaton, Mary Seaton, Mary Carmichael* From the ballad variously known as "Mary Hamilton", "The Queen's Maries", "The Four Marys", etc. (*The English and Scottish Popular Ballads*, ed. Francis James Child, no. 173). The fourth of these ladies in waiting to Mary Queen of Scots was Mary Hamilton, the king's mistress, who murdered their illegitimate child and was hanged after refusing the king's intercession.

7–8 *Charles Lamb* In a footnote to his essay "Oxford in the Vacation", when it first appeared in the *London Magazine* in 1820, Lamb expressed his attitude towards authorial revisions: "There is something to me repugnant, at any time, in written hand. The text never seems determinate. Print settles it. I had thought of the Lycidas as of a full-grown beauty - as springing up with all it parts absolute - till, in evil hour, I was shown the original written copy of it, together with the other minor poems of its author, in the Library of Trinity, kept like some treasure to be proud of. I wish they had thrown them in the Cam, or sent them, after the latter cantos of Spenser, into the Irish Channel. How it staggered me to see the fine things in their ore! interlined, corrected! as if their words were mortal, alterable, displaceable at pleasure! as if they might have been otherwise, and just as good! as if inspirations were made up of parts, and those fluctuating, successive, indifferent! I will never go into the work-shop of any great artist again, nor desire a sight of his picture, till it is fairly off the easel; no, not if Raphael were to be alive again, and painting another Galatea." Lamb's editor believes the essay to have been written in Cambridge (*The Works of Charles and Mary Lamb*, ed. E. V. Lucas (Methuen, 1903), II, 309, 311). A plaque on a building in King's Parade opposite King's College reads "Charles Lamb/Lodged Here/August 1819".

7 *"Saint Charles" said Thackeray* "[Thackeray's] judgments came from the heart rather than the intellect, and it was fortunate when these coincided. 'St Charles', he said to Edward FitzGerald, . . . putting one of Charles Lamb's letters to his forehead, remembering his devotion to his afflicted sister" (Lewis Melville, *William Makepeace Thackeray* (London: John Lane, 1910), I, 180–1).

page 8 *Thackerays Esmond* The manuscripts of *Lycidas* and *Henry Esmond* are in the library of Trinity College, Cambridge. According to Trinity's *Catalogue of Western Manuscripts*, Thackeray's ms was donated by Woolf's father Leslie Stephen, whose first wife was Thackeray's younger daughter. Stephen wrote in his *DNB* life of Thackeray that the ms shows the novel "was written with very few corrections".

9 *baptismal certificate* None of the agnostic Leslie Stephen's children was baptised.

12 ~~*Kreisler played The Kreutzer Sonata*~~ Beethoven's "Kreutzer" sonata for violin and piano (Op. 47), performed here by the popular violinist and composer Fritz Kreisler (1875–1962). The work also gave its title to Tolstoy's famous late story *The Kreutzer Sonata.*

14 *We are all going . . . company* Thomas Gainsborough's dying words whispered to Sir Joshua Reynolds were "We are all going to heaven, and Vandyck is of the party" (*DNB*).

14 *manx cat* The source of Woolf's interest in the symbolism of the tailless cat from the Isle of Man that can walk on the grass prohibited to the female narrator appears to derive from one of the gnomic remarks of Blanche Warre-Cornish, the mother of Woolf's Bloomsbury friend Mary MacCarthy. She was wife of the Vice-President at Eton, and her sayings circulated for years among Etonians and others before finally being privately published in a collection entitled *Cornishiana* by Logan Pearsall Smith in 1935. Of Manx cats she said "No tails! . . . no tails! Like men! How symbolical everything is." Aldous Huxley, a former master at Eton, used Mrs Cornish and her remarks in the novel *Limbo*; Woolf reviewed it in 1920 and quoted the remark (*Essays*, III, 177).

16 *an anthology* Both Tennyson's and Rossetti's poems appear in a favourite anthology of Woolf's, *The Oxford Book of English Verse*, edited by Arthur Quiller-Couch and first published in 1912.

17 *There had fallen a splendid tear* From Alfred Lord Tennyson's "Maud".

17 *My heart is like a singing bird* From Christina Rossetti's "A Birthday".

18 *Grantchester* A village near Cambridge where Rupert Brooke lived and after which he called his famous poem.

23 *Mr Verrall? Mr Sidgwick? Jane Harrison?* A. W. Verrall (1851–1912) was a classicist at Trinity College, well known for his work on Euripides, and first professor of English literature at Cambridge. Henry Sidgwick (1838–1900), also of Trinity, was a distinguished philosopher and strong supporter of women's education at Cambridge; his wife, Eleanor Mildred (Balfour) Sidgwick, was the second principal

page 23 of Newnham. Jane Ellen Harrison (1850–1928), celebrated classicist, and anthropologist at Newnham, later lived in Bloomsbury with Hope Mirrlees. Woolf visited them shortly before Harrison's death in April and later attended her funeral (*Diary*, III, 176, 179–81). The Hogarth Press published Harrison's *Reminiscences of a Student's Life* in 1925.

29 *But you know the story . . . Lady Stanley of Alderley* In *Room* (p. 31) the story of Girton's founding is documented with quotations from Barbara Stephen's *Emily Davies and Girton College* (which Woolf reviewed in 1927) and Ray Strachey's *The Cause: A Short History of the Women's Movement in Great Britain* (1928). Lady Stanley of Alderley (1807–95) was an ardent liberal, an early advocate of women's education, one of the most effective supporters of Davies and Girton, and Bertrand Russell's grandmother.

30 *Miss Clough* Anne Jemima Clough (1820–92), the first principal of Newnham College.

40 ~~*only the names of men encircle the proud dome*~~ Between 1907 and 1952 the following names were painted under the windows around the dome of the Reading Room: Chaucer, Caxton, Tindale, Spenser, Shakespeare, Bacon, Milton, Locke, Addison, Swift, Pope, Gibbon, Wordsworth, Scott, Byron, Carlyle, Macaulay, Tennyson, Browning (P. R. Harris, *The Reading Room* (British Museum, 1986), p. 27).

42 *Dean Inges opinion* William Ralph Inge (1860–1954), Dean of St Paul's and religious writer. In the Twenties and later his journalism earned him the nickname of "the gloomy dean" (*DNB*).

42 *Lord Birkenheads opinion* F. E. Smith, Earl of Birkenhead, (1872–1930) conservative lawyer, politician, opponent of women's suffrage, and Lord Chancellor, 1919–22. In a speech against women's suffrage in 1910 (part of which he reprinted in 1928) Birkenhead perorated "I have never in the course of my observations here or elsewhere founded myself on some assumed intellectual inferiority of women. I do not believe it, but I venture to say that the sum total of human happiness, knowledge and achievement would have been almost unaffected if Sappho had never sung, if Joan of Arc had never fought, if Siddons had never played, and if George Eliot had never written. At the same time, without the true functions of womanhood faithfully discharged throughout the ages the very existence of the race and the tenderest and most sacred influences which animate mankind would have disappeared" (quoted in John Campbell, *F. E. Smith, First Earl of Birkenhead* (London: Cape, 1983), p. 279).

42 *La Bruyères opinion* In *Room* (p. 44) Woolf quoted La Bruyère's opinion as "Les femmes sont extrêmes; elles sont meilleures ou pires que les hommes" ("Women are extreme; they are better or worse than men").

page 43 *Samuel Butler* "It has been said that all sensible men are of the same religion and that no sensible man every says what that religion is. So all sensible men are of the same opinion about women and no sensible man ever says what that opinion is" (*The Note-books of Samuel Butler*, ed. Henry Festing Jones (London: A. C. Fifield, 1912), p. 228).

43 *Thomas Day . . . Mr Edgworth* Thomas Day (1748–89), author of the children's book *Sandford and Merton*, a follower of Rousseau's ideas in *Emile* and friend of Maria Edgeworth's father R. L. Edgeworth (1744–1817) whom he influenced with his educational theories. In writing of Day and Edgeworth in her "The Lives of the Obscure", Woolf mentions that Day urged Edgeworth "to leave his son without education" (*Common Reader 1*, p. 112). There seems to be no evidence that Maria Edgeworth was brought up the same way.

43 *Dr Johnson saying* A footnote in *Room* (p. 45) quotes Johnson's saying to Boswell in *The Journal of a Tour to the Hebrides* "Men know that women are an overmatch for them, and therefore they choose the weakest or the most ignorant. If they did not think so, they never could be afraid of women knowing as much as themselves. . . ."

43 *German tribe* In *Room* (p. 45) Woolf added the following footnote: "'The ancient Germans believed that there was something holy in women, and accordingly consulted them as oracles.' Frazer, *Golden Bough*."

43 *Goethe* Woolf is probably alluding to the famous last line of *Faust*: "Das Ewig-Weibliche zieht uns hinan." ("The eternal feminine draws us onward.")

44–5 *great book on the . . . inferiority of the female ⟨sex⟩* Woolf may be referring here to Otto Weininger's *Sex and Character* (London: Heinemann, 1906), a misogynist and anti-semitic work that influenced Ludwig Wittgenstein, Gertrude Stein, and James Joyce, among others. Weininger, who committed suicide at 23, bears no relation to the personality of Professor X. But it has been pointed out that his book is discussed by Desmond MacCarthy in the 1920 review of a book on women by Arnold Bennett that Woolf read and replied to (Susan Dick "'*What Fools We Were!*': Virginia Woolf's *A Society*", *Twentieth Century Literature*, 33 (Spring, 1987), 53.) MacCarthy wrote of *Sex and Character* "in every human being there were mixed the two elements, 'M' (Man) and 'W' (Woman), just as these characteristics appear physiologically in each sex. To 'M' Weininger attributed all the admirable moral and intellectual qualities and to 'W' all the bad ones" ("Books in General", *New Statesman* (2 October 1920), p. 704).

49 *Come into the garden Maud* From Tennyson's "Maud".

49 *Evening Standard* "Principles: Conservative. Established 1827. A high class evening journal in London and the Home Counties. Its

page 49 news is gathered from all parts of the world. Special pages are devoted to Stock Markets, Ladies Fashions, Sporting News, etc. and its literary articles by leading writers are outstanding features" (*Newspaper Press Directory* (London: Benn, 1927), p. 84). Among these writers in 1929 were Dean Inge and Arnold Bennett, who would review *Room* there under the title "The Queen of the High Brows".

49 *"All, all . . . Hitchen exclaimed"* This quotation is on the verso of 48. Elizabeth Hitchener, whose "Ode to the Rights of Women" begins with this line, was a friend of Shelley's. Woolf cites the line in her review of Shelley's letters to Hitchener in 1908 (*Essays* I, 175) and again in the essay "The Eccentrics" in 1919 (*Essays*, III, 40).

49 *Anger: desire . . . inferior* Written in pencil.

50 *Sir Austen Chamberlain* Foreign Secretary (1924–9), who regularly attended League of Nations meetings in Geneva.

55 *Odyssey was written by a woman* Samuel Butler's theory, argued in *The Authoress of the Odyssey* (1897).

57 *the act . . . giving votes to women* Women were given the vote at the age of 30 in 1918, and at the age of 21 in 1928.

58 *that one gift . . . death to hide* "And that one talent which is death to hide,/ Lodged with me useless, . . ." John Milton, "When I Consider How My Light is Spent".

60 *the Admiralty Arch or The Sieges Allee* The triple Admiralty Arch in London, built in 1910, is at one end of The Mall that leads into Trafalgar Square; the central arch is opened only on ceremonial occasions. The Sieges Allee in Berlin is embellished with statues of Hohenzollern rulers.

65 *to merely* These originally cancelled words have dots under them that apparently indicate they were to be uncancelled.

66 *p. 260–1* The page references are for the quotations from G. M. Trevelyan's *History of England*, first published in London by Longmans in 1926. The next quotations are on pp. 436–7.

69 *The Paston ⟨letters⟩* For the medieval Paston family's letters see Woolf's "The Pastons and Chaucer" in *Common Reader 1*.

69 *⟨lives of the⟩ Verneys & the Hutchinsons* The memoirs referred to by Trevelyan are *Memoirs of the Verney Family during the Seventeenth Century*, compiled by F. P. Verney (1892–9) and Lucy Hutchinson's life of her regicide husband *Memoirs of the Life of Colonel Hutchinson* (1806).

70 *lives of the obscure* Woolf published three essays under this title in *Common Reader 1*.

71 *Robert Trevelyan* A slip of the pen. The poet Robert Calverley Trevelyan, a friend of the Woolfs, was the brother of the historian George Macaulay Trevelyan.

page 72 *all the machinery . . . washing up* These words are on the verso of 71.

72 *Joanna Baillie* (1762–1851); dramatist, poet and friend of Sir Walter Scott who called her "the immortal Joanna" in *Marmion* (*DNB*). In *Room* Woolf changed the object of her influence from Scott to Edgar Allan Poe (p. 69).

72 *Miss Mitford* Mary Russell Mitford (1787–1855), author of, among other works, *Our Village* (1832), a popular collection of stories and sketches. Woolf's three reviews of Constance Hill's *Mary Russell Mitford and her Surroundings* (1920) are incorporated into "Outlines", *Common Reader 1*.

73 *Mary Arden . . . 1564* Arden was the birth name of Mary, the mother of Shakespeare, who was born in 1564.

73 *1582* The year of Shakespeare's marriage.

75 *Nick Greene* A character from *Orlando*, contemporary of Shakespeare, whom he criticizes; based on the pamphleteer and playwright Robert Greene (1558–92) among others.

76 *mute & inglorious Jane Austen* "Some mute inglorious Milton here may rest." Thomas Gray, "Elegy Written in a Country Churchyard" (1751).

81 *Judith* The name of Shakespeare's younger daughter. She and her twin brother Hamnet were born in 1585; she married Thomas Quiney in 1616 and died in 1662 (*DNB*).

83 *Currer Bell, George Eliot, Georges Sand* Pseudonyms of Charlotte Brontë, Mary Ann Evans, and Lucile-Aurore Dupin.

84 *Tacitus* Corrected to Pericles in the typescript. Pericles's comment is from his Funeral Oration in Thucydides's *The Peloponnesian War*.

84 *Cet chien est a moi* "Ce chien est à moi, disaient ces pauvre enfants; c'est là ma place au soleil. - Voilà le commencement et l'image de l'usurpation de toute la terre" ("This dog is mine, said those poor children; that is my place in the sun. - Here is the beginning and the image of the usurpation of all the earth"), Blaise Pascal, *Pensées* (*Oeuvres Complètes*, ed. Jacques Chevalier (Paris: Bibliothéque de la Pléiade 1954) No. 231).

85 *never blotted a line* According to Ben Jonson in *Timber, or Discoveries Made upon Men and Matter* (1640).

86 *Miss Emily Davies* (1830–1921) advocate of women's education and founder of Girton College. See note to p. 29.

87 *Oscar Browning* (1837–1923) Eton schoolmaster then fellow of King's, historian and educator. Anecdotes about Browning's examining Girton students and the stable boy are given in H. E. Wortham, *Oscar Browning* (London: Constable, 1927), pp. 231, 246–7.

88 *Lady Bessborough . . . Lord Granville . . . "notwithstanding"* Henrietta, Countess of Bessborough (1761–1821), principal correspondent

page 88 of the statesman Lord Granville Leveson-Gower (1773–1846), and mother of Lady Caroline Lamb. Her letters, including the one on his maiden speech, are included in Lord Granville Leveson Gower, *Private Correspondence, 1781–1821*, ed. Castalia Countess Granville, 2 vols (London, 1916).

89 *Johnson repeated the phrase* "Sir, a woman's preaching is like a dog's walking on his hinder legs. It is not done well; but you are surprized to find it done at all" (James Boswell, *Life of Johnson*, Oxford Standard Authors (London: Oxford University Press, 1952), p. 327).

89 *A Book About Music* "*A Survey of Contemporary Music*, Cecil Gray, p. 246" - footnote in *Room* (p. 83).

91 *Shakespeare's mind had burnt up all these impediments* Here and in chapter 5 Woolf appears to be echoing to the opening of Sonnet 116: "Let me not to the marriage of true minds/ Admit impediments."

93 *25 . . . How are we fallen!* The page reference is to *Poems by Anne, Countess of Winchilsea*, ed. John Middleton Murry (London: Jonathan Cape 1928). The quotation on that page from "The Introduction" continues "How are we fallen! fallen by mistaken rules,/ And Education's, more than Nature's fools. . . ." Eight lines from the poem are quoted in *Room* (p. 88).

93 *Alas ~~the~~ a woman* The quotation, also from "The Introduction", continues "Alas! a woman that attempts the pen,/ Such an intruder on the rights of men,/ Such a presumptuous creature is esteemed. . . ." In quoting eleven lines of the poem in *Room* (pp. 88–9) Woolf dropped the second line here.

93 *To some few friends* From the last lines of "The Introduction: 'To some few friends, and to thy sorrows sing./ For groves of laurel thou wert never meant:/ Be dark enough thy shades, and be thou there content'." These lines are quoted in *Room* (p. 89).

94 *Nor will in fading silks . . .* Winchilsea, "The Spleen". Also quoted in *Room* (p. 89).

94 *Mr Murry justly says* The critic John Middleton Murry in the introduction to Winchilsea's poems mentioned above.

94 *d of b. 1624? 1674 . . . the Duchess that Lamb loved* The dates of birth and death, written on the verso of 93, are those of Margaret Cavendish, Duchess of Newcastle, whose country home was Welbeck Abbey in Nottinghamshire. Woolf reviewed a biography of the Newcastles in 1911 (*Essays* I, 345–51) and then devoted an essay to the Duchess's character and writings in *The Common Reader 1*. Charles Lamb described her in his "Mackery End, in Hertfordshire" essay in *Elia* as "somewhat fantastical, and original-brain'd, generous Margaret Newcastle".

page 95 *"Women live Bats or Owls . . . civilest"* Woolf quoted these words from Newcastle's *Female Orations* in *Common Reader 1* (p. 73). Among the sources she gives in a note are *The World's Olio, Orations of Diverse Sorts, Accommodated to Divers Places; Female Orations; Plays; Philosophical Letters*, etc. (p. 248).

95 *Milton it is said. . .* "It was whispered by some that [Milton] was obliged for many of the thoughts in his 'L'Allegro' and 'Il Penseroso' to this lady's 'Dialogue between Mirth and Melancholy' . . ." (*DNB*).

96 *37 . . . 1674* The page numbers refer to passages in *The Letters of Dorothy Osborne to William Temple*, ed. G. C. Moore Smith (Oxford, 1928) where she criticizes the Duchess of Newcastle (p. 37). In October 1928, Woolf reviewed the letters that Dorothy Osborne (1627–95) wrote to Swift's friend Temple before their marriage. The review was incorporated in *Common Reader 2*. The page numbers and dates (again, those of the Duchess) are written on the verso of 95.

97 *she was, it is said, the first women to make money by ⟨her⟩ writing* "The importance of Aphra Behn is that she was the first woman in England to earn her living by her pen", V. Sackville-West, *Aphra Behn: The Incomparable Astrea* (London: Gerald Howe, 1927), p. 12.

97 *A thousand Martyrs . . . Love in fantastic triumph sate* Titles of poems by Aphra Behn (1640–89) quoted by Sackville-West and also included in *The Oxford Book of English Verse* under the titles "The Libertine" and "Song".

99 *the Blues* Blue stockings: an 18th century group of learned, literary London women.

100 *Mrs. Carter* Elizabeth Carter (1762–1815) was the subject of an early review by Woolf entitled "The Bluest of the Blue" (*Essays* I, 112–14). She wrote of Carter, "To conquer sleep she had a bell tied to the head of her bedstead to which a string was attached, leading through a 'crevasse' in her window to the garden below. At four or five in the morning a friendly sexton tolled the bell. Elizabeth sprang from her bed and worked at her books till six. . . ." Woolf also made five pages of reading notes on memoirs about Carter in a notebook, the last item of which is her notes for the conclusion to *Room* given in appendix 2.

101 *Monks House Manuscript* See Introduction, p. xiv. The Monks House manuscript (Monks House Manuscripts B.6.e) consists of 20 unpaginated leaves of punched two-hole paper that were found ringed together with a few manuscript pages of "Phases of Fiction" and of the essay "On Not Knowing French" that was published in February 1929. The manuscript is written in purple ink. Its first 14 leaves (pp. 103–16 of the transcript) measure 20.5×26.5 centimetres, with the same printed margin and watermark as the first 90 leaves of

page 101 the Fitzwilliam manuscript. The last 7 leaves (pp. 117–22 of the transcript) are half a centimetre wider and have a drawn border and the same watermark as the second part of the Fitzwilliam manuscript, except that the colour of the margin line is blue instead of black. The Monks House manuscript was noted by Alice Fox and quoted by Jane Marcus, who described it as "holograph draft notes" in *Virginia Woolf and the Languages of Patriarchy* (Bloomington, Indiana: Indiana University Press, 1987), p. 186.

103 *"The supreme head of song"* Algernon Charles Swinburne's description of Sappho in "Ave Atque Vale".

103 *Austen Leighs life* "*Memoir of Jane Austen* by her nephew, James Edward Austen-Leigh" - footnote in *Room* (p. 100).

104 *~~in which~~ Jane Austen wrote* The words *Jane Austen* have dots under them that apparently indicate they were to be uncancelled.

105 *129* Presumably the page number for the quotation from chapter 12 of *Jane Eyre*.

106 *"I never ask anyone"* In the *Common Reader 1* essay on George Eliot, Woolf quoted from her biography, "I wish it to be understood . . . that I should never invite any one to come and see me who did not ask for the invitation" (pp. 165–6).

107 All the marginalia are in pencil.

108 *It is another feather in their cap* Written in pencil.

109 *Sir Egerton Brydges* (1762–1837), editor of Newcastle's memoirs. Woolf wrote in her *Common Reader 1* essay on Newcastle that her language "much perturbed Sir Egerton Brydges. She used, he complained, 'expressions and images of extraordinary coarseness as flowing from a female of high rank brought up in courts'. He forgot that this particular female had long ceased to frequent the Court; she consorted chiefly with fairies; and her friends were among the dead. Naturally, then, her language was coarse" (pp. 76–7).

109 ⟨*So that on [putting pen page]*⟩ and ⟨*herself confined*⟩ Written in pencil.

109 *The current sentence . . . ~~Jane Austen remodelled~~* For examples of the sentence and Austen's remodelling of it, see appendix 3, pp. 181–2.

110 *[antipathies]* Written in pencil. The following passage, written on the verso of 109 in pencil appears to have nothing to do with the manuscript: "She wants to let 4 ~~roo~~ her part of the house wh. contains 4 bds. 2 sittingrooms, kitchen & wcs & bath".

110 *Barbara Leigh Smith* (1827–91), later Barbara Bodichon, campaigned for women's rights, strongly supported Emily Davies and Girton.

114 *Chloe & Olivia* The phrase in the margin is written on the verso of 113.

page 114 *mincing liver* In November, 1928, Woolf described her young, unmarried cousin Janet Vaughan in her diary as "an attractive woman; competent; disinterested, taking blood tests all day to solve some abstract problem" (III, 206). A medical scientist and later Principal of Somerville College, Dame Janet has added that in the course of investigating liver extract as a cure for pernicious anaemia, she borrowed a mincing machine from Woolf, who was fascinated and wanted to know all about what she was doing ("Some Bloomsbury Memories", *Charleston Newsletter*, 12 (September 1985), p. 21).

117 *that what to do* Written on the verso of 116.

118 *The hostess* Written in pencil.

120 *Marshall & Freebodys* Debenham and Freebody as well as Marshall and Snelgrove were well known London department stores.

121 *the anonymous gentleman in Art & Letters* Desmond MacCarthy in *Life and Letters* 1 (August, 1928), 221–2. See Introduction, p. xxx.

122 ⟨I don't think it occurred . . . with it⟩ Written in pencil.

125 *"Highly developed" - "Infinitely intricate"* The quoted words refer to the description of a woman as an organism "so highly developed . . . so <u>*extraordinarily*</u> complex . . ." on p. 117.

125 *no mark on the wall* An echo of Woolf's early story "The Mark on the Wall" (1917).

125 *Debrett* Debrett's *Illustrated Baronage and Knightage* and *Illustrated Peerage* of Britain and Ireland have been published yearly since 1865. Neither they, nor the *DNB* nor *Who's Who* mention anyone by the name of Butts.

125 *Whitaker's Almanac* Published yearly since 1869, it includes a Table of Precedency. The Table is also satirized in "The Mark on the Wall".

126 *Sir William Joynson-Hicks* Known as Jix, active as Home Secretary (1924–9) in the banning of *The Well of Loneliness* in 1928 and the suppressing of D. H. Lawrence's poems in 1929.

129 *for there is no mistaking . . . pricking, the* Written on the verso of 128.

129 *Mary Carmichael* This is the first mention of Carmichael as a novelist in the surviving manuscripts. A novel entitled *Love's Creation* was published in 1928 (London: John Bale, Sons and Danielsson, Ltd) under the name Marie Carmichael by Marie Stopes, the birth-control crusader (Susan Gubar, "The Birth of the Artist as Heroine, . . ." *The Representation of Women in Fiction*, ed. Carolyn G. Heilbrun and Margaret R. Higonnet (Baltimore, Maryland: Johns Hopkins Press, 1983), p. 55). A publisher's note in the novel proclaims Marie Carmichael to be "another facet" of the famous sexologist and

page 129 palaeontologist Dr Stopes. The novel, which opens in a University of London zoological laboratory, tells the story of a young male scientist who marries a female biology student; she is killed shortly after their marriage and he later marries his deceased wife's unscientific sister.

130 *Balaclàva* The 1854 Crimean War battle famous for the charge of the Light Brigade.

132 ⟨*bearing*⟩ Written in pencil.

133 *forged* and *& came to a murky place* Written in pencil.

134 *Give her another hundred . . . the book.* Written in pencil.

137 *ego-centricity* Written on the verso of 134.

137 *26th October 1928* The date of Woolf's Girton talk.

140 *Emily . . . Cayley* Tennyson married Emily Sellwood in 1850 after a ten-year engagement, and Christina Rossetti refused the translator Charles Bagot Cayley in 1866.

143 *Whitehall* Thoroughfare leading to Parliament Square and decorated with statues of statesmen and soldiers. Many government buildings are located along it.

143 *Clearly the mind . . . possibility.* Written on the verso of 142.

147 This page is unnumbered in the Fitzwilliam Manuscript.

149 *This foolish notion . . . the pages*: This passage is circled, possibly for insertion above at the passage beginning "{Whatever I read . . ."

150 *manx cat in the quadrangle* Quadrangle is an Oxford term; previously the cat had appeared in the court, which is the Cambridge term.

151 *Coleridge . . . androgynous mind* In a 1918 review of Coleridge's *The Table Talk and Omniana* Woolf wrote "The same desire to justify and protect one's type led [Coleridge] no doubt to perceive the truth that 'a great mind must be androgynous . . . I have known strong minds with imposing, undoubting, Cobbet-like manners, but I have never met a great mind of this sort'" (*Essays*, II, 221–2).

156 *Churchill* Winston Churchill was currently Chancellor of the Exchequer.

157 *Plain Tales . . . Winkie* Collections of Kipling stories published in the 1890s.

158 *Graphic . . . Tatler* Illustrated London weeklies focussing on celebrities.

158 *The picture will come down* The scene is in *Swan Song* (1928), the third volume of Galsworthy's *Modern Comedy*.

162 *the daughter of a clergyman* These originally cancelled words have dots under them that apparently indicate they were to be uncancelled.

162 *gunandros* or gynandrous, the reverse of androgynous.

164 *Daffodils . . . dares' The Winter's Tale*, IV, 4, 118–19.

167 *Professor . . . at Cambridge "The Art of Writing* by Sir Arthur Quiller-Couch" - note in *Room* (p. 161). The title is actually *On the*

page 167 *Art of Writing*, which was published in 1916. Quiller-Couch succeeded Verrall as the second Professor of English Literature at Cambridge (1912–44). The Hogarth Press published his *A Lecture on Lectures* in 1927.

171 ~~*it may be having . . . to see a*~~ This cancelled phrase is also apparently marked for insertion into the middle of line three above.

172 *Sir Sidney Lee* Succeeded Leslie Stephen as editor of the *DNB*, and wrote the extensive entry on Shakespeare which he then expanded into *The Life of William Shakespeare* (1898).

181 *"The grandeur of their works . . . success".* The source for these sentences has not been identified. It may come from *The Times* newspaper. In *Room* the sentence has "generations" but Woolf has clearly written "generation" in the typescript.

182 *"She examined into . . . family".* From *Pride and Prejudice*, vol. II, ch. 7.

183 *Gertrude Bell* famous travel writer (1868–1926), among whose books are *Safar Nameh - Persian Pictures: A Book of Travel* (1895) and *Amurath to Amurath: Travels in Asia Minor and Persia* (1911). Her letters were published in 1927.

184 *Cassandra* Published for the first time as an appendix to Ray Strachey's *The Cause* in 1928, "Cassandra" was part of the second volume, entitled "Practical Deductions", of Nightingale's unpublished *Suggestions for Thought to Searchers after Religious Truth.*

184 *Harriet Martineau* (1802–1876), social reformer and author of stories, essays, novels, history, social philosophy, and autobiography.

186 *The Slade* The Slade School of Fine Art, University College London.

187 *anonymous gentleman . . . minister to their needs* In her 1927 review of Barbara Stephen's *Emily Davies and Girton College* Woolf quoted from an essay by W. R. Greg (1809–91) entitled "Why are Women Redundant?": "Mr Greg, underlining his words, wrote that 'the essentials of a woman's being are *that they are supported by, and they minister to, men*'" (reprinted in *The Moment and Other Essays* (London: Hogarth Press, 1947), p. 160).

188 *Princess Mary* Princess royal (1897–1965) only sister of the Prince of Wales, later the Duke of Windsor (1894–1972).